HOW TO PASS

HIGHER
MODERN STUDIES

Richard Deakin

Hodder Gibson

Acknowledgements

The Publishers would like to thank the following for permission to reproduce copyright material:

Photo credits

Page 8 © David Cairns/Rex Features; page 12 © Adam Elder/Scottish Parliament; page 27 © PA/EMPICS; page 37 © Eddie Mulholland/Rex Features; page 40 by kind permission of the Conservative Party; page 41 (top) by kind permission of the Labour Party (bottom) by kind permission of the Liberal Democrats; page 42 by kind permission of the Scottish National Party; page 48 © T. Norris/Scottish Viewpoint; page 50 © Allan Milligan/Scottish Viewpoint; page 60 © Leon Neal/AP/Empics; page 67 © Courtesy of the Department for Work & Pensions; page 73 © Purestock X; page 79 © Paula Solloway/Photofusion; page 91 © AP/Empics; page 96 © SR/TS/Keystone USA/Rex Features; page 98 © Richard Lord/The Image Works/TopFoto; page 101 © Bruce Connolly/CORBIS, page 108 © Qilai Shen/Rex Features; page 110 © Vince Streano/CORBIS; page 117 © Stephan Savoia/AP/Empics; page 119 © Sayvid Azim/AP/Empics; page 124 © Omar Torres/AFP/Getty Images; page 127 © Tim Boyle/Getty Images; page 134 © Paul Cooper/Rex Features; page 139 © Lehtikuva Oy/Rex Features; page 144 © Argus/Still Pictures; page 150 © Jorgen Schytte/Still Pictures; page 152 © Paul Grover/Rex Features; page 156 © Charles Onians/AFP/Getty Images; page 159 © Issouf Sanogo/AFP/Getty Images; page 167 © Jean/Marc Giboux/Getty Images; page 171 © Steve Allen/Alamy; page 172 © Peter Morgan/Reuters/Corbis; page 174 © Cristiano Laruffa/Rex Features; page 177 © Elvis Barukcic/AFP/Getty Images.

Acknowledgements

Cartoons © Moira Munro 2007.

Every effort has been made to trace all copyright holders, but if any have been inadvertently overlooked the Publishers will be pleased to make the necessary arrangements at the first opportunity.

Although every effort has been made to ensure that website addresses are correct at time of going to press, Hodder Gibson cannot be held responsible for the content of any website mentioned in this book. It is sometimes possible to find a relocated web page by typing in the address of the home page for a website in the URL window of your browser.

Hodder Headline's policy is to use papers that are natural, renewable and recyclable products and made from wood grown in sustainable forests. The logging and manufacturing processes are expected to conform to the environmental regulations of the country of origin.

Orders: please contact Bookpoint Ltd, 130 Milton Park, Abingdon, Oxon OX14 4SB. Telephone: (44) 01235 827720. Fax: (44) 01235 400454. Lines are open 9.00–5.00, Monday to Saturday, with a 24-hour message answering service. Visit our website at www.hoddereducation.co.uk. Hodder Gibson can be contacted direct on: Tel: 0141 848 1609; Fax: 0141 889 6315; email: hoddergibson@hodder.co.uk

© Richard Deakin 2007
First published in 2007 by
Hodder Gibson, an imprint of Hodder Education,
a member of the Hodder Headline Group
2a Christie Street
Paisley PA1 1NB

Impression number	5	4	3	2	1	
Year		2010	2009	2008	2007	

Cover photo © ESA/K. Horgan/Stone/Getty Images
Illustrations by Jeff Edwards
Typeset in 9.5 on 12.5pt Frutiger Light by Phoenix Photosetting, Chatham, Kent
Printed and bound in Great Britain by Martins The Printers, Berwick-upon-Tweed

A catalogue record for this title is available from the British Library

ISBN-10: 0-340-90696-0
ISBN-13: 978-0-340-90696-5

CONTENTS

AN INTRODUCTION TO HIGHER MODERN STUDIES

Welcome to this Revision Book

The Higher Modern Studies course is a very interesting course that is full of topical issues. The examining body, the Scottish Qualifications Authority (SQA), sets an exam based on these issues. It lays out, in detail, what you need to know and do to pass the exam. The exam tests your knowledge and understanding, and skills. At the beginning of each chapter, there is a list of the topics to be covered, as specified by the SQA. The content of each chapter has been written to follow these guidelines and to make sure you cover all you need to know for the exam.

How to Use this Revision Book

This revision book has been written to help you pass the Higher Modern Studies course after 2006. The SQA changed the content of some topic areas and the structure of the Higher exam; the first exam in the new structure is taken in 2007. This revision book cannot be used on its own. The book will summarise the main topics, give hints on how to pass the exam, how to revise and how to practise writing answers for the final exam. You will also find out the standard expected by the SQA to pass the exam. You are expected to use the book along with your other notes, textbooks, and any relevant websites.

So What is Involved in Passing Higher Modern Studies?

You need to pass a number of unit assessments or internal tests throughout the year as well as the final exam in May in order to get the full certificate. Higher Modern Studies, a National Qualification Course, certificated by the SQA, consists of three Units. Each of the Units is broken down into a number of areas called Study Themes. You may have a choice of which areas to study, although this depends on what you studied with your teacher in class. The lists below show what your choices are:

Unit 1 Political Issues in the United Kingdom

There are four Study Themes:

     Study Theme 1A Devolved Decision Making in Scotland

     Study Theme 1B Decision Making in Central Government

     Study Theme 1C Political Parties and their Policies (including the Scottish Dimension)

     Study Theme 1D Electoral Systems, Voting and Political Attitudes

You have to study **two** out of the four Study Themes and your teacher will have taught two of them in class. Each of these Study Themes is covered in this book.

Unit 2 Social Issues in the United Kingdom

There is only **one** Study Theme here:

> Study Theme 2 Wealth and Health Inequalities in the UK

Everyone must study this.

Unit 3 International Issues

There are six Study Themes in this Unit:

> Study Theme 3A The Republic of South Africa
>
> Study Theme 3B The People's Republic of China
>
> Study Theme 3C The United States of America
>
> Study Theme 3D The European Union
>
> Study Theme 3E The Politics of Development in Africa (with the exception of the Republic of South Africa)
>
> Study Theme 3F Global Security

You must study **two** of the six Study Themes and you will have been taught two of these by your teacher. All six Study Themes are covered in this book.

The Exam

This is the part we all dread but the exam you face in May will be very fair. The papers are based on the syllabus, the teachers teach the syllabus and you answer questions on topics you have been revising. The exam does not try to trick you. The questions you see in the exam will be familiar to you if you have done proper revision. Your job is to learn the content, think about the questions and then try to answer them as well as you can.

The exam consists of two papers.

Paper 1 – The Essay Paper

Time   1 hour and 30 minutes

◆ This paper examines knowledge and understanding covering the course content and also assesses analysis, evaluation and problem solving. (Don't worry about these terms; we will look at what they mean.)

◆ Questions will require an extended response (you will need to write an essay long enough to be worth the marks allocated).

◆ The paper will consist of three sections:

Section A Political Issues in the United Kingdom

Section B Social Issues in the United Kingdom

Section C International Issues

◆ Each question will be worth 15 marks.

◆ Candidates must answer a total of four questions: one question from each Section, and one other from either Section A or Section C.

◆ The paper is worth 60 marks in total.

Paper 2 The Decision Making Exercise

Time   1 hour 15 minutes

◆ This paper consists of a decision making exercise, based on Section B – Social Issues in the United Kingdom.

◆ It contains a series of short evaluating questions worth 10 marks in total, and a report worth 20 marks.

◆ The paper is worth 30 marks in total.

Internal Assessment

You also need to pass the Unit Assessments that occur throughout the year. The questions are taken from the National Assessment Bank (NAB) and cover each part of the course. You have to pass a certain number of these NABs to gain the overall award in Modern Studies. You have to pass one essay question in both the Political Issues Unit and the International Issues Unit and you will be given 35 minutes for each of these. You will also need to pass a Decision Making Exercise Report in the Social Issues Unit and you will be given 60 minutes for that. Once you pass all three of these you will then have gained the Internal Assessment award for Higher Modern Studies. If you fail any of these you will be able to resit them at a later date.

The Marker

Markers are all experienced teachers or tutors of Modern Studies. Their work is carefully controlled and monitored by the SQA and is checked by the SQA to ensure that the same standards are applied throughout the country. These markers get together to discuss answers and they work from the same guidelines when marking papers. The SQA have a number of systems in place to ensure all candidates are treated fairly. The SQA encourages markers to reward candidates whenever possible and markers are keen to see candidates get credit for things they get right.

The Exam Instructions

In the exam paper it is important to make sure you know what you are being asked to do. In the Essay Paper, the SQA will always use the same kind of words in questions. If you understand what these words mean, you are well on the way to answering the question correctly. All of the questions in the Essay Paper are *analyse* type questions. This means that you are expected not just to give information about the topic, but that you have to look at arguments for and against a range of issues. The most common types of questions are listed on page 4.

Key Points

An analysis of the question is important

Discuss … You will usually be given a statement about an issue, then be asked to look at the evidence for and against the statement and comment on both sides.

Example: 'The Prime Minister is the most powerful figure in UK politics.' Discuss.

To what extent … This is similar to the 'discuss' question but is asking you to say how far something is true or not, by looking at supporting evidence.

Example: To what extent has the Scottish Parliament improved democracy in Scotland?

Critically examine the view … Here you are expected to take a particular point of view and look at the evidence both for and against that view.

Example: Critically examine the view that pressure groups are a threat to democracy.

Assess the effectiveness of / consequences of … You are expected to look at what has been done in a certain area and comment on whether or not it has been effective or on what the consequences of those actions have been.

Example: Assess the effectiveness of government policies in South Africa to reduce
social and economic inequalities.

Remember, you are expected to be able to argue different points of view, look at advantages and disadvantages, judge the extent of an issue, or the effectiveness of policies in an area.

In Paper 2, the Decision Making Exercise, you should also know what is expected of you before you sit the exam. For more information on this, see page 187.

UNIT 1

Political Issues in the United Kingdom

STUDY THEME 1A: DEVOLVED DECISION MAKING IN SCOTLAND

What You Should Know

SQA:

Decision making in Scotland: the Scottish Parliament as an arena for conflict, co-operation and decision making; functions; organisation of and procedures for business. The Scottish Executive; the respective roles of the First Minister and the Cabinet. The effects of the electoral system on decision making for Scotland at Holyrood level.

Representation of Scottish interests at Westminster. The distribution of powers between the Scottish Parliament and the UK Parliament; co-operation and conflict between the Scottish Parliament and Scottish Executive and the UK Parliament. The effects of the electoral system on Westminster decision making for Scotland.

Local government in Scotland: role, functions, finance and reform. COSLA, co-operation and conflict with the Scottish Executive. The effects of the electoral system on local authority decision making.

This topic can be split into three main sections:

1   The Scottish Parliament
2   The Relationship between the Scottish and UK Parliaments
3   Local Government in Scotland

1 The Scottish Parliament

The main issues covered in this section are:

◆   Scottish politics
◆   Structure of the Scottish Parliament
◆   Founding principles of the Scottish Parliament
◆   The voting system
◆   Election results
◆   Role of an MSP
◆   The work of Parliamentary Committees
◆   The First Minister
◆   Has devolution improved democracy?
◆   Use of devolved powers

Scottish politics

The Scottish Office for many years was the 'unofficial government' of Scotland. The Secretary of State for Scotland presided over (from London) a number of key areas which allowed a Scottish dimension, including education, health, local government, etc.

Scotland went against many of the political trends of the UK, for example during the 1980s and 1990s when the UK had a Conservative Government. Campaigners for Scottish self-government fell into either the 'independence' camp of the Scottish National Party (SNP), or the 'devolution' camp.

The Scottish Constitutional Convention, which included the Labour Party, had been set up in 1989 and was arguing for greater control through a Scottish Parliament. Issues like the Poll Tax caused many Scots to become disillusioned with rule from London and, by the time of the 1997 General Election, only the Conservative Party in Scotland supported the status quo.

With the huge margin of Labour victory in 1997, proposals for a referendum were soon introduced and, in 1997, the people of Scotland voted to have a Scottish Parliament and to give it tax-varying powers. As a result, legislation was introduced to elect a Scottish Parliament in 1999.

Structure of the Scottish Parliament

The Scottish Constitutional Convention had set out a blueprint for the new Parliament in 1995 and this was used largely as the basis for its introduction. Its main features were:

◆ a devolved **Scottish Parliament** within the UK

◆ some powers to be **reserved** for the UK Parliament

◆ some powers to be **devolved** to the Scottish Parliament

◆ functions of the **Scottish Office** to be taken over

◆ **129 MSPs** elected – 73 constituency, 56 Party List

◆ a Scottish **First Minister** to be elected

◆ financed by a **block grant** from the UK Parliament

◆ power to raise or lower **income tax** by 3%.

Figure 1.1 The Scottish Parliament building in Holyrood, Edinburgh

Founding principles of the Scottish Parliament

When the Scottish Parliament was set up there were a number of principles under which it was supposed to operate.

◆ Accessibility – the Parliament in Edinburgh gives easy access to Scots.

◆ Accountability – Members of the Scottish Parliament (MSPs) are accountable to the electorate.

◆ Transparency – open government is to be seen to be operated.

◆ Equal opportunities – more women and minorities could be encouraged.

◆ Distribution of power – the Committee structure will check ministers.

◆ Representative and participation – a wide range of people will be involved.

◆ Consensus and Co-operation – coalition government will help here.

The voting system

The Scottish Constitutional Convention had recommended that a system of proportional representation (PR) be introduced for the elections. The system chosen was to be the **additional member system (AMS).** This was chosen for a number of reasons:

◆ It's easy to understand as it includes elements of simple majority.

◆ All MSPs are linked to a geographical area.

◆ It provides a broadly proportional result.

Two types of ballot paper were given to the voters. There was one for the **Constituency MSP** (73 areas altogether in Scotland), who was elected on the old simple majority system, used in all British elections before.

The country was also divided up into eight regions (e.g. Central Scotland) and voters had to cast a vote for a **Party List** candidate. Each region elected seven MSPs (a total of 56 MSPs from the Party List). Seats were allocated in each region in proportion to the votes cast, though how well the party did in the constituency ballot was also taken into account. The tables below show the results of the 1999 election.

Election results

Table 1.1 Constituency results 1999

Party	Percentage of vote	MSPs
Labour	39%	53
SNP	29%	7
Conservative	16%	0
Liberal Democrat	14%	12
Ind. (Dennis Canavan)		1
Others	3%	
Total		73

Table 1.2 Regional List results 1999

Party	Percentage of vote	MSPs
Labour	33%	3
SNP	28%	28
Conservative	13%	18
Liberal Democrat	15%	5
Scottish Socialist Party	2%	1
Green	4%	1
Others	5%	0
Total		56

Table 1.3 Total number of MSPs 1999: 129

Lab	SNP	Con	LD	SSP	Green	Ind
56	35	18	17	1	1	1

The results meant that no party had an overall majority in the Scottish Parliament, which reflected fairly well the voting and, as a result, the Labour Party and the Liberal Democrats formed the Scottish Executive together in a coalition. Donald Dewar (Labour) became First Minister and Jim Wallace (Liberal Democrat) became his Deputy. The second election took place in 2003 as there is a fixed term of four years for the Scottish Parliament.

Table 1.4 Constituency results 2003

Party	Percentage of vote	MSPs
Labour	35%	46
SNP	24%	9
Conservative	16%	3
Liberal Democrat	15%	13
Others	10%	2
Total		73

Table 1.5 Regional List results 2003

Party	Percentage of vote	MSPs
Labour	29%	4
SNP	21%	18
Conservative	15%	15
Liberal Democrat	12%	4
Scottish Socialist Party	6%	6
Green	7%	7
Others	10%	2
Total		56

Table 1.6 Total number of MSPs: 129

Lab	SNP	Con	LD	SSP	Green	Ind
50	27	18	17	6	7	4

Table 1.7 Comparison of Scottish Parliament Results 1999 and 2003

Party	1999		2003	
	% vote	MSPs	% vote	MSPs
Conservative	14%	18	16%	18
Labour	43%	56	32%	50
Liberal Democrat	13%	17	14%	17
SNP	27%	35	22%	27
Others	3%	3	19%	17
Total		129		129

It is clear that the main parties, particularly Labour and SNP, lost out in 2003 to the minor parties. This may be because people see they can use their second ballot vote as a kind of protest vote.

Role of an MSP

Each MSP has two basic roles: to represent their constituents in Parliament, and to work in the constituency for the electorate. They can perform these jobs in a number of ways.

Parliament:

◆ attending the sessions in the chamber
◆ taking part in debates

◆ asking questions both written and oral (Question Time)

◆ voting on legislation and motions

◆ working in committees.

Constituency:

◆ holding surgeries for their constituents

◆ attending meetings with various groups (councillors)

◆ writing letters on behalf of constituents

◆ attending functions in the constituency.

Figure 1.2 MPs discussing an issue in the debating chamber of the Scottish Parliament

The work of Parliamentary Committees

The Scottish Parliamentary Committees match the main policy areas of the Parliament and are expected to play a leading role in monitoring the power of the Executive. There are seventeen cross-party committees which have the job of scrutinising legislation as it passes through Parliament. They perform a number of jobs, though there are limits attached to their work.

◆ They hold the Scottish Executive to account by examining its work.

◆ Each law passes through a Committee before it is finalised.

◆ They take evidence from members of the public, experts and ministers.

◆ It is suggested that they are the 'engine room of the Parliament'.

◆ The role of the Petitions Committee is seen as being particularly important.

◆ They have the power to introduce Bills when deemed necessary.

However, the following limit their influence as a moderating force.

◆ The Committees' convenors are chosen by the parties in power.

◆ The parties also have a tight grip on the legislation put through Parliament.

◆ Committees could be seen as merely 'rubber stamping' Executive policies.

The First Minister

The **First Minister** (Jack McConnell) is elected by the Parliament, as is the **Presiding Officer** (George Reid). The Scottish Executive or Cabinet is chosen by the First Minister, with each Minister heading a particular policy area. The role of the First Minister is often chosen as a question topic in the exam. The First Minister has a number of jobs to perform but there are checks on his powers. These same rules apply to the functions of the Scottish Executive.

Role of the First Minister

- Responsible for the policies linked to the devolved powers.
- Has the responsibility to ensure policies are implemented.
- Appoints the Ministers in the Scottish Executive (Cabinet).
- Operates as the link between Westminster and the Scottish Parliament.
- Spokesperson for the Executive in the Parliament.

Checks on the power of the First Minister

- Coalition partners (Liberal Democrats) have a say in formulating policies.
- They have to be accommodated inside the Executive (Deputy First Minister).
- First Minister's own party may not like the compromises made on policies.
- First Minister will be under pressure from his party in Westminster (Prime Minister).
- First Minister is accountable to the Scottish Parliament – many more parties there.

Has devolution improved democracy?

One question likely to be asked in the exam is: has devolution given the Scottish people a greater say in how they are governed? There are arguments for and against this view.

Key Points

For the view that devolution has improved democracy

- There is now an elected Parliament in Edinburgh representing Scots.
- The devolved powers are there to be used by Scots for Scots.
- Holyrood is easier to access than Westminster for most Scots.
- There are many more parties represented in Holyrood.
- Elections are every four years instead of usually five.
- The electoral system (AMS) is a lot fairer, it is argued.

Against the view that devolution has improved democracy

- Many important powers are reserved, and there is great use of Sewel Motions (where the UK Parliament legislates on Scotland's behalf and the Scottish Executive adds this to its own legislation).
- Under the electoral system, parties have too much power over Lists.
- Scottish Parliament still depends on Westminster for finance.
- The AMS has resulted in a coalition that nobody voted for.
- Liberal Democrats came fourth but have a say in government policy.

Use of devolved powers

Another likely question in the exam is related to whether or not the Scottish Parliament has used its devolved powers well. There are arguments for and against this view.

Key Points

For the view that devolved powers have been used well

◆ Many decisions have been made using the devolved powers – on health, education, etc.

◆ Scottish solutions have been found for Scottish problems.

◆ Legislation has been passed a lot more quickly than it would have been in London.

◆ Coalition (with Liberal Democrats) has meant a wider range of issues is considered.

◆ Scottish public show more interest in Scottish affairs – media coverage.

Against the view that devolved powers have been used well

◆ More bills started in Westminster than Holyrood – Sewel Motions.

◆ Scottish legislation still often tagged on to Westminster legislation.

◆ Liberal Democrat effectiveness in getting reform is questioned – limited areas.

◆ Coalition has often meant compromises – this pleases few people.

◆ No major reform of health or education has happened.

Possible questions on the Scottish Parliament

◆ To what extent are there limits on the powers of the Scottish Parliament?

◆ Assess the effectiveness of the committees of the Scottish Parliament.

◆ To what extent are there criticisms of the Scottish Parliament?

◆ The Scottish Parliament has improved democracy in Scotland. Discuss.

◆ Critically examine the role of MSPs in the government of Scotland.

◆ Critically examine the ways the Scottish Parliament has used its powers.

◆ To what extent is the role of the Secretary of State for Scotland important?

◆ Assess the effectiveness of the First Minister in the government of Scotland.

Questions and Answers

SAQ 1   The Scottish Parliament has improved democracy in Scotland. Discuss.

(15 marks)

Here you should analyse whether the Scottish Parliament has improved democracy and consider any criticisms that have been made of the Scottish Parliament.

Questions and *Answers* continued ➢

Answer to SAQ 1

When the Scottish Parliament was set up in 1999, it was given a number of devolved powers in areas such as education, health, local government and social work. The Scottish Parliament is able to make decisions over these matters and this means that the Scottish people have a direct input into these matters. It has passed a number of laws, such as free personal care for the elderly, abolition of tuition fees, bans on fox hunting and smoking, which mean the Scottish situation is different from the rest of the UK. However, there are still reserved powers over which the Scottish Parliament has no say, in areas such as defence, foreign policy, economic policy and immigration. The Scottish Parliament also depends on Westminster for finance.

The Scottish Parliament allows the will of the people of Scotland to be seen a lot more clearly now and this has been reflected in the decisions that have been made. This contrasts greatly with the 1980s and the early 1990s when a Conservative Government in London made all the decisions yet had very little support in Scotland. However, many important decisions are still taken in London and added on to Scottish legislation through Sewel Motions.

The AMS electoral system introduced for the Scottish Parliament elections is a form of proportional representation and it results in a greater correlation between votes and seats, which many people say is more democratic. It also gives smaller parties such as the Greens a much greater chance of being represented in the Parliament. However, it has also resulted in a coalition government between the Labour Party and the Liberal Democrats. The Liberal Democrats came fourth in the elections in 1999 and 2003, yet they have a say in the government of the country. The two parties may also have to compromise on their policies to get agreement, and nobody voted for these compromise policies. Parties also have power over which candidates get to be on the lists.

The two-tier system of MSPs, with constituency MSPs and Regional List MSPs, gives people more contact with their local representatives. There are more opportunities for people to raise matters of concern and to have them pursued in the Parliament. However, it can be a bit confusing to some people who don't really know who their MSPs are, particularly the List MSPs; and constituency MSPs complain that they get landed with a lot more work as a result.

The Scottish Parliament has also introduced procedures that make it a much more accessible place than Westminster. It works normal office hours and has modern working practices that may attract more people into politics. It also has the Petitions Committee that allows ordinary people to bring matters directly to the attention of Parliament. However, you probably still need the support of a large party to get elected and not many petitions have been successfully put into law. The turnout at the Scottish Parliament elections has also been poor, with only around 50% of people voting.

In conclusion, there are arguments to say that the Scottish Parliament has improved democracy in Scotland, though there are still some criticisms.

2 The Relationship Between the Scottish and UK Parliaments

The main issues covered in this section are:

◆ The devolved and reserved powers

◆ The Scottish Executive

◆ Secretary of State for Scotland

◆ Scottish representation at Westminster

The devolved and reserved powers

The Scottish Parliament was given a number of areas to control, which are called the **devolved powers**; there are a number of areas left under the control of the UK Parliament, called the **reserved powers**. These powers are listed in the table below:

Devolved powers	Reserved powers
Health	Defence
Education and training	Foreign affairs
Local government	Central economic polices (taxes)
Social work and housing	Social security
Economic development and transport	Immigration
Law and home affairs	Abortion, firearms, drug control
Environment	
Agriculture, forestry and fishing	
Sport and the arts	

Many of the powers given to the Scottish Parliament used to be under the control of the Secretary of State for Scotland and the Scottish Office. As a result, the post of Secretary of State for Scotland is much less important now and the main part of this job is to negotiate the block grant of money from the UK Parliament.

The Scottish Executive

The Scottish Executive is, in effect, the Scottish Cabinet and, since the formation of the Scottish Parliament in 1999, it has contained members from both the Labour Party and Liberal Democrats in a coalition government. Each department has a Minister and a Deputy Minister to run it, with the main departments being the Education Department, the Enterprise, Transport and Lifelong Learning Department, the Finance Department, the Health Department and the Justice Department. These are all areas that cover the devolved powers given to the Scottish Parliament. The Scottish Executive is led by the First Minister who appoints all the other ministers. You should know who some of the main Ministers are.

The Secretary of State for Scotland

The Secretary of State for Scotland sits in the UK Cabinet and is appointed by the Prime Minister. This used to be an important post in the UK Government before the Scottish

Parliament was set up. In recent years, however, the post is not considered to be as important and, in fact, the present holder, Douglas Alexander (2006), has to combine this job with that of Transport Secretary. The Secretary of State for Scotland has to look after Scottish interests in the UK Parliament on reserved matters such as defence. He also has to be the link between Holyrood and Westminster on matters such as the UK Parliament's funding of the Scottish Government, calculated according to the Barnett Formula. As the same party is in power at the moment in Edinburgh and London, there have been few areas of conflict, but that could change with different parties in power.

Scottish representation at Westminster

Representation of Scottish MPs in the UK Parliament was reduced from 72 to 59 in the 2005 General Election, as a result of the setting up of the Scottish Parliament. The 'West Lothian Question', where Scottish MPs can vote on English affairs but English MPs cannot vote on Scottish affairs, has been debated as a controversial issue. It also seems more likely that Scottish people will turn to their MSP rather than their MP, given the wide range of issues covered in the Scottish Parliament, and the role of Scottish MPs may well be diminished as a result.

Disputes between Edinburgh and London are likely to occur and possible conflicts could cause problems if Scottish MSPs want one thing and London does not. The legislation passed on free personal care for the elderly, the abolition of tuition fees, and the early ban on fox hunting and smoking in public places are all areas where the Scottish Parliament has made the law different in Scotland from the rest of the UK.

Possible questions on the relationship between the Scottish and UK Parliaments

There is an overlap between the first section on the Scottish Parliament and this section so you should look at the possible questions in the last section and make sure you have the knowledge to include parts of this section in your answer.

Questions and Answers

SAQ 2 The Scottish Parliament has important powers, but it is only a junior partner in the government of Scotland. Discuss. *(15 marks)*

Here you should analyse the powers of the Scottish Parliament and compare them to the powers of the Westminster Parliament.

Answer to SAQ 2

The Scottish Parliament was set up in 1999 and was given a list of devolved powers: health, education, social work, housing, local government, transport, law and home affairs, fisheries and forestry, sports and the arts. Since it was set up, the Scottish Parliament has passed a number of laws in these areas, notably free personal care for the elderly, abolition of student tuition fees, a ban on fox hunting and a ban on smoking in public places.

Questions and *Answers* continued ➤

Questions and Answers

The UK Parliament in Westminster retained a list of reserved powers, including, defence, foreign policy, social security, taxation, immigration, economic policy, business and employment legislation and ethical issues like abortion. Only the Westminster Parliament can pass legislation in these areas, and many people consider that these are important aspects of Scottish people's lives which are decided by a majority in Westminster. Since 2005, Scottish representation at Westminster has been reduced from 72 to 59 MPs and so Scottish people have less influence over these matters than they used to.

The Scottish Parliament does have the power to raise or lower income tax by up to 3p in the pound, though, by 2006, this was a power that had not been used. The main party in the coalition government in the Scottish Parliament is the Labour Party and it may well be that it is wary of using this power as the Labour Government in London do not want tax levels in Scotland to be different from the rest of the UK. If this is the case, then it may be a power that is not really worth having since it is unlikely to be used. If there was to be a situation where two different parties were in power in Holyrood and Westminster, then perhaps we might see this power become a lot more important.

Westminster also seems to be able to get Holyrood to accept a lot of Sewel Motions. This is where legislation has been passed through the UK Parliament and the Scottish Executive accepts additions to Scottish legislation to bring Scottish law into line with UK law. Perhaps this is an indication of Holyrood accepting that it is a junior partner in the government of Scotland, or it may just be that the Scottish Parliament agrees to these motions as being sensible decisions to take.

The terms that are used to describe the various parts of the Scottish system perhaps show that it is accepted that the Scottish Parliament is not just a junior partner. The Scottish Executive is so-called to distinguish it from the UK Government. The First Minister is the leader of the Scottish Executive as opposed to the Prime Minister. This appears to give the person holding this post a higher status than the head of a local government structure. Jack McConnell is certainly regarded by many as the head of the Scottish 'government'. The Presiding Officer does a similar job to the Speaker in Westminster. The Scottish Parliament has also adopted many up-to-date modern practices like sensible working hours and electronic voting, which has put it far ahead of the old-fashioned House of Commons.

In conclusion, it can be seen that there are many arguments that seem to suggest that the Scottish Parliament is not just a junior partner in the government of Scotland, but really does have a major role to play. However, there are a number of limitations on its power and Westminster does have the final say on many issues.

3 Local Government in Scotland

The main issues covered in this section are:

- Background to local government
- Changes to the structure of local goverment
- The role of local government
- The role of COSLA
- Powers and responsibilities of local authorities
- Local government finance
- Strengths and criticisms of local councils
- Relationship with the Scottish Executive
- Proposals for change
- STV and local council elections

Background to local government

Scottish local government has gone through two complete re-organisations since 1980 and, with the introduction of the Scottish Parliament, further changes are likely to be introduced. Local government plays a huge part in our lives given the range of services provided by our local councils, yet many people feel alienated from the decision making process involving local councils with, on average, only 40% of people turning out to vote. After May 1999, the Scottish Parliament took over responsibility for local government in Scotland and the McIntosh Commission was set up to look at this new relationship.

Changes to the structure of local government

Between 1975 and 1996 Scotland had a **two-tier** structure of local government. There were 12 large Regional Councils (e.g. Strathclyde Regional Council) with more than 50 smaller District Councils (e.g. Hamilton District Council). Regional Councils provided most of the large mandatory services such as education, police, fire, while the District Councils handled the more local services such as housing or cleansing.

In 1996, a system of all-purpose, **unitary** councils was introduced as the regions and districts were merged into 32 councils over Scotland (e.g. South Lanarkshire Council). These new councils have to provide all the services handed down to local government from central government.

The role of local government

Local councillors

Since re-organisation in 1996, residents have one local councillor responsible for all services. The councillor normally lives in the community and can be seen as the voice of the community. He or she will meet voters at surgeries, attend council meetings, attend party political meetings and other functions in their work as councillors. They are not paid a salary but get allowances and expenses for responsibilities such as chairing council committees. Many councils have tended to become much more party political in recent years.

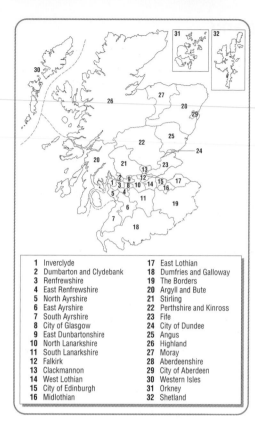

1	Inverclyde	17	East Lothian
2	Dumbarton and Clydebank	18	Dumfries and Galloway
3	Renfrewshire	19	The Borders
4	East Renfrewshire	20	Argyll and Bute
5	North Ayrshire	21	Stirling
6	East Ayrshire	22	Perthshire and Kinross
7	South Ayrshire	23	Fife
8	City of Glasgow	24	City of Dundee
9	East Dunbartonshire	25	Angus
10	North Lanarkshire	26	Highland
11	South Lanarkshire	27	Moray
12	Falkirk	28	Aberdeenshire
13	Clackmannon	29	City of Aberdeen
14	West Lothian	30	Western Isles
15	City of Edinburgh	31	Orkney
16	Midlothian	32	Shetland

Figure 1.3 The 32 local authority regions in Scotland

Local council organisation

The **Leader** of the council is usually a political appointment and can hire and fire council staff and recommend councillors to the chairmanship of important council committees.

The **Group Executive** acts as a disciplined team and ensures the party line is obeyed. It controls the membership of the committees and controls who should speak for the council.

The **Provost** is a civic post and not a political one and is regarded as the first citizen of the council, representing the council at formal functions.

The **committees** play a major role in council business. There are two types of committees – resource committees and service committees.

Resource committees are the most powerful as they deal with general matters affecting the whole council, such as personnel and finance.

Service committees deal with specific council services such as education or social work. The chairperson is usually called the **Convenor**. Where one party dominates a council, this group will dominate council committees and full council meetings can often be no more than rubber stamps.

Council officials are employees of the council and liaise with convenors to provide the best information and advice they can. Each council department will have a Director, and a Chief Executive will head up all the Directors.

The role of COSLA

Local government in Scotland is represented by the Convention of Scottish Local Authorities (COSLA). Formed in 1975, COSLA exists to promote and protect the interests of councils in Scotland by providing a forum for discussion of matters of common concern. COSLA finds out the views of member councils and communicates these to central government, other bodies and the public.

The Convention is the ruling body, which has overall control of COSLA's policy and direction. It consists of representatives from all 32 member councils and political groups represented within Scottish local government. The Convention meets three times a year in different venues throughout Scotland. The main decision making body is the Leaders Meeting, which is held eight times each year and is attended by the political leaders from all member councils.

Powers and responsibilities of local authorities

Local council services

Local councils are responsible for providing a wide range of services for the local community. Some of these services are mandatory services: they have to be provided by the councils, for example education, police, fire services. Other services are discretionary services: they can be provided if the council decides to and if they have the money for them, for example leisure services. The main services are shown below:

- Education
- Social work
- Housing
- Leisure services
- Roads
- Police
- Fire
- Planning
- Environmental services

The Scottish Parliament allocates funds to the local councils, and councils can raise their own finance through means such as Council Tax.

Local government finance

Local government in Scotland is financed in a number of ways:

- **Revenue Support Grant** ('block grant') from the Scottish Parliament. This provides around 80% of councils funding and is very crucial to how councils work
- **Non-Domestic Rates** (taxes on businesses in the local area). Councils can set business rates in their area
- **Council Tax** (local taxation from local residents). Councils can decide the levels of Council Tax for their area, but increases can be controlled by the Scottish Parliament.

Councils also get some income from charges for their services, for example charges for swimming pools, but this forms only a small proportion of their overall income. In the 1980s, the Conservatives cut back on the 'block grant' and forced councils to cut back on their services. The 'block grant' is still the council's main source of income and today councils can only get about 20% of their income from their own sources. Councils were also forced by the Government to sell off or 'privatise' their assets (council houses) and put services out to 'competitive tendering'. The introduction of the Private Finance Initiative (PFI) and Public–Private Partnerships (PPPs) has allowed councils to finance projects (schools and housing) in another way. Councils can also get money through the Challenge Fund and the New Opportunities Fund.

Strengths and criticisms of local councils

You are often asked about the part played by local government in Scotland and you should be prepared to look at the benefits achieved by local councils and the criticisms of their role.

Key Points

Strengths of local councils

◆ Councils provide a wide range of services for their communities.

◆ Councils provide for local democracy in the local area.

◆ Councils work to attract both government and private investment.

◆ Councils must set performance targets and monitor their work to ensure 'best value'.

Criticisms of local councils

◆ Scottish Parliament has taken greater control of councils and services.

◆ Councils have many more administrative posts and greater bureaucracy.

◆ Council Tax is rising more rapidly than inflation – no perceived improvement in services.

◆ Some smaller councils find it difficult to provide services efficiently.

◆ Increase in use of PPPs and privatisation has reduced the role of councils.

◆ There has been evidence of corruption and inefficiency in some councils.

◆ Low voter turnout in council elections could be evidence of apathy.

Relationship with the Scottish Executive

The Scottish Parliament has overall responsibility for legislation and policy concerning local government. The Scottish Executive is also responsible for allocating money to councils and controlling their investment expenditure.

In March 2002, the Scottish Executive published a white paper called 'Renewing Local Democracy – The Next Steps' where they outlined the proposals for improvements in the way local councils represent the communities they serve. They suggested a number of changes – removing some barriers to people who might wish to stand as councillors (reducing the age from 21 to 18), introducing a new electoral system (single transferable vote, STV, from 2007 elections) and discussing the possibility of ending allowances and introducing salaries for councillors. COSLA and other bodies supported the proposals put forward by the Scottish Executive.

The Scottish Executive also gave a commitment to setting up an improvement service for local councils in the document called 'Building a Better Scotland' which also announced increases in spending to improve local services.

There are a number of areas where the Scottish Executive and local councils have come into conflict with each other:

Financial problems

The problems with the Direct Labour Organisations (DLOs) in 1998, where evidence of huge bonuses and overtime payments came to light, caused Donald Dewar to announce an inquiry into all 32 councils' DLOs. Poor financial management was blamed, and councils were ordered to show immediate improvements or face the closure of their DLOs. North Lanarkshire and East Ayrshire were ordered to put out their contracts to private tender from 1999. Since the Local Government (Scotland) Act 2003, local councils have been subject to 'best value' scrutiny by the Scottish Parliament. Local councils have to prove not only that they are seeking the most cost-effective way of providing services, but also that they are providing the highest-quality service too. Councils who do not meet these conditions can be closed down and have their services taken over by the Scottish Executive. In June 2005, Inverclyde Council was given a short time to turn itself round or face being taken over.

Corruption and sleaze

There have been a number of scandals in recent years involving allegations of bribery, criminal activity and general misconduct in local councils. The Glasgow Labour Party investigated allegations of 'cronyism' and votes for trips; nine councillors were suspended including Provost Pat Lally, though he won a legal battle in court against the party. There have also been problems in Renfrewshire and the SNP-run Moray Council, where the Chief Executive was dismissed on the grounds of severe misconduct.

These scandals have shaken public confidence in local democracy and prompted calls for the Scottish Parliament to exercise greater control over the operation of local government. This is being resisted by those in local government who feel centralisation of power would be contrary to the whole devolution process taking place in Scotland.

Lack of accountability

The number of people voting in local elections has been traditionally low, with average turnout being only 40%. Supporters of electoral reform argue that simple majority gives results that are biased in favour of Labour. In Glasgow, for instance, opposition parties won 38% of the vote but only 6 out of 83 seats. This means there is little chance of the opposition scrutinising effectively the council's activities.

To improve turnout, the 2002 elections were put back a year to coincide with the Scottish Parliament elections in 2003. The McIntosh Commission has also recommended a system of PR for local councils, and the Scottish Executive has agreed to this. The STV system will be introduced in the 2007 local council elections. This has caused concern amongst Labour councillors, as many could lose their seats.

Other sources of conflict

Two areas of the provision of council services have caused some controversy in recent years:

Private Finance Initiative (PFI) and Public–Private Partnerships (PPPs)

Councils are restricted in the amount of money they get and they don't want to raise Council Tax, or they or are discouraged by the Scottish Parliament from doing so. One way of starting new projects is to get involved in PFI. This was started by the Conservatives in the 1990s but Labour has continued with what they call Public–Private Partnerships (PPPs). Schools, leisure centres and roads can be built with private sector money and rented back to the councils. There has been opposition and criticism about who would own these facilities and the conditions the workers would have to endure.

Direct Labour Organisations (DLOs)

DLOs employ their own workers to deliver council services such as housing maintenance and road repairs. They hit the headlines in the mid-1990s when two in particular, North Lanarkshire and East Ayrshire, reported substantial losses. Accusations of bad management and even corruption were levelled against them, and the investigations showed that some money could have been saved. More local councils are now planning to be enabling authorities rather than providers and will be shopping around, which may mean the end of more DLOs.

Proposals for change

The McIntosh Commission and the Kerley Committee were set up in 1999 to look at, and attempt to improve and modernise, the relationship between central and local government in Scotland. They made a number of recommendations:

a) Proportional representation (STV) – to be introduced in 2007 elections

b) Standards – a new code of conduct for councillors

c) Selection of councillors – salaries (2007) to attract top candidates, four-year terms

d) Structure – directly elected Provost, council 'cabinets' or executives.

Some of these have been implemented, while other proposals are still under consideration.

STV and local council elections

Starting in 2007, all local council elections will use the single transferable vote (STV) system. Local council wards will be either three- or four-member constituencies, with the existing boundaries of the 32 local councils staying the same. There had been criticism for some time about the dominance of some councils by one party, especially in central Scotland, and the corresponding low turnout levels for local elections. The Liberal Democrats had also been looking for some move to proportional representation and this was the price paid by the Labour Party for the continuation of the coalition government in Holyrood. It is likely that some councillors, who could take their seat for granted in the past, will find it more difficult now that more power is in the hands of voters because of the preferences of STV. There are likely to be a few more coalition governments in council areas as well.

Possible questions on local government in Scotland

◆ Critically examine the changes made to system of local government in 1996.

◆ To what extent does local government provide an effective service for the people of Scotland?

◆ Assess the effectiveness of the structure and organisation of local government in Scotland.

◆ Local government in Scotland plays an important part in people's lives. Discuss.

◆ Assess the effectiveness of attempts to improve participation in local government.

◆ Examine the way local government in Scotland is financed.

◆ To what extent are there criticisms of local government in Scotland?

◆ Critically examine any issues of conflict between local and central government.

◆ There is disagreement between Scottish Executive and local authorities. Discuss.

Questions and Answers

SAQ 3 To what extent does local government provide an effective service for the people of Scotland? *(15 marks)*

Here you should analyse the job that local councils do in Scotland and give a developed conclusion stating how effective the service is.

Answer to SAQ 3

In 1996, local councils in Scotland were re-organised, from two-tier authorities to 32 single-tier councils. The administrative costs of moving from one structure to another were quite considerable and there were many more executive posts created within the new structure, though the number of councils was reduced.

The old Regional Councils, such as Strathclyde Regional Council, were said to be large enough to provide many of the services on an efficient basis. Even though some of these services are still provided by Joint Boards, e.g. Strathclyde Police and Fire Services, many of the smaller councils find it very difficult to provide the full range of services. It is arguable whether some of these smaller councils are viable.

The cost of running all these councils seems to be rising every year. Council Tax rises are invariably higher than inflation and many people complain that they don't see any improvement in the services. In fact, there have been a number of cuts in council services in key areas such as community care services and education. The abolition of councils, however, would not necessarily mean a reduction in the cost of providing services.

The setting up of the Scottish Parliament has seen more and more power put into the hands of Holyrood. The Scottish Executive decides how much money councils get, they can ensure councils act within government policies and they set targets for 'best value'. Some people would argue that this means the role of local councils is a lot less important now. However, it is argued that local councils are an important part of democracy.

The Scottish Parliament has also promoted the idea of Public–Private Partnerships (PPPs) for many council building programmes in areas such as schools and housing. This has reduced the ability of local councils to co-ordinate and plan services as effectively as they once did and has led some people to say local government is a lot less important now than it used to be. However, it is local councils who monitor and evaluate these PPP schemes.

There has also been evidence of corruption and inefficiency in local government. North Lanarkshire Council, West Ayrshire Council and Inverclyde have all been criticised for the way they have conducted their affairs. It is not surprising perhaps that the turnout at local elections has been as low as 12% in some areas. This is an indication of apathy on the part of local people where their local councils are concerned. However, the vast majority of local councils are seen to provide valuable services to their community with little hint of trouble.

In conclusion, it can be seen that there are a number of criticisms that can be made of local government in Scotland. However, local councils still provide for many people the best way of delivering local services to local areas.

STUDY THEME 1B: DECISION MAKING IN CENTRAL GOVERNMENT

What You Should Know

SQA:

The Executive; the respective roles of the Prime Minister and Cabinet; accountability to Parliament; the role of senior civil servants in the UK political system.

Parliament (House of Commons and House of Lords) as an arena for conflict, co-operation and decision making; functions; organisation of and procedures for business.

Influences on the decision making process in the UK: the extent of these pressures, their impact and legitimacy.

This topic can be split into three main sections:

1   The Executive (Prime Minister and Cabinet)

2   The Houses of Parliament

3   Pressure Groups.

1 The Executive (Prime Minister and Cabinet)

The main issues covered in this section are:

◆   Powers of the Prime Minister

◆   Checks on the power of the Prime Minister

◆   Role of the Cabinet

◆   Role of the Cabinet Minister

◆   Relationship between the Prime Minister and the Cabinet

◆   Role of senior civil servants and special advisors.

Powers of the Prime Minister

After an election, the leader of the winning party takes on the post of Prime Minister and then has the job of governing the country. In Britain, the Prime Minister is head of the Executive branch of government (the decision making function) and also has a part to play in the Legislative branch (law making function), as leader of the largest party in the House of Commons.

The Prime Minister's powers

◆   **Power of appointment**. The Prime Minister (PM) has to appoint the members of the Cabinet, who are the leading ministers in the Government. He or she can also reshuffle the Cabinet at any time and is able to appoint other junior ministers in the Government, civil service posts, create life peers, and award honours.

◆ **Controlling government business**. The PM usually sets the agenda at Cabinet meetings. Prime Ministers also set up Cabinet sub-committees, and appoint their own advisers and policy units.

◆ **Policy development and presentation**. The Cabinet originates all policies and the PM is at the heart of this. He or she is the spokesperson for the Government, and leads the party in the House of Commons. The PM also controls how these policies are presented through the PM's press office, in party briefings and the use of the media.

◆ **Represents the UK abroad**. The PM attends summit meetings such as Commonwealth and EU meetings with other world leaders. He or she also plays a key role in foreign and economic policy.

◆ **Calls a general election**. The PM can decide the date of a general election and is able to capitalise on favourable publicity at any particular time.

In all of these areas, it is important to remember that how these powers are used depends heavily on the style, personality, leadership qualities, and handling of PM's Question Time, of the individual concerned. Margaret Thatcher was a very strong personality, who did not suffer many alternative viewpoints, a fact that probably brought about her downfall. John Major was much more prepared to listen to others and go with the majority view, again probably contributing to his defeat. Tony Blair seems to have tried to stay above party politics as far as possible and make the role of the PM more presidential.

Figure 2.1 Prime Minister's Question Time at the House of Commons in London

Checks on the power of the Prime Minister

Prime Ministers appear to have considerable power over the decision making process, but there are a number of limits to their powers:

◆ **Party support**. The PM must continue to carry the support of Members of Parliament (MPs) as PMs need to stand for re-election each year. The challenge to Margaret Thatcher in 1990 led to her stepping down from the leadership as many MPs thought the party would not win the next election with her as leader.

◆ **Powerful colleagues**. The PM may be forced to include powerful party figures in the Cabinet who do not share the same views on political matters. This binds them through collective responsibility into supporting the PM and stops them being the focus of opposition on the backbenches.

◆ **Power of the media**. Media coverage may strengthen or weaken the PM's position. Given the power of the media in determining the result of elections, it is important that the PM is seen to be in control. John Major suffered through his lack of control of certain ministers over Europe. Tony Blair, on the other hand, was seen as keeping everyone 'on message' most of the time.

◆ **Power of the electorate**. Every PM has to seek re-election at least every five years, and unpopular parties will not be re-elected. PMs who lose general elections will normally lose leadership of their parties, as happened with Major in 1997. Margaret Thatcher lost the leadership in 1990 due to the belief that the party might not win the election.

Role of the Cabinet

As the leading institution of the Government, the Cabinet:

◆ decides the major policies of the Government

◆ plans the legislative calendar of business of Parliament

◆ settles disputes between government departments

◆ ensures that government departments follow policies

◆ reviews and evaluates the work of the Government.

These various functions can be performed within the Cabinet itself or through the Cabinet sub-committees. There are also an increasing number of informal groups set up by the Cabinet to help with the formulation of policy.

The Cabinet Office also exists to assist in decision making. You should also be aware of the doctrine of collective responsibility.

Role of the Cabinet Minister

Each individual Cabinet Minister also has responsibilities outwith their role as a member of the Cabinet.

◆ They head an important department and make the day-to-day decisions.

◆ They put forward legislative proposals for their department.

◆ They fight for the best funding they can get for their department.

◆ They work closely with the civil servants in their department.

◆ They answer questions in Parliament and committees about the department.

Relationship between the Prime Minister and the Cabinet

Typical questions in this section look at the role and powers of the Prime Minister in relation to colleagues in the Cabinet. How powerful is the Prime Minister and what limitations are there on his powers?

Key Points

Prime Minister: strengths	Cabinet: challenges
Elected by the party as leader	Can challenge for leadership of party
Chooses the members of the Cabinet	Can form groups or factions around them
Seen as the Head of the Government	Can use media to brief against some policies or individuals
Has overall view of Government policy	Have the expertise of their departments behind them
Has many powers of patronage	

The roles of senior civil servants and special advisors

The Civil Service consists of full-time professional employees who are supposed to assist the Government in implementing policy and offering advice. Civil servants have a number of responsibilities:

◆ They provide information to help Ministers run departments.

◆ They develop expertise in the work of their department.

◆ They help Ministers with written and oral questions in Parliament.

◆ They draft reports and strategy documents for the Minister.

Civil servants are supposed to be impartial when offering help and advice. There are a number of difficulties with this role, which can mean that civil servants may not offer impartial advice all the time:

◆ Civil servants may have built up a number of years expertise and knowledge, whereas the Minister may only be in post for a short time.

◆ If civil servants have worked for one party in government, they may have difficulty in adapting to new political masters.

◆ Top civil servants may share social and educational backgrounds with Conservative MPs and may find it hard to work with other parties.

◆ The career structure of the civil service may mean that civil servants who wish to enhance their careers will aim to 'please' ministers with their advice.

Possible questions on the Prime Minister and the Cabinet

◆ The Prime Minister is the most powerful figure in UK politics. Discuss.

◆ Critically examine the powers of Cabinet Ministers.

◆ Assess the effectiveness of the part played by civil servants in the UK.

Questions and Answers

SAQ 1   The Prime Minister is the most powerful figure in UK politics. Discuss.

(15 marks)

> Here you should analyse the powers of the Prime Minister and the
> limitations there may be on them.

Answer to SAQ 1

In the UK system of government, the Prime Minister is elected by MPs in Parliament. He or she is likely to be the leader of the winning party after the election. The winning party usually has a majority in Parliament and this means the PM will have a strong base to carry out policies throughout the term of Parliament. The PM can, however, face leadership challenges during their term in office. In 1990, Margaret Thatcher faced a leadership challenge while PM and eventually was forced to resign due to a lack of support among Conservative MPs.

The PM chooses the other ministers in the Cabinet and he or she can set the agenda for Cabinet meetings. The PM also has a great deal of power through patronage when appointing to other posts. This means the PM can usually appoint friends or like-minded people into positions of power in the Government. These people owe their position to the PM and the doctrine of collective responsibility means they will usually support the PM and the Government. However, there may well be important or influential figures within the party that the PM feels he or she cannot leave out of Government. It may be better to include some people in Government rather than have them attacking from the backbenches.

The PM also has the Cabinet Office to back him or her up. The PM may also have a large number of personal advisers who owe their position to the PM alone and who can usually be relied upon to be loyal and trustworthy. However, the PM has no one else to blame if these people make mistakes or errors of judgement.

The PM today is also the focus of the attention of the media. He or she is the spokesperson for the nation, and major statements of policy are often announced by the PM. During an election campaign the PM is at the centre of things. He or she will gain the credit if things go well. However, he or she can also be blamed for any defeats or if any of the party's policies become unpopular. If, near an election, the PM's popularity is declining, the party may well consider removing him/her in order to win.

The PM is in a position to have an overall view of government policies. This may give him an advantage if individuals challenge him on any areas. However, the PM may not know the details of policy in individual departments, and Ministers in these departments may be more aware of how things are.

In conclusion, the PM does have a lot of power in the UK political system. However, there are a number of checks and balances on this power.

2 The Houses of Parliament

The main issues covered in this section are:

◆ Role of the House of Commons

◆ Role of an MP

◆ Demands on an MP

◆ How representative are MPs?

◆ Role of the House of Lords

The UK Parliament consists of three elements: the House of Commons, the House of Lords and the Monarchy. All three have to work together to ensure the legislative process of government is carried out.

Role of the House of Commons

The House of Commons has 646 members elected by simple majority with the Government being the 'winning' party. The House of Commons has four main functions:

◆ **Controlling finance**. The Chancellor of the Exchequer outlines the Budget – the Government's **income and spending** plans. The House of Commons debates this, votes on it, and checks it through the Public Accounts Committee.

◆ **Scrutinising the work of the Government**. Select Committees can call witnesses to explain department policies. Each Minister can be asked questions in Parliament. They can give written answers or can appear at **Question Time** in the House of Commons. Prime Minister's Question Time is every Wednesday. There are also Adjournment Debates and Opposition Days.

◆ **Protecting individuals**. Any citizen of the UK can petition the House of Commons and ask for protection; individual MPs must also make themselves available for consultation with constituents who may **lobby** them at the House.

◆ **Making laws. Legislation** is the main business of the House of Commons. Bills go through a number of stages in the Commons before also going through the Lords and then getting the Royal Assent.

Role of an MP

Members of Parliament (MPs) are chosen by the people of a constituency to represent them in the decision making process. The duties of MPs can be split into two main areas, which are closely linked to the places they can expect to be at certain times of the week. From Monday to Friday, an MP is most likely to be in Parliament and will perform a number of duties. At weekends/holidays, an MP is in the constituency.

Parliamentary work

◆ MPs can ask questions at **Question Time** – Wednesday PM's questions.

◆ MPs can take part in **debates** on important issues – e.g. Iraq War.

◆ MPs can **vote** in Divisions on Laws – e.g. ban on handguns.

◆ MPs can attend **Committee Meetings** – e.g. Select Committee on Defence.

◆ MPs can attend meetings of their own **Parliamentary Party.**

◆ MPs can deal with the **mass media** – e.g. give television interviews.

◆ MPs can meet with **'lobbyists'** – e.g. constituency groups, professionals.

Constituency work

◆ MPs can hold monthly **surgeries** to hear complaints – from e.g. local people.

◆ MPs can reply to **letters** sent to them by constituents – e.g. local issues.

◆ MPs can be the **link** between central and local government – e.g. local councils.

◆ MPs can hold meetings with their local **Constituency Party** – e.g. selection.

◆ MPs can maintain a **high profile** in the area – e.g. attend functions, appear in local papers.

Demands on an MP

MPs are representatives, not delegates; they are free to decide which way to go on any issue. There are, however, a number of demands on MPs that they need to take into account:

◆ **The party**. MPs are normally elected as candidates for a party. The party will expect each MP in return to support it – this is known as the whip system. Some backbench MPs may feel strongly enough about certain issues to vote against the party, but this is rare: e.g. some Labour MPs voted against a Labour Party proposal for 90 day detention for terror suspects.

◆ **Constituency matters**. MPs need to remember that their local constituency has to be looked after and, at times, the interests of their constituency may conflict with the interests of their party.

◆ **National interest**. At times issues of national security arise, or issues to do with the interests of the country, e.g. the Gulf War, European Union, etc.

◆ **Conscience**. There are issues where the party may not have a set view and MPs have a free vote – e.g. on abortion, divorce, capital punishment.

◆ **Pressure groups**. MPs are continually being lobbied by various pressure groups and may even be paid as consultants for some.

How representative are MPs?

In the past it was clear that the system provided us with MPs that were mostly white, male, middle-aged, highly educated professionals. It was seen as an 'old boys network' where narrow sectional interests were put forward. Recently, changes to this picture of the typical MP have emerged.

Ethnic minorities

The first ethnic minority MPs were elected in 1987; they were four Labour MPs. This increased to six in 1992, nine in 1997, and twelve in 2005. Mohammed Sarwar (Glasgow Govan) became the first Muslim MP in 1997. Ethnic minorities make up 5% of the population, but still account for under 2% of MPs, so although there has been an improvement the balance is still not representative of the population.

Women MPs

In 1983 there were 23 women MPs, in 1987 this increased to 41 women MPs, in 1992 it increased further to 60, but the big increase was in 1997 when 120 women MPs were elected, 101 of them from the Labour Party. Although 1997 marked a major change in electing women MPs, women are still only around 18% of the total.

Average age

The average age of MPs up until 1997 was in the range 50–60. Conservative MPs had been in office for a long time and it was traditional to have to 'serve your apprenticeship' before you became a candidate. New Labour chose a lot of younger candidates in 1997 to appeal to a wider range of voters and, with their landslide victory, a lot more of them were elected than even the party thought possible. The average age is much lower now than it was in the past.

Highly educated professionals

MPs in the main still come from the professions, though there has been a shift from the Conservative professions of directors, lawyers and consultants to the Labour professions of lecturers, teachers and journalists, with the New Labour victory in 1997. There are also fewer MPs from public schools and Oxford and Cambridge universities, and a lot more from comprehensive schools and the new universities, set up by Labour in the 1960s. Many of these new Labour MPs are first-generation middle class.

Role of the House of Lords

The House of Lords has gone through several changes in recent years. Up until 1999, all of the hereditary peers (not elected but holding titles they inherited) could sit in the House. The 1999 House of Lords Act reduced the number of hereditary peers to 92, alongside 527 life peers, 26 bishops and 28 law lords. Most countries around the world have a legislature that has two chambers – usually an Upper and a Lower Chamber. The Lower Chamber is usually stronger than the Upper Chamber, but the House of Lords, like many Upper Chambers, has a number of functions:

◆ It carries out tasks that the Lower Chamber (House of Commons) does not have the time to do, like tidying up legislation that has been passed through the House of Commons.

◆ It gives minority groups representation they may not get elsewhere, by allowing debates on issues of public interest.

◆ It can act as a delaying and steadying influence on the Lower Chamber through Question Time, Select Committees and debates.

◆ It has the highest court in the land and considers the last stages of appeals in the court system.

Reform of the House of Lords

In 1999 the Wakeham Commission, set up to look into the reform of the House of Lords, reported that the House of Lords should remain a largely appointed house of about 600 members with a few elected members, around 120. Supporters of a more democratic chamber were disappointed that the parties would still control a lot of the appointments.

Possible questions on the Houses of Parliament

◆ To what extent is Parliament able to limit the powers of the Government?

◆ Critically examine the role of MPs in the UK system of government.

◆ Assess the effectiveness of the House of Lords in using its powers.

Questions and Answers

SAQ 2 To what extent is Parliament able to limit the powers of the Government?

(15 marks)

Here you should look at the ability of Parliament to limit the powers of the Prime Minister and the Cabinet, analysing this in a balanced way.

Answer to SAQ 2

In Parliament, there are a number of opportunities for parties and individual MPs to control the power of the PM and Cabinet. Each week, MPs get the chance to question the PM and other Ministers during Question Time. This is an opportunity for them to put the PM on the spot and raise questions about Government policy or constituency matters. However, the PM usually comes well prepared with answers written by his advisers or the Cabinet secretariat and it is unusual to catch him unawares.

Similarly, during debates, individual MPs and the Opposition spokespersons can challenge the Government. There are debates on issues of national importance and debates on legislation going through Parliament. However, the PM and other Ministers may only stay for the start of the debates, and individual MPs may not get called to speak at that time. The Government also controls the agenda in Parliament and the time allowed for debates so the Opposition may not get many opportunities.

If the Government has a large majority in Parliament, as it had in the 1997 and the 2001 Governments, then it would be unlikely that the Government would suffer any defeats in the House of Commons. Any threat of a vote of no confidence could also be met by a threat of dissolution. Few MPs would like the prospect of standing in an election midway through a Parliament.

If the Government does have a large majority, some Government backbench MPs may think rebelling is a relatively safe option. However, the whip system is very strong and there is an incentive for MPs to toe the party line if they want any kind of promotion or advancement in Government.

The House of Lords has opposed the Government from time to time, but its powers are very limited and the Government can usually overcome any opposition by passing the legislation through the House of Commons.

In conclusion, the Houses of Parliament have a number of opportunities to limit the power of the PM and the Cabinet, but there are ways for the Government to get round these.

3 Pressure groups

The main issues covered in this section are:

◆ Types of pressure group

◆ Pressure group activities

◆ Pressure groups and democracy

◆ Mass media influence

Types of pressure groups

Being able to influence the decisions taken by a government is a healthy sign of a democracy at work. Groups of people who wish to influence Government will come together to improve their chances of doing so. They are often called pressure groups. They fall into different categories.

◆ **Cause**. These pressure groups tend to have a particular cause that they try to promote. They can be either sectional or attitude groups.

– **Sectional** groups are concerned about the way the Government deals with the less fortunate members of society. Examples: Shelter, Age Concern, Child Poverty Action Group.

– **Attitude** groups are concerned about the effects of modern life on our environment and promote a point of view. Examples: Greenpeace, Friends of the Earth, RAC, AA.

◆ **Interest**. These pressure groups represent the interests of people involved in business in general or in a certain business or industry.

Examples: Confederation of British Industry (CBI), Institute of Directors, Transport and General Workers Union (TGWU).

Pressure group activities

The extent to which a pressure group can promote its interest depends largely on whether it is an insider or outsider group. Insider groups use more consultation, while outsider groups rely more on direct action to generate public opinion.

There are a number of ways that pressure groups can apply pressure; these are listed below in order of likely effectiveness.

◆ **Government**. The pressure group may be asked by the Government to provide expert advice on its area of concern. Through this direct contact with Ministers, its ideas may be more easily accepted. Professional lobbyists could be used.

◆ **Parliament**. If the pressure group is unable to get direct access to the Ministers who make the decisions, they may try to influence MPs. MPs have the chance to introduce Private Members Bills, can act as sponsors of groups, and be consultants for groups.

◆ **Public opinion**. Pressure groups may mobilise public opinion behind their cause and so exert pressure on the Government in this way.

◆ **Organisation**. By having good levels of subscriptions, good public image, good leaders to speak for them, and a sound organisation, the pressure group may promote its cause more favourably.

Pressure groups and democracy

Pressure groups can be viewed as an essential part of a healthy democracy as they allow participation in decision making between elections. Some people argue that not all groups have the same opportunities to influence decisions.

Key Points

Arguments for the effectiveness of pressure groups

◆ They provide expert information and can guide policy development.

◆ They add to the process of open and effective government.

◆ They can ensure minority opinions are reflected.

◆ They provide opportunities for citizens to participate in the political process.

Arguments against the effectiveness of pressure groups

◆ Insider groups can influence the Government before formal policies are known.

◆ Well-resourced groups who represent the privileged have a big advantage.

◆ Many discussions are behind closed doors and are not 'open' government.

◆ Government policies may be compromised to suit the views of some groups.

Pressure group effectiveness

In the 1960s and 1970s, the government met regularly with powerful economic pressure groups such as the trade unions and the CBI. The Conservatives under Margaret Thatcher, however, followed their own policies without much consultation, and the importance of these groups declined. New Labour appears to be adopting a more inclusive policy as far as pressure group consultation is concerned, although we are unlikely to return to the days of heavy influence, as in the 1960s and 1970s.

Those groups likely to have any influence with the government are insider groups, or groups which share the following characteristics:

◆ They represent powerful economic and professional interests.

◆ They are well-resourced, with sound leadership, administration and finances.

◆ They have been successful in attracting members, particularly middle class.

◆ They have a high level of expertise in their chosen field.

◆ They can generate public opinion in their favour through direct action.

The influence of pressure groups and the strategies they employ is to a great extent dependent on whether they are insider or outsider groups.

Insider groups

Insider groups are those which the Government thinks may help in the decision making process; they will be asked for their views and opinions. Examples are the Police Federation and the National Farmers Union. Most are powerful economic groups though some cause groups may have the Government's attention because of public opinion on a particular issue. Insider groups share the following features:

◆ They may have expert information – e.g. Howard League for Penal Reform.

◆ They may have a large middle-class membership, and a good structure.

◆ Their policies are in line with the current Government's thinking.

◆ They have powerful sanctions and political leverage – e.g. trade unions, CBI.

Outsider groups

Outsider Groups are either at odds with the Government's views on an issue or deliberately reject insider status as they want to have a free hand to influence decisions. They often favour highly co-ordinated public campaigns to mobilise public opinion. Examples are Greenpeace, CND, Friends of the Earth.

Mass media influence

The influence of the mass media on voting has become an important issue. This subject is examined in further detail on pages 58–61.

Figure 2.2 Greenpeace protesters disrupt a keynote speech by the Prime Minister

Possible questions on pressure groups

◆ Critically examine the view that pressure groups are a threat to democracy.

◆ To what extent do pressure groups have a role to play in a democracy?

◆ Assess the effectiveness of the influence of the mass media in a democracy.

Questions and Answers

SAQ 3 Critically examine the view that pressure groups are a threat to democracy.
(15 marks)

Here you should look at the role of different types of pressure group in a democracy, and whether or not they are a threat to democracy.

Questions and Answers continued ➤

Questions and Answers

Answer to SAQ 3

In a democracy, groups of people are free to organise themselves in order to be able to influence the Government. At election time, people are able to have their say by voting for the party they think will do the best job of running the country. In between elections, and this could be as long as five years, people have to have other ways of influencing government decisions. Many people do this through membership of pressure groups. There are many cause groups, such as Shelter and Age Concern, or Greenpeace and Friends of the Earth, who have their own areas of influence. There are also many sectional groups such as the CBI and UNISON who also represent their members' interests.

Some pressure groups provide the public with expert information and can help the Government to formulate policy on an educated basis. The British Medical Association often helps the Government with expert views and opinions on how the National Health Service could be improved. However, many discussions take place behind closed doors, and alternative views and opinions that the Government does not like may be ignored completely.

By consulting with pressure groups in this way, the Government may add to open and informed comment on policies before they are decided upon. But those pressure groups that are well financed and resourced may have a much bigger say in policies than other groups. They may, for instance, be able to employ professional lobbyists, which many people regard as having a corrupting effect on Parliament and on MPs. Insider groups are considered by many as having too much influence as they have direct contact with Ministers that other groups might not have.

Pressure groups also allow minority views and opinions to be heard, which is one of the cornerstones of a democracy. However, these minority views may carry a lot more weight than they should if the minority group serves strong and powerful interests. These minority views may also be shown through direct action, which often involves the use of illegal tactics. Anti-motorway protesters involved in digging holes or tree-sitting may be regarded by many as having no place in a democracy.

Leaders of many pressure groups are un-elected and unaccountable to the public, and the groups often have a relatively small active membership. They can sometimes be financed by secret donors and there has been concern recently over the links between pressure groups and their support for political parties. However, they can often get information from the Government that would otherwise be difficult for individuals to get and there are safeguards in place to ensure the Government is not swayed secretly through donations or loans.

In conclusion, there are many arguments to say that pressure groups are good for democracy; however, there are a number of opposing arguments as well.

STUDY THEME 1C: POLITICAL PARTIES AND THEIR POLICIES

What You Should Know

SQA:

Political parties: ideology, membership, organisation and finance; influences on the decisions within parties and on the formulating of party policies; the role of party leaders, MPs, party members, the media and voters.

Conflict and consensus within and between parties; ideological differences within and between parties; reasons for changes in party ideologies and/or policies. Electoral success.

Party policies on taxation, law and order, education and Europe: trends and differences.

The topic can be split into three main sections:

1 Party Organisation and Structure

2 Parties and Electoral Success

3 Parties and their Policies.

You must refer to the four main Scottish parties in the context of the SQA exams.

1 Party Organisation and Structure

The main issues covered in this section are:

◆ Ideology and policy

◆ Organisation, finance and decision making

◆ Party leaders.

Ideology and policy

Political parties are groups of people who have similar views on a wide range of issues and who want to gain power to put in place their own policies to address these issues in practice. They want to govern the country. We will look at where the main parties lie in relation to each other in terms of how they want the country to be governed.

You will often hear the terms 'left wing' and 'right wing' being used to describe a political party in relation to certain ideologies.

A simple way of explaining this is to say that 'left wing' parties want to see the Government being involved a lot in the way people live. The terms socialism and communism are often used to describe the ideology of these types of party. On the other hand, 'right wing' parties prefer governments to stay out of people's lives and allow individuals and private organisations freedom to look after their own affairs. The terms capitalism and conservatism are often used to describe the ideologies of these types of party. The diagram below shows where the main British parties lie in relation to each other on the political spectrum.

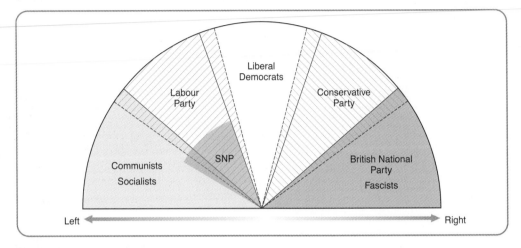

Figure 3.1 The place of British political parties on the left–right political spectrum

Organisation, finance and decision making

We will look at each of the main parties in turn and examine how it is organised, what its main sources of finance are and how decisions are made.

The Conservative Party

When people join the Conservative Party, they join a local Constituency Association. It is responsible for recruiting members, selecting candidates, fund-raising and campaigning. It is also responsible for choosing delegates to attend the party annual conference. Scotland has a separate organisation which has at its head the Scottish Conservative and Unionist Council.

Figure 3.2 The Conservative Party logo

Central Office is the headquarters of the Conservative Party and is in London. There is also a Scottish Central Office in Edinburgh. Central Office is run by the party chairman, who is appointed by the party leader. Its job is to run the day-to-day party machine and act as a link between the ordinary party members and the party leaders. It does this through a Board of Management which is run by the 'director general' who is appointed by the party chairman. The party chairman also has the job of planning and running election campaigns.

The party conference is held each year and is an opportunity for party members to give their views and opinions on issues. It is also a chance for the leader to address the party and lay out his or her vision for the party. The party conference does not make policy in the Conservative Party. This is the job of the party leader.

The party leader is elected in two stages. First, MPs can vote for any candidates, with the bottom candidates falling out each time, until there are two main challengers left. The party leader is then chosen from the last two candidates by the party membership at large. This is how David Cameron was chosen as party leader in 2005. The party leader of the Conservatives has a lot more power than most other party leaders. He or she has total control of all appointments, in or out of government and appointments to all full-time positions within the party. He or she also has the final say on party policies, although he or she will consult the Cabinet or Shadow Cabinet.

The Conservative Party is mainly financed through donations from private individuals or private companies. The local associations are also involved in various fund-raising activities in the local area and members pay a small membership fee each year.

The Labour Party

The members of the Labour Party fall into a number of categories. Firstly, individuals can join the Constituency Labour Party (CLP) in their local constituency. They can also be members of the party through 'affiliated organisations' such as trade unions, socialist societies and fabian societies. These groups make up what is known as the 'grass roots' membership of the party. The main function of the CLP is to choose the candidate for the constituency and to put forward delegates for the annual conference. The affiliated organisations can also choose delegates.

Figure 3.3 The Labour Party logo

The history of the Labour Party explains why MPs, trade unions, and CLPs are involved in decision making at the party conference. Despite the introduction of 'one man, one vote' (OMOV) for some decisions, the trade unions, CLP and other organisations still have some say in decision making, for example, in the selection of the leader. The leader is chosen by an electoral college representing the three main elements in the party – MPs, constituency parties and trade unions.

The party conference used to be able to tie leaders down to particular policies. In recent years, however, successive Labour leaders have succeeded in increasing the power of the Parliamentary Labour Party (PLP) when it is in government. The Labour Shadow Cabinet is selected by a vote of the PLP, but the Prime Minister is free to choose his or her own Cabinet when in government. Labour leaders also have a lot more say over policies than they had.

The ordinary members also elect a National Executive Committee (NEC), which is responsible for the day-to-day running of the party.

The Labour Party is mainly financed through the subscriptions of its members. Since trade union membership is still quite large in this country and most of those trade unions are affiliated to the Labour Party, this is a major source of finance.

The Liberal Democrat Party

The main body which is responsible for the organisation of the party is the Federal Party. It is responsible for the preparation of UK-wide policy, parliamentary elections and fund-raising. England, Scotland and Wales separately are responsible for the operation of local parties, selection procedures for prospective parliamentary candidates, the arrangements for

Figure 3.4 The Liberal Democrat Party logo

collecting and renewing party memberships and policy matters relating specifically to their state – though they can request the Federal Party to look after the development of policy matters in particular fields.

The Liberal Democrats choose their leader through the single transferable vote (STV) electoral system; this process was used when Charles Kennedy resigned in early 2006 and Menzies Campbell was chosen as the new leader. They are also keen to see proportional representation (PR) being introduced for other elections and were instrumental in introducing STV for local elections in Scotland in 2007, as part of the coalition government in the Scottish Parliament.

The Liberal Democrats' main source of finance is through party memberships and donations from individuals. Since they do not have as many members as either the Labour or Conservative Parties, they do not have as much money to help them.

The Scottish National Party

The aim of the Scottish National Party (SNP) is clearly seen in its name, that is, the establishment of an independent Scotland. This has been refined in recent years to mean an independent Scotland in Europe, to show that, despite being a small country, Scotland could still prosper in the European Union. The SNP describes itself as a moderate left-of-centre party,

Figure 3.5 The Scottish National Party logo

to try to gain political support based on more than just the aim of independence. It is organised in much the same way as the other main parties in Scotland, with branches in each constituency containing the grass roots membership, an annual conference, a National Council, which has a major say in forming policy, and a leader elected by the ordinary members.

Possible questions on party organisation and structure

◆ To what extent has ideology declined as an influence on the policies of the two main parties in the UK?

◆ Critically examine the way the main parties in the UK formulate policies.

◆ Ordinary party members have little effect on decision making in the main parties in the UK. Discuss.

◆ Assess the effectiveness of the methods used by the main parties to choose their leaders.

Questions and Answers

SAQ 1 To what extent has ideology declined as an influence on the policies of the two main parties in the UK? *(15 marks)*

Here you should analyse the part played by ideology in influencing the policies of the Conservative and Labour Parties.

Questions and *Answers* continued ➤

Answer to SAQ 1

The Labour Party in the 1980s and early 1990s had to change its policies greatly as it was in danger of becoming unelectable. With John Smith and later Tony Blair, New Labour was formed and it moved the old Labour Party more into the centre ground of British politics. One of the major changes made by the Labour Party was the dropping of the old Clause 4, which effectively ended the association of the Labour Party with socialism. This meant a major decline in the influence of ideology in the Labour Party.

The Labour Party is now much more prepared to accept a market economy approach to business and monetary policy. It keeps tight control of inflation, keeps business taxes down and does not intend to raise income tax levels to pay for social reforms. The trade unions have seen their influence decline and public–private partnership (PPP) has been advanced in many areas, notably in health and education. However, the Labour Party still displays some of its old style policies related to social welfare. It is committed to increased spending on the NHS, on education and social inclusion and to tackling child poverty.

The Conservative Party, having been in office for so long in the 1980s and 1990s, also found itself in the position of having to re-invent itself after two landslide victories for New Labour in 1997 and 2001. The problem it had, however, was that New Labour had taken over much of the middle ground, particularly on taxation and the economy. It needed to move more into the centre and not further to the right to avoid major decline.

The Conservatives have retained a lot of their more traditional right-of-centre polices, in education, law and order and immigration, but they have become more tolerant of issues that the public seem to care about that used to clash with their ideology. Examples of this would be their changing attitude to the NHS and support for the more vulnerable groups in society like the poor and the disadvantaged. David Cameron's election as party leader in 2006 saw an attempt by the Conservative Party to put forward a more caring and tolerant face. However, on the right wing of the party, there are areas where ideology is still considered to be important. The old right-wing attitudes on Europe and on immigration and asylum seekers remain and they could well prove to be difficult obstacles for a party trying to get back into government to overcome.

In conclusion, the Labour Party seems a lot less inclined to let ideology guide the policies of the party than it used to. However, there are areas where the social conscience of the old Labour Party is still important. On the other hand, the Conservative Party has not abandoned ideology in the same way Labour has, although it is trying to soften its approach to certain topics to attract more voters.

2 Conflict Within Parties and Electoral Success

The main issues covered in this section are:

◆ Conflict and consensus

◆ Electoral success.

Conflict and consensus

Each of the main parties has large groups or factions within it who have their own particular slant or view as to how the party should best move forward. How well these groups can work together or how well the leader can contain different views within a party may well decide whether the party can win and keep office. We will look at the main factions within each party, and how divisions can occur.

The Labour Party

As the name suggests, the origins of the Labour Party lie in the working-class movement and the original party constitution contained Clause 4, which stated that industries and businesses should be nationalised – taken into state control. This remained a part of the socialist traditions of the Labour Party throughout the 1980s. The Conservative landslide victories in the 1980s under Margaret Thatcher persuaded some members to modify the Labour Party's stance and so New Labour was born. John Smith and later Tony Blair moved the party more to the centre of British politics, with the revision of Clause 4 and a more liberal economic policy. New Labour had to appear to be a united party to win power in 1997 and the 'Blairites' within the party achieved a great measure of control over party policy and appointments. Since 1997, there have been a few examples of the more socialist wing of the party going against New Labour policy, on, for example, social security, defence and taxation. The party's large majority up to 2005 has meant the rebellions have had little impact. The Blairites, for the moment, seem to have a grip on the party and as long as they are in power they may not be seriously challenged. Other divisions within the Labour Party have been over the Iraq war, foundation hospitals, top-up fees for university education.

The Conservative Party

Under Margaret Thatcher, the Conservative Party moved more to the right and succeeded in winning four elections in a row through to the 1992 election. The 'Thatcherites' adopted right-wing economic and social policies and held on to power for 18 years. Divisions in the party centred around the debate over Europe between the 'Europhiles' and the 'Eurosceptics'. When Margaret Thatcher was finally ousted as leader, the party found it hard to rally round another leader. After John Major, who lost the 1997 election, there came William Hague, Iain Duncan Smith, Michael Howard and then David Cameron. There seem to be three factions within the party: the modernisers aligned with Michael Portillo, the traditionalists aligned with David Davis, and the pro-Europeans aligned with Kenneth Clarke. The ideology of the far right on Europe and immigration is important in the party.

The Liberal Democrat Party

The old Liberal Party of the early twentieth century saw itself as a centre party of British politics. It was sometimes a radical alternative to Labour and a moderate alternative to Conservatives. In 1988 it merged with the Social Democratic Party, which had broken away from Labour and it became the Liberal Democrat Party. It covers a wide range of views within the party and its main policies are a commitment to electoral reform (supporting PR), a commitment to a federal Europe and constitutional reform including more devolution and a reform of the House of Lords. It does not tend to have the same kind of factions that exist in the other two main parties, though the recent leadership election in 2006 brought some of these out into the open.

The Scottish National Party

The SNP, like most large political parties, has a number of factions within it. The two main factions are based on those who believe that the party should adopt a gradual approach to independence working through the Scottish Parliament to start with, and those who believe the party should go straight to independence as quickly as possible. With the success of the SNP in the Scottish Parliament, as the main opposition party to the Executive, there are many in the party happy to take this route to independence.

Electoral success

We will look firstly at the UK election results in four recent general elections. Note the successes and failures of the main parties in these elections:

Table 3.1 UK general elections 1992–2005

	Conservative		Labour		Liberal Democrats	
	% vote	Seats	% vote	Seats	% vote	Seats
1992	42%	336	34%	271	18%	20
1997	31%	165	43%	418	17%	46
2001	32%	166	41%	412	18%	52
2005	32%	198	35%	356	22%	62

Note in particular the link between votes and seats and how the two-party system appears to be supported by the results. Note how the 'first past the post' (FPTP) electoral system favours the Labour Party, in particular in Scotland.

Table 3.2 UK general elections – Scotland

	Conservative		Labour		Liberal Democrats		SNP	
	% vote	Seats	% vote	Seats	% vote	Seats	% vote	Seats
1992	26%	11	39%	49	13%	9	21%	3
1997	17%	0	45%	56	13%	10	22%	6
2001	16%	1	43%	56	16%	10	20%	5
2005	16%	1	39%	41	23%	11	18%	6

Scottish Parliament results

The additional member system (AMS), which is a PR system, is used to elect MSPs to the Scottish Parliament. The main parties, particularly Labour and SNP, lost out in 2003 to the minor parties (see page 11, Table 1.7). People may have used their second ballot vote as a protest vote.

For the European Parliament results 2004 (Scotland) see page 53, Table 4.6.

Possible questions on conflict within parties and electoral success

◆ To what extent is there conflict between groups in the main parties?
◆ Critically examine the electoral success of the main parties in the UK.

3 Parties and their Policies

The main issues covered in this section are:

◆ Taxation policies
◆ Law and order policies
◆ Education policies
◆ Policies on Europe

You should remind yourself of the ideology of the main parties that we covered earlier in this chapter. This obviously has an influence on the types of policies the main parties will adopt. Remember, the exam board tells you which areas it is likely to be asking questions about when it comes to policies. These are listed above. Remember also that policies of parties are likely to change and adapt fairly regularly and you will have to keep up to date with any changes as they happen.

Taxation policies

In the past, the Conservatives were traditionally the party of low taxes and low government spending, while the Labour Party increased taxes to spend more. In recent years, however, the Conservatives have not been so keen to promise tax cuts and the Labour Party has promised not to increase taxes. The table below summarises the main parties' policies on taxation:

Table 3.3 Party policies on taxation

Conservative Party	Labour Party	Liberal Democrats
Against increases in 'stealth' taxes – e.g. National Insurance rises.	Promise not to increase income tax since 1997.	Replace council tax with local income tax.
Reduce business taxes.	Tax relief for 'hard working families'.	Introduce 50% tax rate on high earners.
Council tax cuts for pensioners.	Spending plans 'affordable without tax rises'.	Raise stamp duty.
Cuts in inheritance tax and stamp duty.		Replace fuel tax with road user charge.

Law and order policies

Table 3.4 Party policies on law and order

Conservative Party	Labour Party	Liberal Democrats
Increase number of police officers.	Increase number of police officers.	Increase number of police officers.
Tough on young offenders.	Tougher sentences for persistent offenders.	Tackle drug dealers more.
Criminals to serve full sentences.	Anti-social behaviour laws.	Tackle 'yob' culture.
Tougher measures on drugs and drug offenders.	On-the-spot fines for 'yobs'.	Let communities decide sentences for minor crimes.
	Victims to have better support.	

Education policies

Table 3.5 Party policies on education

Conservative Party	Labour Party	Liberal Democrats
Restore grammar schools in England.	State schools 'specialise' in areas.	Cut class sizes for youngest.
More power for parents.	Tuition fees in England.	Children taught by qualified teacher in each subject.
Endowments for universities.	More money to successful schools.	Scrap university fees.
Encourage 'staying-on'.	Encourage 'staying-on'.	No 'unnecessary' tests.
Vocational training.	Vocational training.	

Policies on Europe

Table 3.6 Party policies on Europe

Conservative Party	Labour Party	Liberal Democrats
Against new constitution for Europe.	Conditionally in favour of new constitution for Europe.	Back EU constitution to clarify position of Brussels power.
Reform of Common Agricultural Policy (CAP) and fisheries policies.	Reform of CAP and fisheries policies.	Join Euro under right conditions but referendum first.
Keep EU rebate for Britain.	Will join euro when conditions are right.	Basically pro-Europe.
Not keen on euro. Keep the pound.	Had to give up part of EU rebate.	

The Scottish National Party

The SNP has its own policies on all of the main areas, like the other main parties. However, as its name suggests, it looks at every issue with a particularly Scottish slant and this is reflected in its stance.

Table 3.7 SNP policies

Taxation	Law and Order	Education	Europe
Full tax freedom for Scottish Parliament.	More police officers (1000).	Reduction of class sizes.	Independent Scotland would sit at Europe's top table.
Scottish business taxes set lower.	Attack on youth crime.	Scrap all tuition fees.	Constitution is a bad deal for Scotland.
Higher taxes for higher earners.	Scrap private prisons.	Replace public–private partnerships with non-profit trusts.	Fisheries policy is a disaster.
Reduced fuel duties.	Independence will allow attack on real causes of crime – poverty.	Independence will create investment.	

Possible questions on parties and their policies

All of the questions you are likely to be asked in this area are going to be on the differences or similarities that exist between the main parties in the areas specified below. They can come in any combination and for any of the main parties. You should prepare for this in your revision.

◆ To what extent are there policy differences between the main parties in the following areas?

   Taxation   Law and Order   Education   Europe

POLITICAL PARTIES AND THEIR POLICIES

STUDY THEME 1D: ELECTORAL SYSTEMS, VOTING AND POLITICAL ATTITUDES

What You Should Know

SQA:

The UK, Scottish, European Parliamentary and Scottish local government electoral systems; effects on the distribution of power within and among parties, in elected bodies and between the electorate and the elected.

Voting patterns; explanations of voting behaviour.

The shaping of political attitudes through the media; opinion polls; referenda; voter participation.

This topic can be split into three main sections:
1   Elections and Electoral Systems
2   Voting Behaviour
3   The Media and Voting.

1 Elections and Electoral Systems

The main issues covered in this section are:

◆   Advantages and disadvantages of simple majority (FPTP)

◆   Electoral reform

◆   Proportional representation (PR)

◆   Advantages and disadvantages of PR

◆   Comparing PR systems

◆   Links between election results and electoral systems.

Advantages and disadvantages of simple majority (FPTP)

First past the post (FPTP) or simple majority is the name given to the system of election we use in UK general elections. There are 646 separate battles in constituencies and the party that wins most MPs or seats in the House of Commons is asked to form the Government. There are a number of advantages and disadvantages to this system.

Figure 4.1 A ballot paper for a simple majority system of voting

Advantages of simple majority

◆ The system usually elects governments that have a clear majority in the House of Commons. For example, in 2005 Labour had a 66 majority. This allows the Government stability to carry out its policies over five years.

◆ The Government is usually only of one party and therefore does not have to compromise on its policies as a coalition might.

◆ The system has been tried and tested, is easy to understand and is relatively cheap to run. It is straightforward for voters to understand, and so may encourage voters to turn out.

◆ The system provides a direct link between the constituency and an MP. This makes the MP highly accountable to the electorate: your own MP.

◆ Extreme parties such as the British National Party and the Communist Party do not usually get much representation in the House of Commons, so they have no MPs. Small parties in the Commons also don't get to hold the balance of power.

Disadvantages of simple majority

◆ Majority governments can be formed on the basis of minority support in terms of votes. In 2005 Labour has a 66 majority on only 35% of votes.

◆ Individual MPs can be elected on the basis of minority support. In Inverness in 1992 (a four-way marginal) the winning candidate got only 26% of the vote.

◆ Smaller third parties do not do well under the system. It leads to a two-party system. The Liberal Democrats in 1997 got 17% of vote but only 7% of seats.

◆ There is poor proportionality between seats and votes. This brings in the issue of 'wasted' votes and 'tactical' voting.

◆ There are regional imbalances. Labour is very strong in Scotland, Wales and the north of England. The Conservatives are strong in the Midlands, and south of England. In 1997 no Conservatives were elected in Scotland or Wales.

Electoral reform

Because of the disproportionate nature of the results in elections under the system of simple majority, more attention has been paid in recent times to electoral reform. The Plant Committee was established by the Labour Party and in 1993 it recommended a move towards proportional representation (PR) for European elections, Scottish and Welsh assemblies and an elected Second Chamber. The Labour Party decided to introduce PR for the European elections in 1999 using a Regional Party List. It also decided that it would elect some MSPs to the Scottish Parliament in 1999 using the same method.

Systems suggested to replace the simple majority fall into two main categories.

Majority systems are where winning candidates have to get 50% of the vote.

Proportional representation (PR) is where seats are allocated in proportion to votes cast.

Proportional representation (PR)

With the PR system the representation of parties is directly linked to the support the parties get in the country. We will look at three main systems.

1 The additional member system

The additional member system (AMS) is an attempt to bring PR and simple majority together. Some MPs are elected in simple majority constituencies and some are elected in regional party lists. This is the system that the Scottish Parliament uses, with 73 constituency MSPs and 56 regional party list MSPs using the 8 European constituencies in Scotland with 7 MSPs from each.

2 The party list system

Each party prepares a list of candidates for the election in order of the party's preference, and voters simply choose which party they want to vote for. Seats are then allocated in proportion to the votes a party gets. This system is used in European Parliament elections in the UK, where Scotland is one region electing seven MEPs from party lists. Spain, the Netherlands and Israel also use this system.

Figure 4.2 A ballot paper for the European Parliament elections in Scotland

3 Single transferable vote (STV)

Voters choose their candidates and parties in order of preference. A fair percentage or quota for a candidate to be elected is worked out. First preferences are calculated to see if the quota has been reached, second preferences are then worked out and added to first preferences, and so on until all the seats have been filled. This is the system proposed for Scottish local council elections in 2007. It is also used in Ireland and Australia.

Advantages and disadvantages of proportional representation systems

Advantages of PR

◆ PR systems give a much fairer representation of the voters' wishes. No majority governments with a minority of votes can be elected. Labour in 2005 got only 35% of votes.

◆ Smaller parties like the Liberal Democrats are more likely to get a fairer representation in Parliament, which more closely reflects their support.

◆ Voters in constituencies have a much better chance of being represented by an MP of their choice. There are multi-member constituencies used under PR and the MPs are likely to be from different parties.

◆ PR may improve participation, as 'wasted' votes are less likely and tactical voting is not necessary because every vote 'counts'.

◆ PR encourages consensual politics as there is a strong likelihood that parties will have to work together after the election.

Disadvantages of PR

◆ Coalition governments are likely and could lead to instability. Italy had around 50 governments in 50 years using the party list system.

◆ Multi-member constituencies may weaken the link between the MP and the voters. List systems take the choice of candidate away completely.

◆ Small parties could become 'kingmakers'. The parties' original policies may become diluted through compromise. Extremists become more important as they may hold the balance of power.

◆ Some systems are difficult to understand and may cause confusion. At first, there seemed to be a problem with two ballot papers in the Scottish Parliament elections in 1999.

◆ Extremist parties, such as the BNP or the Communist Party, may get a foothold in the Parliament even though their support is small.

Comparing PR systems

Since there are a number of different PR systems, three of which are being used in Scotland, you may be asked to compare the strengths and weaknesses of each system against the others. The table below shows this:

Table 4.1 Strengths and weakness of different PR voting systems

PR system	Strengths	Weaknesses
AMS	Retains the link between MP and constituency	It still has many of the faults of simple majority
	Gives a fairly proportional result in votes and seats	The list MPs are accountable to the party and not voters
	It produces strong, stable governments – Scotland	It creates two types of MP who might not be treated equally
	It gives the voter at least one vote that counts	The parties still have power over selecting all candidates
Party list	It is the most proportional of all the PR systems	Voters have little or no choice over candidates
	It is very easy for the voters to understand and use	Groups traditionally under-represented are not helped
	It gives equal weighting to every vote that is cast	There is no connection between MPs and an area
	Voters have to choose from only a small number of parties	Party leaders have all the power in their hands
STV	Power is in the hands of the voters – preferences	This system is the least proportional of all three
	It is simple for voters to use and there is no need for tactical voting	Constituencies are much larger but with more MPs
	It keeps MPs linked to an area that voters identify with	MPs may have to spend more time dealing with local matters
	It produces governments with more than 50% of votes	Disliked by politicians many of whom could lose safe seats

Links between election results and electoral systems

Since we have looked at how the various electoral systems worked, we should now look at what kind of results we get using these systems. We will look at the UK General Election 2005 (simple majority), the Scottish Parliament Election 2003 (AMS) and the European Parliament Election 2004 (regional list). You should also look at the local council elections in 2007 (STV).

UK General Election 2005

Table 4.2 Election results 2005

Party	Votes (%)	Seats
Labour	35.3%	356
Conservative	32.3%	198
Liberal Democrat	22.1%	62
SNP	1.5%	6
Others	8.8%	24
Total	100%	646

Scottish Parliament Election 2003

Table 4.3 Constituency results 2003

Party	Percentage of votes	MSPs
Labour	35%	46
SNP	24%	9
Conservative	16%	3
Liberal Democrat	15%	13
Others	10%	2
Total	100%	73

Table 4.4 Regional List results 2003

Party	Percentage of votes	MSPs
Labour	29%	4
SNP	21%	18
Conservative	15%	15
Liberal Democrat	12%	4
Scottish Socialist Party	6%	6
Green	7%	7
Others	10%	2
Total	100%	56

Table 4.5 Total number of MSPs: 129

Lab	SNP	Con	LD	SSP	Green	Ind
50	27	18	17	6	7	4

European Parliament results 2004 (Scotland)

Table 4.6

Party	Percentage of votes	Seats
Labour	26.4%	2
Conservative	17.8%	2
Liberal Democrat	13.1%	1
SNP	19.7%	2
Green	6.8%	0
UKIP	6.7%	0
SSP	5.2%	0
Others	4.3%	0
Total	100%	7

You should look again at the different strengths and weaknesses of the electoral systems and use some of the facts from the actual results to support these.

Possible questions on elections and electoral systems

◆ The advantages of the 'first past the post' electoral system far outweigh the disadvantages. Discuss.

◆ To what extent do particular PR systems improve representation?

◆ Assess the effectiveness of the AMS electoral system used in Scotland.

Questions and Answers

SAQ 1 The advantages of the 'first past the post' electoral system far outweigh the disadvantages. Discuss. *(15 marks)*

Answer to SAQ 1

The simple majority or 'first past the post' electoral system has been used in UK general elections and council elections for a very long time. It is based on the fact that the person with the most votes wins and the party with the most seats becomes the Government. The UK elects 646 MPs, each representing a particular constituency, and parties will try to put up candidates in as many seats as they can. The FPTP system has a number of advantages and disadvantages.

Questions and **Answers** continued ➤

Questions and Answers continued

Answer to SAQ 1 continued

Under the FPTP electoral system, a government is usually elected that has a majority in Parliament. In the last three general elections in the UK, the Labour Party had majorities of 177, 165 and 66, which allows them to carry out their legislative programme with little trouble. However, on each occasion, the Labour Party had less than half the people in the country voting for them. In 2005, in particular, Labour only got 35% of the total vote. Many people would argue this is unfair and unrepresentative. This is sometimes called an 'elected dictatorship'.

The voting procedures under FPTP are very straightforward, the results are known quickly, and this system is well-known to the British public. Many argue this increases turnout and participation. However, there are a lot of wasted votes under this system as many people live in very safe seats and if they don't support the winner they are unlikely to see their vote count for anything. There may also be tactical voting in safe seats to stop someone winning, which is not very democratic.

FPTP encourages voters to choose between the two main parties as they are the only ones likely to form a government. The two main parties in the past offered two different ideologies for voters to choose from. However, the main parties are a lot closer to each other now and smaller parties are discriminated against. The Liberal Democrats had 22% of the vote in 2005 yet only gained 62 seats, which is around 9% of seats.

FPTP keeps the link between one MP and one constituency. The MP knows he or she has to represent all of the people in the area, and everyone knows who their MP is. However, an individual MP's share of the vote can be as low as 30% and this means that 70% of the people in the constituency did not get who they voted for. Many would argue that this is very unfair.

In conclusion, there are arguments to say that FPTP is a good system for electing a government. However, there are arguments against the system also.

2 Voting Behaviour

The main issues covered in this section are:

◆ Long-term factors – social class, age, gender, ethnicity, geography, ideology gap
◆ Short-term factors – rational choice, issue voting, competence, leadership style, election campaigns and party image.

Voting behaviour is very complex and can be dependent on a number of factors, some long-term and some short-term.

Long-term factors

A number of social factors influence voting behaviour: age, ethnicity, family, gender, religion and region (geography). It does seem, however, that social class itself is the most important long-term influence.

Social class

Up until recently, the Registrar General defined social class in terms of a six point scale which classified people into groups according to their likely income. In 2002, the Registrar General decided to change the classification of the population into groups that were more closely associated with their occupations, and increased the number of groups to around nine. However, the older categories are often still used, grouping people as professional and managerial (AB), middle class (C1), skilled working classes (C2), and unskilled working class or unemployed (DE); electoral information can still be classified in this way.

Social class and voting

From 1945 to 1970, there was a clear link between voting and class, with 65% of the working class voting Labour and 85% of the middle class voting Conservative. However, there have always been working-class people who vote Conservative and what are called middle-class radicals who vote Labour.

Since 1970, there has been a decline in the importance of class as the main determinant of voting behaviour. One cause of this has been the decline in the numbers of people who could be called working class. This fell from 47% in 1970 to 34% in 2006. The working class itself, however, can perhaps now be split into traditional working class and new skilled working class, who own their own homes, work in the private sector and are not trade union members. As a result, there has been what is sometimes called class de-alignment in voting patterns. The Labour Party lost heavily in the working-class group in 1987 and 1992, though the policies of New Labour allowed the party to recapture this ground in 1997 and 2001. The tables below show this.

Table 4.7 1992 General Election: Class percentages

Party	AB	C1	C2	DE
Conservative	56	52	38	30
Labour	20	25	41	50
Liberal Democrat	22	19	17	15

Table 4.8 1997 General Election: Class percentages

Party	AB	C1	C2	DE
Conservative	42	26	25	21
Labour	31	47	54	61
Liberal Democrat	21	19	14	13

The figures above show that class seems to play a much less important role now than it did. The Conservative lead in AB voters over Labour was 36% in 1992 compared with only 11% in 1997. In group C1, Labour support doubled over two elections, while Conservative support halved. However, class is still the single most important long-term factor which affects voting behaviour. The 2001 figures are similar to 1997. In 2005, the Labour Party's lead in these areas was pulled back by the Conservatives.

Age

In the past, older voters were more likely to vote Conservative than Labour, with the Conservatives leading Labour in 1992 in all age groups except 18–24. In 1997, however, Conservatives only led Labour in the over 65s group, and Labour did particularly well with middle-aged voters in the 30–44 and 45–64 age groups, showing their broad-based appeal.

Gender

Until recently the evidence seemed to suggest that women were more likely than men to vote Conservative, with a gap of around 3% in 1992. In 1997, however, Labour eliminated the gender gap, perhaps due to its policies appealing to women and the high number of women candidates, resulting in 101 women Labour MPs.

Ethnicity

A large percentage of ethnic minorities in Britain vote Labour, though Asians in non-manual work may not be so inclined.

Geography

A number of strong regional factors can be seen in voting behaviour. Scotland, the north of England and Wales have become predominantly Labour strongholds. In 1997, the Conservatives won no MPs in either Scotland or Wales, despite gaining 17.5 % of the vote in Scotland and 20% of the vote in Wales. These areas have been the traditional industrial areas of Britain which have been in decline. The south of England used to be Conservative dominated, but inroads made there by Labour in 1997 reduced the Conservatives to a rural English party. The 2001 figures were similar to 1997, though in 2005 the Conservatives fought back in the south of England and the Midlands.

Ideology gap

The Labour Party in the 1980s seemed to have policies which did not appeal especially to the new working-class voters, and successive party leaders, Neil Kinnock, John Smith and Tony Blair, worked to make New Labour a modern party with broad-based support. The commitment to improve society without the need to increase taxation was part of the strategy for the 1997 election and proved to be very successful. The same strategy applied in 2001, although other factors did come into play in 2005, such as the Iraq War. The gap between Labour and Conservative is a lot closer than ever before.

Short-term factors

There is evidence that class and party alignment have become less important now than they were. Attention, therefore, has been focused on short-term factors that cause changes in voting behaviour. Between 1992 and 1997, the Labour Party gained almost 2 million votes, while the Conservatives lost over 4 million and the Liberal Democrats lost nearly 1 million. This means there were a lot of floating voters (voters who switch from one party to another) and this is very important, as floating voters are the ones who usually determine who becomes the Government. The 1997 General Election revealed an unusually high number of voters who were willing to switch directly from Conservative to Labour (about 1.4 million). There could be a number of reasons for these short-term choices.

Rational choice

An increasing number of voters may look at the policies of the parties and decide which party is most likely to protect and advance their interests. Policies on health, education, taxation, foreign policy and immigration are all important to voters when deciding how to vote.

Issue voting

In the 1980s, many voters considered that the Conservatives had a range of policies that were likely to increase their material prosperity, while Labour had unpopular policies on defence and taxation. New Labour tried to rid itself of this 'tax and spend' image and still persuade voters it could develop education, the NHS and employment, without high taxes.

Competence

The Labour Party's image from the 1970s, of high inflation and trade union unrest, was difficult to overthrow and many people believed the Conservatives would manage the economy better. New Labour changed its policies, and voters no longer considered that the 'feel good' factor of the 1980s and early 1990s was enough to make them vote Conservative.

Leadership style

John Major had been seen as being more trustworthy than Neil Kinnock in 1992, though Tony Blair and New Labour boosted Labour's opinion poll ratings through to the 1997 election. This was maintained in 2001, though the Labour Party's vote fell back in 2005 as did Tony Blair's popularity.

Election campaigns and party image

Gaining extensive media coverage and improving the party image has become an extremely important matter for parties. Press conferences, spin doctors, sound bites, all play a part in the modern campaign. The Conservatives could not shrug off the 'sleaze' factor in 1997 and divisions within the party over Europe gave the impression of disunity. 2001 was similar to 1997. In 2005, the Labour Party tried hard to play down the importance of the Iraq War and play up its record on domestic issues.

Possible questions on voting behaviour

◆ To what extent is social class the most important influence on voting behaviour?

◆ Critically examine the factors that influence voting behaviour.

Questions and Answers

SAQ 2 To what extent is social class the most important influence on voting behaviour? *(15 marks)*

Here you should analyse the importance of social class on voting behaviour and compare it with other factors, giving as many examples of other influential factors as you can.

Questions and Answers continued ➤

Questions and Answers continued

Answer to SAQ 2

In the past, there was a very strong correlation between a person's natural class and voting. Up to the 1950s, around 85% of classes A and B (the middle classes) voted for the Conservatives and around 65% of classes D and E (the working class) voted for Labour. However, in recent years there has been some class dealignment (a breaking up of the old class system) and the correlation between class and voting is not as strong. The Conservatives made inroads into the C, D and E vote in the 1980s and the Labour Party made inroads into A and B voters in the 1990s.

There always have been a number of working-class Conservatives and middle-class radicals who did not vote with their natural class party. Working-class Conservatives are attracted to strong policies on law and order and have been drawn to support a party that encourages them to improve their standard of living through lower taxes and the sale of council houses. Middle-class radicals may work in the public sector and support the policies of the Labour Party to increase spending in these areas, or they may be first-generation professionals who still remember their working-class roots.

Despite this, it has been estimated that the number of people who vote according to their natural class party has fallen to around 47% of voters. This is still a relatively high number of people who vote with their natural class party and this is the single biggest influence on voting. However, many of the other long-term factors said to influence voting behaviour, such as education, location, ethnicity and religion, are very closely linked to social class. Social class may be less important than initially thought.

There has been an increase in the importance of short-term factors on voting in elections in recent years. Issues have become more important to a better-educated electorate. The way the campaign is conducted, the image of the party and its leader, the influence of the media and tactical voting have all become more important. The number of voters who change their vote from one election to the next has increased, showing long-term factors like social class are not as important.

In conclusion, there is still evidence to say that social class is an important factor in voting behaviour. However, it may not be the most important factor any longer.

3 The Media and Voting

The main issues covered in this section are:

- The media and politics
- The press
- Television
- Extent of media influence on voting

The media and politics

As old party loyalties based on social factors are breaking down and, as politicians realise there are a lot more floating voters, a great deal more attention has been given to the importance of the mass media in influencing the way people vote. A number of factors should be recognised.

Interpreting the news

News is not only reported but interpreted by the media. Most people get their information about elections from the media, and the role of the media as an opinion former is very significant. Current affairs TV programmes such as *Question Time* have become very important to both voters and parties.

Ownership

Ownership of the press is concentrated in the hands of a few companies, and many of these companies have invested heavily in the satellite and cable revolution. These bodies will seek to advance their own interests and positions, and will use their businesses to support or undermine certain political parties.

The media and democracy

The media ensure the public is made aware of the views and activities of their elected representatives and so uphold the democratic traditions in this country. However, the media can also manipulate news to suit its own powerful commercial interests. Parties also try to manipulate the media through spin doctors and other methods because they recognise that the media is a powerful influence in the political system.

The press

Popular and quality press

In Britain, the press can be divided into popular/tabloid papers and quality/broadsheet papers. Readers of tabloid papers are mostly working class and may have a limited interest in politics, relying more heavily on TV for their news. Readers of quality papers are more likely to be middle class and may have a higher level of political interest and participation.

Ownership

News International owned by Rupert Murdoch accounts for 35% of the newspaper market, with Mirror Newspaper Group and United Newspapers being the other major players. Since the press is independent of government control, it is in a powerful position to influence public opinion.

The press and influence

Tabloid journalism has meant that some newspapers have focused on personalities rather than on policies, with journalists being under pressure to obtain exclusive stories. There has been an increasing emphasis on the sensational and the trivial.

Newspapers and elections

Newspapers seem to have more influence on voting behaviour than they did in the past. The *Sun*'s campaign in 1992, 'It's The Sun Wot Won It' appeared to be very successful. In 1997 it switched support to Labour, 'It's the Sun Wot Swung It'.

The 1997 Election

In the 1997 election, 60% of Britain's national dailies advised people to vote Labour. John Major's policies on Europe, the 'cash for questions' scandal, and Tony Blair's New Labour, all persuaded Rupert Murdoch to put the *Sun* behind Labour, as well as News International's *News of the World* Sunday newspaper. The quality press is also influential because they cover the political issues in detail and are often used by politicians to respond to points made in them. In 2001 and 2005, this press support for politicians stayed more or less the same.

ELECTORAL SYSTEMS, VOTING AND POLITICAL ATTITUDES

The lobby system

The major political parties have increasingly used 'spin doctors' to get favourable media coverage and limit any damage likely to come from stories. The Lobby System in Parliament allows parties to give out unofficial information, which might otherwise not be available. It could be said that this allows the Government to manage the news and reinforces the position of 'spin doctors'.

The press and privacy

The tabloid press, in particular, seize on stories about the private lives of politicians, and any politicians who become the subject of this kind of coverage often find themselves losing the support of a large number of voters. The methods used by journalists to find such stories have been increasingly condemned, and the Labour Government is looking at outlawing some of their activities. It must be careful, however, not to restrict the freedoms enjoyed by the press in this country. The Official Secrets Act has been widely condemned as having too wide a scope and it allows Ministers to maintain secrecy by claiming national interest.

Television

As television is thought by many adults to be more accurate, reliable and trustworthy than the press, a significant number of people rely on it for their main source of information. The BBC and ITV authorities are required by law to ensure an unbiased approach to politics.

Political coverage

Around 20% of total television coverage is devoted to current affairs, though this increases in the run-up to a general election. The BBC and ITV tend to ensure the three main political parties receive broadly equal coverage, though this may tend to put many viewers off as it may appear bland and uninteresting. It may well be, however, that as many as 70% of people have already decided how they are going to vote before the election coverage begins. Despite this, politicians are very sensitive to the idea that television should be as impartial as possible, because of the role that television can play in promoting a positive image of the party.

Information technology and television

Cable, satellite and the advent of digital television have meant that viewers can now access a much wider range of programmes than that offered by the BBC and ITV. Concerns have been expressed over the ownership of many of these new stations in the hands of a few major players and it remains to be seen how effectively they can be controlled.

Figure 4.3 Tony Blair makes a statement to the media at 10 Downing Street, London, 25 April 2006

Television and political parties

The increasing importance of television has radically altered the way political parties deal with television. This can be seen in a number of ways:

◆ **The importance of image**. The image of the party, as seen through the personalities of the leaders, has clearly outlined what kind of person is deemed to be 'suitable' as leader. Tony Blair was seen as young, fresh, and full of life, compared with John Major.

◆ **Media events**. Events of national importance are arranged by the party headquarters, with national celebrities and sports personalities.

◆ **Sound bites**. Concise statements are issued by the party leaders and will be given prominence in televised news broadcasts, e.g. 'Time for a change'.

◆ **Spin doctors**. Professional media managers or 'spin doctors' will try to maximise positive political coverage through photo-opportunities, party news conferences, and spokespersons being 'on message'. Alistair Campbell and Peter Mandelson both did this job well for Labour.

◆ **Narrowing the focus**. Using your best performers on television, and concentrating on a narrow range of issues during the campaign, are strategies adopted partly because of the demands of television.

Extent of media influence on voting

Key Points

Strong influence

◆ For many the media is their only source of information on politics.

◆ The media reports all the campaign issues and the results of opinion polls.

◆ The parties spend more and more time organising how they use the media to campaign for power – spin doctors, sound bites.

◆ The press claimed in 1992 and 1997 to have won the election for the Labour party.

◆ Campaigns are becoming more and more presidential and party leaders spend more time appearing in the media – especially TV.

Exaggerated influence

◆ Many people know the press is biased and don't let this affect them when voting.

◆ It could be argued that people choose their party first and read a newspaper that only confirms what they already believe.

◆ In the weeks before an election as many as 52% of people claimed they had seen little or no coverage of the election.

◆ There are a whole wide range of long-term and short-term factors which can affect voting behaviour.

◆ The person with the best image does not always win the election.

Possible questions on the media and voting

◆ To what extent do the media influence voting behaviour?

◆ Critically examine the way the main parties use the media during elections.

Questions and Answers

SAQ 3   To what extent do the media influence voting behaviour?   *(15 marks)*

Here you should analyse the importance of the media on voting behaviour and compare it with other factors.

Answer to SAQ 3

Many people say that the media is their only source of political information. This is especially important around election time as the media will report the results of opinion polls and will give information on the main issues of the election. However, it could be argued that the saturation coverage of the election may actually turn off some of the electorate and persuade them not to turn up and vote.

The press can be particularly partisan during election time. The *Sun* claimed to have won the election for the Conservatives in 1992 when they campaigned against Neil Kinnock, and then to have swung the election for Labour in 1997 when they switched their allegiance to Tony Blair. However, it could be argued that many people buy a newspaper that already supports their political views and opinions and that the newspaper is merely confirming their views.

The broadcasting media have to be a lot more impartial in their political coverage. TV in particular has to be very careful of the coverage it gives to all parties. However, there can still be some bias in the broadcasting media as they can choose which stories to air and which headlines to use, and many politicians and parties have complained of bias in the past.

Politicians attach a great deal of importance to the media during campaigns. Sound bites, spin doctors, press conferences and party political broadcasts all have their part to play in creating the image of the party or the leader. With the two main parties a lot closer to each other in their policies and ideologies, image has become a much more important issue in recent campaigns. In 1997, Tony Blair was seen as the fresh young leader compared with tired old John Major. In 2001, Tony Blair's image was still an important factor, though his popularity fell in 2005 perhaps due to the Iraq War. The election of David Cameron as leader of the Conservative Party in 2006 probably had a lot more to do with image rather than policies.

Despite all of these arguments to suggest that the media is an important factor in influencing elections, there are many other long- and short-term factors that play their part. Social class, education, gender, ethnicity and age are all long-term factors to consider. Short-term factors such as the issues of the day, the competence of the party leader, the funding of the parties and the handling of the campaign by the party are also factors that affect voting behaviour.

In conclusion, there are arguments that show that the media does have an important part to play in influencing voting behaviour. However, there are other factors that have to be taken into account.

UNIT 2

Social Issues in the
United Kingdom

STUDY THEME 2: WEALTH AND HEALTH INEQUALITIES IN THE UNITED KINGDOM

What You Should Know

SQA:

The principles of the Welfare State. The debate over the provision of and funding of health care and welfare; individual and collective responsibility.

Evidence of inequalities in wealth and health; causes of inequalities in wealth and health; consequences of inequalities in wealth and health.

With reference to ethnicity and gender: the extent of social and economic inequalities; the nature and effect of government responses to deal with these inequalities.

This topic can be split into three main sections.

1. The Welfare State – Wealth and Health Issues
2. Inequalities in Wealth and Health
3. Government Responses.

1 The Welfare State – Wealth and Health Issues

Background

During the Second World War, the Government looked ahead to the kind of society it wanted for its returning soldiers and the people of a country that had gone through a long war. It set up the Beveridge Commission to look into this and report on what the Government should do to make sure people in the UK could get the best possible living standards the country could afford. The Beveridge Report, published in 1942, laid the groundwork for the Welfare State, where the Government would guarantee that every person in the UK would be given a minimum standard of living. Beveridge identified five areas called 'the five giants', which stood in the way of social progress. These 'five giants' had to be tackled if people in the UK were to see improvements in their standard of living. The various departments of the Government were given the job of reforming the services they provided to eliminate the major problems that existed in the five areas. The five giants were:

♦ Want – Social Security would reform services to eliminate poverty.

♦ Disease – A National Health Service would be created in the UK.

♦ Ignorance – Education services would be improved.

♦ Squalor – Housing conditions of people would be improved.

♦ Idleness – Policies would be introduced to deal with unemployment.

The Beveridge Report used phrases like 'a safety net', where the Government would prevent anyone from falling below a certain level in living standards. It talked about 'from the cradle to the grave' showing that the Government would look after citizens all through their lives. The new Labour Government elected in 1945, after the war, set about introducing all of these ideas. This was the start of the Welfare State.

Wealth in the UK

There are a number of different ways we can measure the wealth of a country or of individuals in that country. Sometimes we can look at gross domestic product (GDP) per capita, that is, the total value of all the country's goods and services divided by its population. This allows us to compare how well one country does against another. Gross national product (GNP) adds the value of any investments made overseas by UK citizens. As far as individuals are concerned, it is more usual to measure wealth by looking at people's incomes. Most people in the UK get their main source of income from employment, though there are some who earn money from benefits, shares, savings, rents and investments.

Gap between rich and poor

Obviously there are high wage earners and low wage earners. In 2004, the top 20% of wage earners received an average of £63,000 per year, before taxes and benefits, while the bottom 20% received £3,700 on average. The types of households that gain most from the redistribution of income through taxation and benefits are single-adult households with children, and retired households. Cash benefits such as Income Support, Child Benefit, Incapacity Benefit, and the State Retirement Pension play the largest part in reducing income inequality. They mostly go to households with lower incomes. Cash benefits make up 61% of gross income for the poorest 20% of households, 37% for the next group, falling to 2% for the top 20% of households. We will look at these differences in more detail later.

Social class structure in the UK

The Registrar General had classified the UK population into groups based on their occupations:

I	Professional occupations	A
II	Managerial and technical	B
III	Skilled occupations	
	Non-manual	C1
	Manual	C2
IV	Semi-skilled occupations	D
V	Unskilled	E

In 2001, the National Statistics Socio-economic Classification was introduced by the government to replace the old Registrar General's list.

It is an occupationally based classification but has rules to provide coverage of the whole adult population. The following table shows its main classes:

Table 5.1 National Statistics Socio-economic Classification

1	Higher managerial and professional occupations
	1.1 Large employers and managerial occupations
	1.2 Higher professional occupations
2	Lower managerial and professional occupations
3	Intermediate occupations
4	Small employers and own account workers
5	Lower supervisory and technical occupations
6	Semi-routine occupations
7	Routine occupations
8	Never worked and long-term unemployed

Using these classification groups, it is possible to measure changes and trends in society to do with employment and income, and how these changes have affected different groups. The Government can then examine what it needs to do to improve the standard of living of people in the UK in terms of education, health and employment.

Provision and funding of welfare

With the introduction of the Welfare State after the Second World War, the Government was determined to improve the standard of living of the poorest sections of society. The Welfare State was to be funded by general taxation and, through a system of benefits and other measures, the state would guarantee this 'safety net' for the people of the UK. The Department for Work and Pensions (formerly called the Department of Social Security) is responsible for deciding who gets benefits. Some benefits are paid to all those who are entitled to them, regardless of income. Most benefits, however, are means-tested, that is, they are only given to those who don't have sufficient income or wealth to rely on. There are a whole range of benefits available to people in the UK, and you should be familiar with these. You need to know who is entitled to them and under what circumstances they are paid. We will look at these in more detail later.

Health in the UK

The National Health Service (NHS)

The introduction of the NHS was seen as 'the jewel in the crown' of the Welfare State. The health of people in the UK was considered to be the most important part of the Welfare State. No longer would the health of an individual be dependent on whether they could afford treatment or not. The Government was determined that, if an NHS was to be introduced, it should be done properly and it laid down a number of founding principles or aims under which the NHS would be organised:

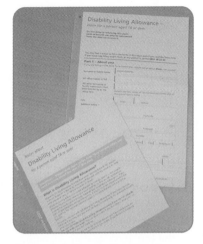

Figure 5.1 An application for benefit from the Department for Work and Pensions

♦ Collectivist – the state would provide and organise a state-run system.

♦ Universal – the whole population would get free health care services.

♦ Comprehensive – every aspect of the nation's health was covered.

♦ Equality – there would be a uniform standard of care for all people.

Funding of the NHS

Originally it was thought that, if the NHS was successful, it would cure a lot of illnesses, and people would become more healthy, so the cost of the NHS would not rise very much. With hindsight, this did not take into account the demand for new services as they became available, and the fact that more degenerative illnesses had to be treated as the population grew steadily older. As a result, the demands on the NHS have become almost limitless, though the income available is not. As the NHS was financed through general taxation, it had to compete with other government departments for finance. Very quickly, charges were introduced for services like prescriptions, dentistry and spectacles, though this clearly breached the commitment for a free service. Finance today, for both income and expenditure, is a major issue in the NHS. There have been a number of reforms in how the NHS is organised (see below) and some debate over issues of finance.

Structure of the NHS in Scotland

The NHS is run by Health Boards, which are appointed by the Government and are under the control of the Scottish Parliament in Scotland. There are 15 Health Boards in Scotland, such as Greater Glasgow, Lothians and Lanarkshire Health Boards. There are three main types of services organised by the Health Boards. Hospital services are provided through General Hospitals in every Health Board area and some specialist hospitals in the larger cities. Primary health care services, including GPs, dentists, opticians and pharmacists, are separately managed in the communities they serve. There are also some local authority services such as district nurses, health visitors, midwives, and special clinics, which are organised in the local community.

Reform of the NHS

When the Labour Party came into power in 1997 it inherited a system called the Internal Market from the Conservatives. The Conservatives believed that the NHS could be run a lot more efficiently if hospitals competed with each other for patients sent to them from GPs. The Labour Party did not think competition worked and instead introduced a system based around co-operation rather than competition. Hospital Trusts were set up in Health Boards to organise hospital services for that area. Primary Care Trusts and Local Health Care Co-operatives (LHCCs) were also set up to allow GPs to have a bigger say in how services are to be run.

2 Inequalities in Wealth and Health

Evidence of inequalities in wealth

Income and wealth

There is a lot of evidence to suggest that there are major inequalities in the UK when you look at the income and wealth of people. The National Statistics Office states that in 2003 the top 10% of earners had around £700 a week of disposable income while the bottom 10% had around £150 a week.

The distribution of wealth is also uneven. In 2001 50% of the population had around 5% of the wealth of the country, with the richest 1% having 23% of the wealth. In 2003, a third of all adults had some form of debt (personal loans, overdraft, credit cards) with 13% owing £10,000 or more. One definition of low income is where a household has an income below 60% of average disposable income. In 2002–03, 17% of the population lived in households with income below this level (£194 per week). This compares with a peak of 21% in 1991–92.

Working-age adults were generally at lower risk than the population as a whole of being on a low income, though those living in workless households were at much greater risk. Children were also at greater risk of living in low-income households than the population as a whole. In 2003 around one in five children (2.6 million) were living in low-income households. A similar proportion of pensioners were living in low-income households in 2003, though this had fallen from one in three in 1991.

Gender and income

The average weekly income for individual women in Great Britain in 2003–04 was £161. This was 53% of the average income for men, which was £303 per week. Between 1996–97 and 2003–04 women's individual income increased from 46% of men's to 53%. Individual income for women rose 31% in real terms, more than twice as fast as the 13% increase for men.

The main factors which influence both women's and men's individual incomes include age, economic activity status, children and whether they are single or have a partner. The largest increase was for single women with children, with total individual incomes rising by 50% over the period in real terms.

Among couples, 67% of total family incomes came from the total individual incomes of men, and 32% from the individual incomes of women. However, for 21% of all couples, women's individual incomes contributed over 50% of family incomes.

Lone-parent families

Since the early 1970s, there has been a doubling in the proportion of households in the UK headed by a lone parent with dependent children, to 6% in 2002. Up to the mid-1980s a large part of the rise was due to divorce. More recently, the number of single, lone mothers has grown at a faster rate, because of the rise in the proportion of births outside marriage. Lone mothers headed the majority of lone-parent families in spring 2002, with just one in ten headed by a lone father. Nearly half of lone mothers are single (never married). Lone parents receive a high priority for social sector housing and are more likely than any other type of household to be renting from this sector. Half of lone mothers with dependent children live in social sector housing. Lone mothers are more likely than lone fathers to be living in any sort of rented accommodation, while a higher proportion of lone fathers, who tend to be divorced, are owner-occupiers. A smaller proportion of lone mothers are in the labour force than mothers who are married or cohabiting. In spring 2003, 56% of lone mothers were economically active, compared with 72% of married or cohabiting women with dependent children.

Education

It is not just in monetary terms that we see inequalities. There are also inequalities when we compare educational attainment with social class categories (see Table 5.1 on page 67).

National statistics show us that, in 2002, 77% of the children in higher professional households gained five or more passes A to C in GCSEs, compared with just 32% of the children in routine households, though the gap between them is closing.

In 2002, 87% of 16-year-olds with parents in higher professional occupations were in full-time education. This compares with 60% of those with parents in routine occupations, and 58% with parents in lower supervisory occupations.

There is a clear relationship between higher qualifications and higher earnings, and the earnings premium for having a degree is particularly high. The average gross weekly income of full-time employees in the UK with a degree was £632 in spring 2003. This was more than double the weekly income of £298 for those with no qualifications. The likelihood of being employed is also higher for those with higher qualifications. In spring 2003, 88% of working-age adults with a degree were in full-time employment compared with 50% of those with no qualifications. Education is also a key factor in explaining the inequality gaps between advantaged and disadvantaged groups in terms of health, living standards and social participation.

Work

There are a number of disadvantaged groups when it comes to getting a job. Older people, minority ethnic groups, lone parents, those with low qualifications and disabled people all experience difficulties, though in recent years they have seen an increase in their employment. Labour market experiences also differ by gender. The male working-age employment rate declined from over 90% in the early 1970s to just below 80% in 2003. For women, participation in employment increased from 56% to just under 70% over the same period.

Children affect the economic activity of women more than that of men. In 2003, 48% of women with a child under two were in employment compared with 90% of men with children of this age. The working-age unemployment rates of those facing some disadvantage are also higher than in the general working-age population.

Minority ethnic groups, lone parents and people without formal qualifications had an unemployment rate of about 10% in 2003. This was roughly twice the rate for the total working-age population. Among the 7 million people of working age who had a disability, the unemployment rate was 8%.

Disadvantaged groups, particularly the disabled, are more likely to be inactive than the general working-age population, and the likelihood of inactivity increases with more disadvantages. Reasons for inactivity vary by sex and age. Men have been hardest hit by a decline in demand for low-skilled workers, and are also most likely to be inactive due to long-term sickness or disability. Older men are also more likely than older women to take early retirement. Women are more likely to be inactive for family reasons, and form the bulk of lone parents.

Living standards

Access to consumer goods and services is one indicator of people's living standards. For those goods that only became available in the last decade or so there is a strong link with household income. In 2002, 86% of households in Great Britain in the highest income group (weekly disposable income of £1,000 or more) had access to a home computer. This was almost six times the proportion for households in the lowest income group (£100 to £200 per week: 15%). The gap was even wider for internet connections. The proportion for the higher income group (79%) was almost eight times greater than that for the lower income group (10%).

More established goods such as washing machines and central heating, once regarded as luxuries, are now more common across all income groups and household types. However, they are still less likely to be found in lower-income than in higher-income households. On average, 91% of households had central heating in their homes in 2002. However, single-pensioner households are the least likely to have central heating, despite being one of the groups most vulnerable to the effects of cold indoor temperatures.

Car ownership is closely related to income, as well as to sex, age and location. In 2002, 59% of households in the lowest income 20% did not have access to a car. This was around seven times the proportion in the top 20% group (8%). High proportions of households without access to a car were found among single pensioners (69%), student households (44%) and lone parents (43%).

For many people, lack of access to a car can cause difficulties in getting to the shops or health services. In 2001, 11% of households without access to a car said they had difficulty in accessing their GP. This compares with 4% who had access to a car.

Causes of inequalities in wealth

In 1997, the Prime Minister, Tony Blair, set up the Social Exclusion Unit. Its main job was to find out the main causes of inequalities in wealth and to suggest policies to tackle the problem of poverty. Poverty is often defined as those households whose incomes are less than 60% of the national average, which in 2005 was around £425 a week. The Government listed a number of poverty indicators that were said to be the main causes of social exclusion. These are closely linked to the evidence of inequalities shown above.

According to the Social Exclusion Unit, the main causes and consequences of social exclusion are:

- poverty and low income
- unemployment
- poor educational attainment
- poor mental or physical health
- family breakdown and poor parenting
- poor housing and homelessness
- discrimination
- crime
- living in a disadvantaged area.

The Unit maintains that: 'The risk factors for social exclusion tend to cluster in certain neighbour-hoods, but not everybody at risk lives in a deprived area.'

We will look at the policies of the Labour Government to tackle wealth inequalities in the next section.

Evidence of inequalities in health

The health of the population has been improving steadily over the last century. However, despite this general improvement, the gap in the main causes of death between those in the advantaged and disadvantaged groups widened in the latter part of the twentieth century. Those in disadvantaged groups are more likely to die earlier and to be in poorer health compared with the rest of the population.

The reasons for these health inequalities are complex. There are links with people's social and demographic circumstances, such as their educational attainment, occupation, income, type of housing, sex, ethnicity and where they live. There are also factors relating to poor lifestyles such as smoking, drinking, drugs, diet, exercise and risk taking.

The Government has produced a lot of information through the National Statistics Office to give evidence of health inequalities. Some of this evidence is outlined below:

Social class inequalities

The Black Report (1980), The Health Divide (1987), Greater Glasgow Health Board (1995), and the Acheson Report (1998) were all of the view that social class or poverty was the main cause of inequalities in health in the UK. National Statistics 2001 tells us that there are substantial variations in reported health status by social group. Among those in employment, rates of 'not good' health for people in routine occupations were more than double those for people in higher managerial and professional occupations (8.6% and 3.4% respectively). Those who had never worked or were long-term unemployed had even higher rates of 'not good' health (18.5%).

Other indicators of social position, such as housing tenure, also point to a social divide in health status. In 2001 those living in council housing had the highest rates of 'not good' health, twice as high as those who rent privately, and three times higher than owner-occupiers.

When we look at the main illnesses causing death, such as cancer and heart disease, we see that socio-economic status plays a part. Survival rates for cancer vary by type of cancer and by a number of factors including sex, age and socio-economic status.

Lifestyle

There is evidence to show that the lifestyle of a person can have a major impact on their health. The main lifestyle issues are smoking, drinking, drugs, diet and exercise.

Smoking

Among adults aged 16 and over in the UK, one in four (25%) were cigarette smokers in 2004 – with a slightly higher proportion of men (26%) than women (23%). People in routine and manual households were more likely to smoke than those in managerial and professional households (31% compared with 18%). Smoking fell substantially in the 1970s and the early 1980s – from 45% in 1974 to 35% in 1982. After 1982 the rate of decline slowed and then levelled out from 1992, at around 27%. Smoking is the main cause of lung cancer, responsible for nine out of ten cases, and it contributes to a range of other diseases and conditions, such as heart and respiratory diseases. It is estimated that between 1998 and 2002 on average 106,000 people a year died from smoking-related causes in the UK – around one in six of all deaths.

Drinking

Among adults in the UK in 2004 nearly one in three (30%) exceeded the recommended daily intake (of no more than four units for men and three units for women) on at least one day during the previous week. Men were more likely to exceed the intake than women – 39% of men compared with 22% of women. Drinking above the recommended guidelines leads to increased risk of harm, both immediately and in later life. It is estimated that there were 5,500 alcohol-related deaths in England and Wales in 2000, the majority from chronic liver disease such as cirrhosis.

Each year there are also approximately 3,500 deaths on UK roads, of which around one in six are alcohol related. Drink-drive fatalities have fallen by two-thirds since the late 1970s. In 2003, Department of Transport estimates showed there were still 580 fatalities and 2,600 serious injuries where at least one of the drivers involved was over the legal limit.

Drugs

According to the most recent government figures more than a third of people have taken drugs in their lifetime and more than 10% did so in the past year. The fact that drug use is relatively high does not mean it is increasing at an alarming rate – the most recent figures suggest that overall usage is stable. However, drug taking is not the easiest subject to get solid information on. Users of recreational drugs are shy at admitting their habits and people addicted to hard drugs tend to have chaotic lifestyles meaning they are difficult to count. One recent trend has been the rise in the use of cocaine. The rise in cocaine use has concerned health professionals – a 2003 study at St Mary's Hospital in London found that one in three young men who attended Accident and Emergency clinics with heart pains had cocaine in their system. Crack and heroin have relatively few users compared with cocaine – the British Crime Survey puts the estimates at 55,000 for crack and 43,000 for heroin, about 0.2% of the population in England and Wales. But these figures are almost certainly underestimates as the survey tends not to reach groups which have a high proportion of users of these drugs – including sex workers and homeless people.

Diet

Obesity in the UK has increased among both adults and children since the mid-1990s. In 2002 it was similar for both sexes, the rate for boys and girls was 17% and for adults was 23%. In 1995 the equivalent figures were 10% for boys and 12% for girls, 15% for men and 18% for women.

Exercise

In 2003 the percentage of adults meeting the recommendations for physical activity in the UK declined with age for both sexes. Men were more active than women in every age group and their activity levels declined steadily with age. For women, activity levels remained the same until the 45 to 54 age group, and then declined.

Figure 5.2 Persuading people to exercise regularly is one way to improve people's health

Since the early 1990s there has been a steady increase in the use of cars and a decrease in walking and cycling to school or to work in the UK. Among children aged five to ten, the proportion who walked to school fell from 61% in 1992–94 to 52% in 2002–03. Among children aged 11 to 16, the proportion of journeys to school by car increased from 16 to 23% over the same period, reflecting the combined decrease in journeys on foot or by bicycle. For adults aged 17 and over, the number of journeys to work by car rose from 66% in 1989–91 to 71% in 2002–03. During the same interval, journeys that were mainly on foot fell from 13 to 10%.

Gender inequalities

There is evidence to show that there are inequalities in health between men and women. National Statistics show that in 2001 the average life expectancy at birth of females born in the UK was 80 years, compared with 76 years for males. However, the gap is smaller in terms of the number of years they can expect to live in good health. Healthy life expectancy for women in 1999 averaged 69 years, compared with 67 years for men. Consequently, while women can expect to live longer than men they are also more likely to have more years in poor health.

Causes of death vary between the sexes. Cancers are now the most common cause of death in women and the second most common cause in men, accounting for only slightly fewer deaths in men than circulatory disease (which includes heart disease and stroke). However, as a result of greater falls in deaths from other illnesses, the proportion of deaths caused by cancer has risen. In 2001 cancers were responsible for 28% of male deaths in England and Wales and 24% of female deaths, compared with 16% among both males and females in 1951.

The trends in lung cancer deaths are closely linked to the prevalence of cigarette smoking among men and women in the UK. The decline in smoking among men has led to a reduction in lung cancer deaths. The male lung cancer death rate fell sharply from the mid-1970s, halving between 1976 and 2001. In contrast, the rate among women rose from the 1970s before levelling off in the late 1980s.

In 2001, although obesity was at similar levels for both men and women, nearly half of men were considered overweight compared with a third of women. Men are almost twice as likely as women to exceed the recommended daily intakes for consumption of alcohol. Around 50% of young men in the UK exceeded the recommended number of daily units on their heaviest drinking day in 2001, compared with around 40% of women. In 1974, 51% of men and 41% of women in the UK reported that they were regular cigarette smokers. The gap narrowed so that by 2001 the proportions had fallen to 28% of men and 26% of women.

Young men are more likely than young women to take drugs. Cannabis is the most commonly used drug in the UK. In 2001, around a third of men aged 16 to 24 and a fifth of women aged 16 to 24 had used the drug in the last year. Class A drugs (including heroin, cocaine and ecstasy) were used less frequently, but again men were far more likely to use these drugs than women (12% of young men compared with 5% of young women).

Ethnicity inequalities

There is evidence to show that in a number of areas, the ethnic background of a person can have an impact on their overall health.

Pakistani and Bangladeshi men and women in England and Wales reported the highest rates of 'not good' health in 2001.

Pakistanis had rates of 'not good' health of 13% (men) and 17% (women). The rates for Bangladeshis were 14% (men) and 15% (women). These rates, which take account of the difference in age structures between the ethnic groups, were around twice that of their White British counterparts. Chinese men and women were the least likely to report their health as 'not good'.

Reporting poor health has been shown to be strongly associated with use of health services and mortality. Pakistani women had higher GP contact rates than women in the general population. Bangladeshi men were three times as likely to visit their GP than men in the general population.

There were marked variations between different ethnic groups in rates of long-term illness or disability which restricted daily activities. Pakistani and Bangladeshi men and women had the highest rates of disability. Rates were around 1.5 times higher than their White British counterparts. Chinese men and women had the lowest rates.

In some groups the difference between men and women in their rates of disability was much greater than in others. In the Indian, Pakistani, Black Caribbean and Black African groups, women had higher rates than men.

Bangladeshi men were the most likely group to smoke cigarettes (44% in 1999), followed by Black Caribbean men (35%). Men from each of these ethnic groups were more likely to smoke than men in the general population (27%). Chinese men (17%) were the least likely to smoke.

Black Caribbeans were most likely to drink above the government guidelines for alcohol consumption (5%): 27% of Black Caribbean men and 17% of Black Caribbean women did so. Other minority ethnic groups were much less likely than the general population to have consumed alcohol in excess of the daily guidelines. Less than 10% of men and women from the Pakistani, Bangladeshi and Chinese groups drank more than these recommended amounts on their heaviest drinking day. Very few Indian women exceeded the guidelines but 22% of Indian men drank above this level.

Geography
There is evidence to show that health varies from one part of the UK to another. Scotland has a higher rate of heart disease and cancer than other parts of the UK. However, there seems to be a close correlation to social class inequalities in those areas that suffer most.

Causes of inequalities in health
There are a number of reasons put forward to explain why there are inequalities in health. No one cause can be identified, but it is more likely to be a combination of factors. The two main schools of thought centre around social class and lifestyle as being the two most important causes of inequalities. They tend to be opposing viewpoints. Is it poor social class setting that causes you to be more unhealthy, or do individuals choose to lead unhealthy lifestyles? We will look at these factors in a bit more detail.

Social class or socio-economic status
Social class or socio-economic status is one way of measuring how good your standard of living is. The Government gives us health statistics based on a person's social class group. As we have seen, the Registrar General's classification changed in 2000 and moved from six to nine groups, now more closely linked to employment, status, pay level, responsibility and

skill. There are a number of reports and surveys that suggest that, the poorer your social class group, the poorer your health is likely to be. Some of these are listed here:

1980 – 'Black Report' confirmed link between social class and ill-health.

1987 – 'The Health Divide' by Health Education Council confirmed this.

1994 – Greater Glasgow Health Board, study of Bearsden and Drumchapel.

1998 – 'Acheson Report' and 'Working Together for a Healthier Scotland'.

Lifestyle

Some people do not accept that poor economic conditions are the main reason for poor health. They argue that people are not forced to smoke, drink, take drugs, have a poor diet and take little exercise. They choose to live this unhealthy lifestyle and it is no surprise that their health is poorer as a result. The James Report in 1993 showed links between the poor Scottish diet and poor health. The effects of smoking, excessive drinking, taking drugs, eating a poor diet and having little exercise on a person's health are well known. It is argued that individual people should be persuaded to adopt more healthy lifestyles to improve the health of the nation.

Two rival theories are put forward to tackle these inequalities. Those people who think that social class is the main problem argue for the Collectivist theory. It says that the state should improve social conditions (unemployment, low income, social exclusion) to improve the health of all poorer people.

Those people who think lifestyles are the main problem argue for the Individualist theory. It says that each person is responsible for their own health and therefore only they can choose to lead healthy lifestyles. The Government's job should be to persuade individuals to live more healthily.

3 Government Responses to Inequalities in Wealth and Health

Government responses to inequalities in wealth

One way the Government can tackle these inequalities is to improve the income of people who are disadvantaged; it does this by paying out benefits. There are a wide range of benefits available.

Welfare benefits

You should be aware of the difference between **universal** benefits and **means-tested** benefits. Universal benefits are those available regardless of income or circumstances, for example Child Benefit, which is paid to those who have children. Means-tested benefits are only paid to people who are eligible for them in terms of income, such as people on a low income, the disabled, or the unemployed; examples are Income Support, Disability Living Allowance and Jobseekers Allowance. Means-tested benefits are designed to target people on low incomes and raise their standard of living to a more acceptable level. Most of the benefits available from the Government are means-tested benefits. We will look in more detail at some of these benefits.

Jobseekers Allowance

This benefit is paid to unemployed people who are aged between 18 and 65 and who are capable of working, available for work and actively seeking work. They must attend interviews with Jobseeker personnel and agree a Jobseekers Agreement, where they will state how they are going to get into work. The weekly rate (2005) is £44.50 for 18 to 24 year olds and £56.20 for over 25s. Jobseeker Direct is a phone service related to this benefit.

Income Support

This is a means-tested benefit available to people aged 16 to 60 who are living on a low income and who are not working, or working less than 16 hours a week. Lone parents, people who are sick or disabled, people who are caring for someone, or people who are registered blind can claim Income Support. If you have savings of more than £16,000 you cannot get Income Support. Savings between £6,000 and £16,000 may affect the amount you get. The weekly rate (2005) is £33.85 for 16 and 17 year olds, £44.50 for 18 to 24 year olds, and £56.20 for over 25s. Couples aged 18 and over get £88.15 a week and dependent children get £43.88 until their 19th birthday. Pensioner couples get £78.90 a week and there are extra payments for disabled, single parents, carers, and in cases of bereavement.

Housing Benefit

Housing Benefit is sometimes called rent rebate or rent allowance and is payable to people on a low income who are paying rent. It is paid by the local council and is means-tested. Again if you have between £6,000 and £16,000 of savings, or more, this will affect your entitlement. The amount you get depends on your income, your savings and your circumstances, such as your age, number and ages of your children, if anyone living with you can help pay the rent and so on. The amounts are similar to Jobseekers Allowance and Income Support.

Council Tax Benefit

This is payable to someone who is on a low income and who is eligible to pay Council Tax. It is paid by the council as a rebate on your Council Tax bill and again it is means-tested. The amount you get depends on your income, your savings and your circumstances, such as your age, number and ages of your children, if anyone living with you can help pay the council tax and so on.

Social Fund

The Social Fund provides lump sum payments, grants and loans to people on a low income. It is for things you may need in your home, such as beds, fridges, cookers, that you may find hard to pay for out of your own income. It is means-tested and any savings you have may affect the amount you get. You may also be able to get a Social Fund Crisis Loan in an emergency or disaster. If it comes in the form of a loan, it has to be paid back.

Child Tax Credit

Child Tax Credit is the main way that families get money to look after their children up to age 16, and 16–18 year olds in full-time education. The amount you get is based on your income. You can claim whether or not you are in work. It has replaced the old tax credits and benefits with a single system – so all families with children, with an income up to £58,000 a year (or up to £66,000 a year if there is a child under one year old), can claim in the same way. In 2006, the amount for one child was £545 a year for high earners, up to £2420 for those on low incomes, with extra money for young children and disabled children. It is paid to the main carer of the child or children.

Child Benefit

This is a universal benefit paid to people who are bringing up children. It is paid for each child usually up to the age of 16, though children in full-time education can still qualify, and it is not affected by income or savings. In 2006 the amount for the eldest child was £17.45 per week and each other child £11.70 per week.

Working Tax Credit

Working Tax Credit is a payment to top up the earnings of low-paid working people (whether employed or self-employed), including those who do not have children. Working Tax Credit helps to make work pay for low-income workers. In most cases, the employer pays it alongside wages or salary, although the self-employed get paid directly. The 'childcare element' of Working Tax Credit is paid directly to the main carer of the child or children along with Child Tax Credit. The amount you get depends on your income; with the £16,000 limit in place. Low-paid workers in 2006 would get up to £1410 a year for a single worker aged 25 and over and up to £3005 for a couple earning less than £8,000 a year.

Incapacity Benefit

This is a benefit paid to workers who have become ill and cannot work for more than four days in a row, and who are not entitled to Statutory Sick Pay (SSP). SSP is paid by employers to people who have paid National Insurance contributions, but is only payable for 28 weeks. If an employee has not paid NI contributions, or is sick for more than 28 weeks, they may be entitled to Incapacity Benefit. In 2006, the amount paid was £68.20 between 28 and 52 weeks off, and £76.45 for over 52 weeks.

Disability Living Allowance

Disability Living Allowance (DLA) is a tax-free benefit for children and adults under 65 who need help with personal care or have walking difficulties because they are physically or mentally disabled. There are two parts to DLA: a care component, if you need help looking after yourself or supervision to keep you safe; and a mobility component, if you can't walk or need help getting around. In 2006, the highest care component was £62.25 a week and the highest mobility component was £43.45 a week. Adults over 65 may claim Attendance Allowance which has a weekly rate of £62.25.

Pension Credit

Everyone in the UK is entitled to a state pension when they reach the age of 60 for women (though this is changing in 2020 to 65) and 65 for men. Pension Credit boosts the income of pensioners living on a low income. At the moment the basic state pension is £82.05 (2005) for a single pensioner and Pension Credit will increase the income of pensioners to a minimum of £109.45 a week for single pensioners and £167.05 if they have a partner. It is means-tested on the basis of savings of up to £6,000 and £16,000, as before. Some pensioners can also get Winter Fuel Allowances.

Social inclusion – Welfare to Work

As well as paying benefits to those who did not have sufficient income to live on, the Labour Government elected in 1997 was determined to tackle the causes of poverty as well as the consequences. The previous Conservative Government believed that the best way to create wealth was to develop a free market economy. The success of private companies would create jobs, and individuals would improve their own chances of becoming better-off through these jobs. The Labour Party did not think the individual approach was the best way to tackle poverty. It believed in the idea of social inclusion. The state would tackle the causes of poverty to make sure all individuals had the chance of being lifted out of poverty. Not only did inequalities in employment have to be tackled, but inequalities in education, health, housing and environment had to be tackled also.

A Social Exclusion Unit was set up by the Government in 1997 to look at the issues. In its own words:

> Social exclusion happens when people or places suffer from a series of problems such as unemployment, discrimination, poor skills, low incomes, poor housing, high crime, ill health and family breakdown. When such problems combine they can create a vicious cycle. Social exclusion can happen as a result of problems that face one person in their life. But it can also start from birth. Being born into poverty or to parents with low skills still has a major influence on future life chances.

As a result of this view, the Government set about introducing policies aimed at improving the life chances of all individuals, but especially those who suffered from social exclusion. The phrase 'Welfare to Work' is sometimes used in connection with those policies aimed at the unemployed.

We will look at a number of the social inclusion policies introduced in recent years to tackle the problems of poverty.

The New Deal

The Government believed that work was the best way for individuals to get out of poverty. They introduced a number of New Deal schemes, such as New Deal for Young People, New Deal for Lone Parents, New Deal for 25 plus, New Deal for 50 plus, and New Deal for Disabled. Every person on New Deal has a personal adviser who helps them to plan the best way back into work. Employers are encouraged to take on New Deal workers and can get up to £75 a week subsidy for doing so. New Deal workers themselves are told what benefits

Figure 5.3 A New Deal trainee

and tax credits may be available to them when they go on New Deal. There may be penalties in the form of lost benefits if they don't accept.

National minimum wage

In 1999, the Labour Government introduced a national minimum wage (NMW) as it realised that it would have to protect vulnerable groups of low-paid workers if it was to get rid of poverty. People who were unemployed would need some encouragement to move from welfare to work. It was also recognised that certain groups of workers, such as women, the young and those in service industries like hospitality, retail and social care, were more likely to be in low pay than other workers. The Government set up an independent Low Pay Commission in 1997 to report on low pay and to set the levels it felt should be given to low-paid workers. At first, workers aged 16 and 17 were exempt from the NMW, with workers aged 18 to 21 getting a minimum of £3.00 an hour and workers over 21 getting a minimum of £3.60 an hour. Eventually, the Government accepted that 16 and 17 year old workers should be included. In October 2006 the rates were £5.35 for over 21s, £4.45 for 18 to 21 year olds, and £3.30 for 16 and 17 year olds.

Dealing with child poverty

The Government came into power in 1997 determined to 'eradicate child poverty by 2020'. The main method it has used to do this is through employment schemes to help the parents of children back into work. Tax credits were also introduced and schemes like Sure Start introduced to help parents with young children. The Government has had some success in reducing the number of children living in poverty by 700,000 since 1997, but there are still some problems to overcome.

Child care is something that has to be addressed. Early years care and education is known to improve children's future educational achievement and health, but almost all childcare services for children under three are private sector arrangements for those whose parents can pay. There are 600,000 children under three living in poverty and only 42,740 free or subsidised childcare places for disadvantaged families.

Work is not an option for all families, especially if they are caring for a disabled child or have health or disability problems themselves. The Child Tax Credit established a guaranteed minimum income level for families in work, but there are no minimum levels for those on benefit. For those who do not have paid work, income can be far below the poverty line. Weekly income support for a couple with two children is around £178, compared with £253 in earnings at poverty level. For a single parent with two children, income support is £147, compared with £175 in earnings at poverty level.

The key factors which suggest that children will fail to break free of the poverty cycle include: missing periods of school, being in care, being known to the police, misuse of drugs, teenage parenthood, and being out of education, employment or training between the ages of 16 and 18. Today, in the UK, one in four children is still living in poverty. In some regions, child poverty is even higher: rising to 54% in inner London. There are some wards in the UK where over 90% of children live in poverty.

'Breaking the Cycle' Report 2004

The Social Exclusion Unit was asked by the Prime Minister to prepare a report in 2004 after seven years of government policies, to say what success the Government had had in dealing with poverty and to outline the challenges the Government still faced. The Report said the Government's successes were as follows.

Successes of the Labour Government

◆ There has been significant progress, particularly in tackling **poverty and unemployment**.

◆ **A reduction in child poverty.** In 2003 there were 700,000 fewer children living in poverty than in 1997. It is estimated that by 2005, if the Government had taken no action, 1.5 million more children would be in poverty.

◆ Expansion of **nursery education** and **childcare services**. Sure Start Local Programmes are now available to 400,000 children.

◆ There were also 500,000 fewer **pensioners** living in relative poverty in 2003 than in 1997, and 1.8 million fewer living in absolute poverty.

◆ **There are now 1.85 million more people in work than in 1997**, and there have been faster than average increases in employment among some disadvantaged groups including lone parents, people with disabilities and those over 50 years old. Long-term unemployment amongst those aged 18–24 halved between 1997 and 2003.

◆ **Educational attainment** has risen. There have been improvements for most ethnic minority groups, and progress in schools in the most disadvantaged local authority areas has been even faster than elsewhere.

◆ The number of **homeless people** sleeping rough has fallen by 70% and there has been a 99.3% decline in the use of Bed and Breakfast for housing homeless families with children since March 2002.

◆ **Youth offending** has reduced and juvenile reconviction rates fell by a fifth between 1997 and 2001. The conception rate for girls under 18 has fallen by 9.4%.

◆ There has been a reduction in **crime** and the fear of crime, including among older people.

◆ The gap between the most **deprived** local authority areas and the rest of the country is narrowing on some indicators, such as rates of employment, educational attainment and teenage conceptions.

◆ Further improvements can be expected as programmes which show encouraging early signs – like Sure Start, Education Maintenance Allowances and Connexions – become more established.

◆ The effects of more recent policy measures like **Child Tax Credit** will not yet have shown up in national data.

The Report did say, however, that there were still some major challenges ahead and that the Government should not become too complacent. The main challenges were as follows.

Major challenges that still face the Labour Government

◆ The report identified five key problems that continue to cause social exclusion:

  – low educational attainment among some groups

  – economic inactivity and concentrations of worklessness

  – health inequalities

  – concentrations of crime and poor quality environments in some areas

  – homelessness.

◆ Progress made by individuals can also be fragile, and is not always sustained. For example, 40% of participants who get a job after participating in the New Deal for Young People return to claiming Jobseeker's Allowance within six months. Progress in other areas of life – like giving up drugs or turning away from crime – can also be undermined easily.

The Report laid out the Government's strategy to meet these challenges in the future.

Meeting the challenges

◆ **Continuing to reduce child poverty.** The *Child Poverty Review* was announced in July 2004. This identifies the next steps across the entire range of policies to improve the life chances of poor children. There will be continued efforts made to increase employment opportunities for parents and to make work pay, as well as support for families where parents are unable to work.

◆ **Continuing to increase investment in early years.** Good early years services will continue to play a vital role in supporting families in their parenting role.

♦ **Tackling educational under-attainment, and supporting the transition into work.** The Government is committed to making continued progress on raising standards in schools and closing the gap in achievement between some groups of children.

♦ **Keeping up pressure on the economic causes of social exclusion,** particularly stubborn concentrations of unemployment.

♦ **Narrowing unjustifiable inequalities in poor health.** New targets to reduce the main cuases of health inequalities – particularly cancer, heart disease and smoking in lower socio-economic groups and a new target to reduce childhood obesity.

♦ **Reducing the level of homelessness.** Increasing the supply of affordable housing to tackle homelessness, including an increase in the number of homes in the social rented sector.

♦ **Tackling crime and poor living conditions in the most deprived areas.** There will be a drive to tackle crime and anti-social behaviour in the highest crime areas, which have a significant overlap with deprived areas.

Government responses to inequalities in health

Since the setting up of the NHS in 1948, there have been impressive social, economic and health improvements in Britain. People from every class and region are healthier and living longer than ever before. Unfortunately, not everyone is able to share the benefits of these improvements. Tackling health inequalities is a top priority for the Government, and it is focused on narrowing the health gap between disadvantaged groups, communities and the rest of the country, and on improving health overall. Since health in Scotland is a function of the Scottish Parliament, you should be aware of the policies brought in by the Scottish Executive to deal with health inequalities.

The 1999 White Paper, *Towards a Healthier Scotland*, set the framework for Scottish public health and health improvement policy. The White Paper recognised that health improvement policies should consider life circumstances, lifestyles, and priority diseases such as heart disease and cancer.

The Executive's 2003 paper on improving health, *Improving Health in Scotland – The Challenge*, highlighted the need for all of the NHS to work as a partnership to improve health. The aims outlined in the paper are to improve the health of all people in Scotland and to narrow the health gap. It recommended the use of 23 indicators to monitor health inequalities, and had a specific objective to improve life expectancy and healthy life expectancy and also 'to reduce inequalities between the most affluent and most deprived groups'.

Targets for reducing health inequalities are also integrated with the Scottish Executive's current social inclusion policy – *Closing the Opportunity Gap*. Since socio-economic conditions have a big effect on health, any policies to tackle gaps between rich and poor will also have an impact on health. There are six health specific indicators (selected from the 23 originally set out in the *Challenge* paper):

♦ smoking during pregnancy – 10.0% reduction in the most deprived areas between 2003 and 2008

♦ adults smoking (aged 16–64) – 10.9% reduction between 2003 and 2008

♦ coronary heart disease mortality (for under 75s) – 27.1% reduction between 2003 and 2008

- teenage pregnancy (aged 13–15) – 33% reduction between 2000–02 and 2007–09
- suicides in young people (aged 10–24) – 15% reduction between 2001–03 and 2007–09
- cancer mortality rates (for under 75s) – 10.1% reduction between 2003 and 2008.

Possible questions on wealth and health inequalities

Any questions on this topic are likely to include aspects of all the issues discussed above. It is unlikely that you will get a question that only looks at one part of this Unit as most of the issues in wealth and health are related to each other. Remember that, as well as showing your knowledge of a topic, you are expected to analyse the topic, looking at the arguments for and against a particular point of view. Here are some likely question areas to prepare for.

- To what extent are the original aims of the Welfare State still being met?
- Critically examine the funding of the Welfare State in the UK.
- Collective responsibility is no longer the best way to provide welfare in the UK. Discuss.
- To what extent do people in the UK suffer from inequalities in wealth / health?
- Assess the effectiveness of government policies in dealing with race / gender inequalities in wealth / health.
- Critically examine the view that gender / race inequalities in the UK have become less important in recent years.

Questions and Answers

SAQ 1   To what extent are there inequalities in wealth in the UK?   *(15 marks)*

Answer to SAQ 1

There have always been inequalities in wealth in the UK. Some people have very good standards of living because of the large incomes they have, while others are not so well off. In any developed country, these inequalities should be kept at an acceptable level and there should be policies in place to make sure no person suffers unduly as a result of poverty.

The Government set up the Welfare State after the Second World War, to make sure the citizens of the UK had an acceptable minimum living standard. It was based on the Beveridge Report, which identified five main areas of need that people might want help with if they could not manage on their own. These 'five giants' were want, disease, ignorance, squalor and idleness. The Government set up departments to deal with each of these areas. The National Health Service (NHS), the Department of Social Security, the Housing Department, the Department of Employment, and the Department of Education were all given the task of making sure that people in the UK had a minimum standard of living. The Government would provide a 'safety net' and look after its citizens 'from the cradle to the grave'.

Has the Welfare State kept inequalities in wealth at an acceptable level in the UK, or are there still groups of people who suffer greatly as a result of poverty?

Questions and *Answers* continued ➤

UNIT 2: SOCIAL ISSUES IN THE UNITED KINGDOM

Answer to SAQ 1 continued

There is a lot of evidence to suggest that there are major inequalities in the UK when you look at the income and wealth of people. The National Statistics Office tells us that, in 2003, the top 10% of earners had around £700 a week of disposable income while the bottom 10% had around £150 a week. The distribution of wealth is also uneven. In 2001 50% of the population had around 5% of the wealth of the country with the richest 1% having 23% of the wealth. In 2003, a third of all adults had some form of debt (personal loans, overdraft, credit cards). One definition of low income is where a household is below 60% of average disposable income. In 2003, 17% of the population lived in households with income below this level (£194 per week).

Working-age adults were generally at lower risk than the population as a whole of being on a low income, though those living in workless households were at much greater risk. Children were also at greater risk of living in low-income households than the population as a whole. In 2003 around one in five children were living in low-income households. A similar proportion of pensioners were living in low-income households in 2003.

Access to consumer goods and services is one indicator of people's living standards. In 2002, almost six times as many households in Great Britain in the highest-income group had access to a home computer in comparison to households in the lowest-income group. The gap was even wider for internet connections.

More established goods such as washing machines and central heating, once regarded as luxuries, are now more common across all income groups and household types. However, they are still less likely to be found in lower than in higher-income households. Single-pensioner households are the least likely to have central heating, despite being one of the groups most vulnerable to the effects of cold indoor temperatures.

Car ownership is closely related to income, as well as to sex, age and location. In 2002, around seven times as many households in the lowest-income group (20%) did not have access to a car compared to the top 20% group. High proportions of households without access to a car were found among single pensioners, student households and lone parents.

Another group likely to suffer inequalities in wealth is women. The weekly average individual income for all women in Great Britain in 2003–04 was £161. This was 53% of men's individual average income, which was £303 per week.

Around 90% of lone-parent families are headed by women and many of them are likely to be living in poverty. Half of lone-parent families are likely to be in social sector housing.

There are a number of disadvantaged groups when it comes to getting a job. Older people, minority ethnic groups, lone parents, those with low qualifications and disabled people all experience difficulties, though in recent years they have seen an increase in their employment. Labour market experiences also differ by gender. The male working-age employment rate declined from over 90% in the early 1970s to just below 80% in 2003. For women, participation in employment increased from 56% to just under 70% over the same period.

Questions and *Answers* continued ➤

Questions and Answers continued

Answer to SAQ 1 continued

In conclusion, there is evidence to suggest that inequalities in wealth can still be seen in the UK, particularly amongst certain groups. However, there is also evidence to suggest that poverty does not have as large an effect on people in the UK as it did in the past. Recent government policies have succeeded in lifting many people out of poverty.

SAQ 2   Assess the effectiveness of government policies in dealing with gender inequalities in the UK in recent years.   *(15 marks)*

Answer to SAQ 2

There is a lot of evidence to show that there are a number of areas where men and women do not experience the same levels of opportunities in the UK. The Government has attempted to improve the situation in a number of ways, but it could be argued that, although things have improved in recent years, women still tend to lag behind men in a number of areas.

In wealth, the average income of women is around 53% of that of men. Women tend not to get as many promoted posts as men. Women tend to work more in part-time, low-paid jobs. The number of women who head lone-parent families is around 90%, and these families tend to have poorer incomes, tend to live in poorer housing and rely a lot more on benefits.

In health, the life expectancy of women is around five years longer than that of men. Women tend to report more illness than men, though this may be as a result of men avoiding going to the doctor when faced with a problem. There are likely to be more elderly women than men using the services of the NHS and the local council, and women tend to get more prescriptions than men.

To tackle all of these inequalities between men and women, the Government has used a number of initiatives. Wealth inequalities have been addressed by paying various benefits. Some of these benefits are universal, in that everyone gets them regardless of their circumstances, for example Child Benefit. Most benefits, however, are means-tested. This means that a person will only get them if they don't have the means to look after themselves, for example, if they are living on a low income. Benefits like this include Income Support, Housing Benefit and Child Tax Credit.

The Government has also tried to tackle inequalities by bringing in a number of policies. New Deal was introduced to help people 'from welfare to work'. The National Minimum Wage was introduced to make it more worthwhile for people to stay in work. The Government has also been addressing the issue of child poverty through a number of initiatives, including schemes like Sure Start, investing in early years services, and tackling things like homelessness.

Questions and Answers continued ➤

Questions *and* Answers *continued*

Answer to SAQ 2 continued

In health, the Government has continued to spend very large sums of money on the NHS and on trying to improve the health of all people. It is trying to tackle the main causes of death, such as heart disease and cancer. It is also hoping that its policies to improve social conditions and tackle the issue of lifestyle will bring long-term benefits to people's health.

What effect have all these policies had on gender inequalities? There is no doubt that the income of women has improved. From 1997 to 2004, women's average income rose from 46% of men's to 53%. Individual income for women rose 31% in real terms, more than twice as fast as the 13% increase for men. The largest increase was for single women with children, with total individual incomes rising by 50% over the period in real terms. However, women still do not have the same rates of pay that men do. Nevertheless, the male working-age employment rate declined from over 90% in the early 1970s to just below 80% in 2003. For women, participation in employment increased from 56% to just under 70% over the same period.

Around 90% of lone-parent families are headed by women. These women are much less likely to be in employment than women with children who have a partner. Their incomes are also likely to be lower and they are more likely to be living off benefits. Women who head lone-parent families are also more likely to be in social housing, where they rent their homes. On the other hand, men who head lone-parent families are more likely to be owner-occupiers. However, the Government has been introducing many policies designed to help women on low incomes, particularly those with children. Schemes like Sure Start and other initiatives to improve early years services are helping women with children to improve their chances of employment and also improve their standard of living.

In health, the Government has been concerned about the levels of illness caused by things like heart disease and cancer. Men suffer more from these illnesses than women. The Government has been trying to improve social conditions through its welfare to work polices, New Deal, National Minimum Wage and others. It is hoping to improve social class inequalities in the long term in this way. It has also tried to improve the number of men who go to health services for checkups. Well-women clinics have been long established, and now the Government wants more men to become aware of the advantages of early prevention.

In conclusion, the Government has adopted a number of policies to tackle wealth and health gender inequalities in the UK. Some of these polices are beginning to show signs of success. However, there are still major inequalities in terms of gender in a number of areas. There are also new challenges the Government will have to face.

UNIT 3

International Issues

STUDY THEME 3A: THE REPUBLIC OF SOUTH AFRICA

What You Should Know

SQA:

The South African political system: the role and powers of the South African government at national, provincial and local levels.

Political issues: participation and representation. Political parties and support from different groups. Political trends.

Social and economic issues: the nature and extent of social and economic inequalities; demands for change; the effectiveness of government responses and the consequences among and within different racial groups.

This topic can be split into two main sections:

1 South African Politics
2 Social and Economic Issues in South Africa.

Background

Although you will not be asked to answer any questions on Apartheid – the system run by the South African whites up until 1990 – you will need to know a bit about it to understand the main problems facing South Africa today.

Apartheid 1948–1990

Afrikaners in South Africa (descendants of white settlers mostly from the Netherlands) set up a system called Apartheid, based on the race of individuals. Apartheid is an Afrikaans word meaning 'separation'. The idea was to ensure that whites in general, but especially Afrikaners, would have the best possible standard of living by keeping power in their hands and restricting what non-whites could do.

Dividing the population
The population was split into four main racial groups by the law which classified people at birth: the Population Registration Act 1950. The Mixed Marriages Act 1949 and the Immorality Acts 1950 and 1957 tried to make sure that the 'purity' of the whites was maintained.

Dividing the land
The National Party (the main Afrikaner party) declared that 87% of the land would be 'white South Africa' and the other 13% would be divided up amongst the black tribes, who would each be given a Homeland. Kwazulu was to be the main Zulu Homeland. This allowed the

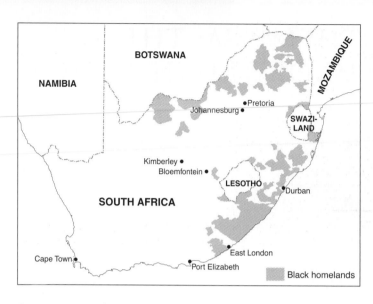

Figure 6.1 South Africa during Apartheid, showing the areas allocated as black homelands

Government to claim that blacks were not really South African citizens, but rather were citizens of their Homeland. It also gave the Government the excuse to forcibly remove blacks from 'white' South Africa.

Controlling the non-white population

The Government hoped to weaken any attempts to unite against Apartheid. It relied on harsh and oppressive laws to control blacks. The Pass Laws meant every non-white person had to carry identity documents, which were proof that they were entitled to be in 'white South Africa'. The Terrorism Act and Internal Security Act gave the police and security forces tremendous powers. People could be banned and held in detention almost indefinitely. Schools were segregated on the basis of race, as was housing and employment. The media was censored by the Government. Only whites were allowed to vote in elections. You should be aware of the effects this system had on the living standards of non-whites in the country.

De Klerk's reforms

F. W. De Klerk, the Afrikaner leader of the National Party, was confirmed as President by the white voters in September 1989 and this allowed him to carry out a reform programme. He was one of many Afrikaners who came to the conclusion that the white population had to 'adapt or die'. There was increasing pressure from opposition inside the country, and many sanctions had been imposed on South Africa from other countries worldwide in protest at Apartheid. The system of Apartheid was falling apart and its leaders decided that the best strategy was to negotiate with the blacks and try to salvage as much of their lifestyles as they could. The main steps in the process leading to the dismantling of Apartheid and the establishment of a democratic government are described below.

Dismantling of Apartheid

In 1990, the ban on the activities of the African National Congress (ANC), the main opposition group, was removed and Nelson Mandela, its leader, was released from prison. The ANC agreed to 'suspend' its armed struggle in response to this. From 1990 to 1994 the ANC and National Party held talks to decide the future structure of the South African Government. They agreed a new Constitution and in April 1994 the first ever multi-racial elections took place in South Africa. The ANC won the election and Nelson Mandela became the first black President of South Africa.

Figure 6.2 Nelson Mandela being released from prison in February 1990

1 South African Politics

The main issues covered in this section are:

◆ The South African political system

◆ Election results

◆ Political parties

◆ Democracy in South Africa

The South African political system

When the National Party and the ANC sat down together after 1990, they had to agree a new political structure for the country before elections could be held. The features of the South African political system are outlined below.

Federal state

The South Africans have a federal state where there is a central government in Pretoria to look after national affairs like defence and foreign policy, and there are nine Provinces that each have their own government. There are also local councils within each Province. The Federal Government has an Executive with a President, Deputy President and Cabinet Ministers. Its Parliament consists of two houses: the National Assembly, whose members are chosen by the people, and the National Council of Provinces (NCOP). The NCOP consists of 54 permanent members and 36 special delegates. Each of the nine provinces sends ten representatives to the NCOP.

Elections

National elections take place every five years. The system used for the national elections is the PR system of National List. In the first election in 1994 the ANC took a majority of the vote, but there was a temporary agreement that said the first government would be a power-sharing one to ease the transition from Apartheid to democracy. Later elections in 1999 and 2004 saw the ANC strengthen its position and the power-sharing arrangements no longer had to be applied.

The President

The Constitution states that the National Assembly chooses the President, who is the Head of State. The first President was Nelson Mandela of the ANC, who served from 1994 to

1999. He was succeeded by Thabo Mbeki of the ANC, who is still President. He can serve two full terms of office, but after that he must stand down. The President appoints the Vice President, currently Phumzile Mlambo-Ngcuka, the first woman Deputy President of South Africa, again of the ANC. The President also appoints the Cabinet.

The provinces

Similar to the USA state structure, South Africa has nine provinces: Eastern Cape, Gauteng, KwaZulu-Natal, Mpumalanga, Northern Cape, Limpopo, North West, Free State and Western Cape.

In the 2004 provincial elections, the ANC won seven out of the nine Provinces. Each of the provinces has its own parliament, elected by the List system of proportional representation. Instead of a Governor (as in the USA), the provinces have a Premier and an executive Council.

The provincial parliaments can make decisions over a wide variety of local issues, including agriculture, education, housing, police, public transport and tourism. The laws of the national Parliament take precedence.

Figure 6.3 South Africa today, showing the nine federal provinces

Election results

The 1994 Election

The ANC won a majority of votes (63%) and seats in the national elections, with the National Party getting 20% (almost the total of white voters). Inkatha got 10% of votes, mostly in KwaZulu-Natal. The ANC also won seven of the nine provinces. The National Party gained the Western Cape (lots of coloured voters who mainly speak Afrikaans) and Inkatha won KwaZulu-Natal (despite allegations of electoral fraud). The real losers were extremist parties on both sides who got little support.

The 1999 and 2004 election results

The table below shows the results of the first election in South Africa and the next two elections. You should note the similarities and differences between the three elections.

Table 6.1 Results of 1994, 1999 and 2004 elections

Party	1994 % vote	Seats	1999 % vote	Seats	2004 % vote	Seats
ANC	63%	252	66%	266	69.7%	279
Democratic Party	1.7%	7	9.5%	38	12.4%	50
Inkatha Freedom Party	10%	43	8.6%	34	6.9%	28
New National Party	20%	82	6.8%	28	1.6%	7
United Democratic Movement	–	–	3.4%	14	2.3%	9
Others	5.3%	16	5.7%	17	7.1%	23
Total	100%	400	100%	400	100%	400

Political parties

African National Congress (ANC)

The ANC got over 60% of the vote each time, increasing its share in 1999 and again in 2004. This gave it a majority in the National Assembly. Nelson Mandela was the first President followed by Thabo Mbeki. It had a clear mandate to carry out its policies. The ANC governs seven of the nine provinces and is in coalition in the other two: KwaZulu-Natal with the IFP and Western Cape with the NNP.

New National Party (NNP)

The re-branded National Party, the party of Apartheid, retained the support of most whites in 1994, but fell into decline by 1999, and by 2004 it had become almost irrelevant. It lost credibility amongst whites during the first spell of government after revelations in the Truth Commission. It does remain in power in Western Cape Province where it is in coalition with the ANC.

The Democratic Party (DP)

The Democratic Party had been a small liberal party supported mostly by whites in 1994, but it benefited from the decline of the NP in 1999 and became the main opposition party under its leader Tony Leon in 2004.

Inkatha Freedom Party (IFP)

Inkatha had around 10% of vote in 1994, mostly from Zulus, and managed to retain most of this support in 1999, though it fell back a bit in 2004. Under its leader, Chief Buthelezi, it is a regional party with support in Kwazulu-Natal, where it is in coalition with ANC.

United Democratic Movement (UDM)

This new party formed after the 1994 election and claims multi-racial support. It did well to get just over 3% of the vote in its first election, though it fell back a bit in 2004.

Democracy in South Africa

An important question that could come up in an exam is: Has democracy been firmly established in South Africa or are there still difficulties the country has to face? Below is a summary of the issues and facts.

Key Points

Evidence that democracy is stable

◆ Written Constitution with bill of rights, rule of law, freedom of press, etc.

◆ Elections in 1994, 1999, 2004, including wide range of parties.

◆ Large turnout at elections, especially 1994, though down to 77% in 2004.

◆ Party List electoral system giving fair proportional results.

◆ Thirteen parties represented in National Assembly.

◆ Wide acceptance of elected Government by population.

Difficulties for democracy

◆ ANC has dominated the Government – some groups feel disenfranchised.

◆ Democratic Party represents only whites – ANC seen as black party.

◆ Still some political violence in township areas, though declining.

◆ Corruption, especially at local level, is a big problem.

◆ Some groups fear for the future if the ANC is not checked.

Possible questions on South African politics

◆ Critically examine the view that South Africa has remained a stable democracy since the end of Apartheid.

◆ To what extent does the ANC dominate politics in South Africa?

◆ There has been little desire for autonomy from different groups in South Africa since the ending of Apartheid. Discuss.

Questions and Answers

SAQ 1 Critically examine the view that South Africa has remained a stable democracy since the end of Apartheid. *(15 marks)*

Here you should analyse evidence to show that South Africa is a stable democracy now, and also any evidence to suggest that there are problems.

Questions and *Answers continued* ➤

Questions and Answers continued

Answer to SAQ 1

With the ending of the Apartheid system in 1994 and the first multi-racial elections in South Africa, many non-whites had the chance to vote for the first time. People turned out in huge numbers to vote, and expectations, particularly in the black community, were very high. There are arguments both for and against the view that South Africa has remained a multi-racial democracy since the election of the Government in 1994.

The country now has a written Constitution, which includes a Bill of Rights, and the rule of law, freedom of the press and freedom of association all play a major part in every South African's life. The transition from Apartheid to democracy has been made very smoothly and peacefully, despite the fears of many people who warned of violence. Large numbers of people have come to accept that choosing the Government through the ballot box is now the system in South Africa.

There have been three elections, in 1994, 1999 and 2004. The turnout of people in 2004 was quite high at around 77%, though not as high as the first election in 1994. These elections have been open to all South African citizens and they can be assured that the Government chosen on each occasion is a lot more inclusive than in the years of Apartheid, especially since the National List system is used. However, the ANC won a majority of the seats at each of the elections and many people argue that it is able to dictate terms to those not represented by the ANC.

The most recent elections in 2004 were contested by as many as 16 parties, which suggests that democracy is now well established in South Africa. However, there is still political violence in areas like KwaZulu-Natal, where extremists of both the far right whites and the radical blacks of the Pan-African Congress do not want to share in this political process. There were also claims that the ANC were involved in targeting key activists from rival parties during the campaign.

As well as national elections, each of the nine provinces elects its own government. This allows people to have a say in what goes on in their local area. In 1994, however, the ANC won seven of the nine provinces and since then have become partners in the other two provinces, Western Cape and KwaZulu-Natal. This means they are very dominant in both local and national politics, though that is what people voted for. There have also been many accusations of corruption at national and particularly local level. Jacob Zuma was forced to resign his post as Deputy President in 2005 because of allegations of corruption, though he was cleared of those charges.

In conclusion, there is a lot of evidence to suggest that South Africa has remained a stable democracy since the ending of Apartheid in 1994, though there are those who question the dominance of the ANC and what this will mean in the future.

2 Social and Economic Issues

In this section we will look first of all at the problems inherited by the ANC when it came into office in 1994. We will then look at the solutions the ANC attempted to improve things for poorer South Africans. Lastly we will look at how well South Africans are doing more than ten years after the multi-racial democracy began. The main issues covered in this section are:

◆ Social and economic problems after Apartheid

◆ Attempted solutions

◆ Success of policies

Social and economic problems after Apartheid

◆ **Health care**. Life expectancy for whites was 73 and for blacks 63. The infant mortality rates for whites was 7 per 1,000 and for blacks was 52 per 1,000. The legacy of Apartheid and poor living conditions meant problems for many poor South Africans.

◆ **Education**. The literacy rate amongst blacks was only 50%, and only 16% of blacks completed school, compared with 85% of whites. 1.7 million blacks aged 6 to 17 did not attend school. Only 25% of black teachers were qualified.

◆ **Housing**. 9 million blacks were homeless, 10 million had no access to running water, 21 million did not have adequate sanitation, 23 million had no access to electricity. Conditions in townships were very poor.

◆ **Crime**. Unemployment and poverty were the main reasons for high rates of crime. Car jacking and violent crimes were particularly bad.

◆ **Land redistribution**. Around 3.5 million people were forcibly removed from their land during the Apartheid years. 55% of blacks lived in rural areas and were farmers, but had little land of their own. White farmers were unlikely to give up 'their' land easily. Blacks needed training, tools and financial help.

◆ **Employment**. Black incomes were one-tenth of white incomes. Unemployment stood officially at 46% but was probably much higher. 40% of the black population of 28 million was under 14 and would need jobs in the near future.

Figure 6.4 Slum housing in Soweto, one of South Africa's townships

Attempted solutions

There were two main areas that the Government had to tackle: firstly, the economic and social conditions of the majority of blacks compared with the whites, and secondly, the political stability of the country. Here we will look only at the strategies to improve social and economic conditions.

Social and economic conditions

After the 1994 election, the Government started a Reconstruction and Development Programme (RDP) which aimed to achieve, in the first five years,

◆ 2.5 million new jobs

◆ 1 million new houses

◆ electricity to 2.5 million houses

◆ free education for all children

◆ free health care for children under 6

◆ redistribution of 30% of the land.

This proved to be far too ambitious and the Government revised its programme and brought in GEAR (Growth, Employment and Redistribution). The Government also tried to encourage black enterprise through the Black Economic Empowerment Act in 2003, which hoped to improve black living standards through the success of black-owned businesses and companies. To succeed with these policies, the Government had to satisfy the hopes of its supporters and at the same time try not to alienate the whites.

Success of policies

Health

Free health care for children under 6 and pregnant women was established in 1994. A clinic building and upgrading programme was also implemented. A National Health Insurance system was introduced, which is long term, but only 7% blacks were covered compared with 69% whites in the early 1990s. More than 5 million children get the 'Mandela sandwich' every day. A Primary Health Care programme offers free immunisation to children under 6. Problems like malaria are getting better, though the problem of HIV/Aids is still a major issue, with around 5 million cases.

Education

A more realistic time-scale for reducing class sizes was introduced. A new curriculum was introduced in January 1998 to try to promote a culture of learning. However, staffing levels are still a problem in black schools. The reduction in qualifications for black teachers is also worrying, as is the level of salaries. Enrolment in primary schools is increasing, around 70% of blacks now get their matric (school leaving certificate), and a greater number of blacks go on to further education.

Housing

1.8 million houses (mostly starter homes) have been built since 1994, though 7.5 million people still lack access to adequate housing. By 2005, over 3.5 million homes had electrical supply and it was estimated that 71% of homes had electricity. In 2005, 32 million South Africans (66%) had access to a free water supply, though basic sanitation had only been provided to 8 million people. In Johannesburg, 200,000 people still live in shacks, there are 235 inner-city 'bad buildings' that have been condemned and there are over 250,000 people on the city's waiting lists.

Figure 6.5 New housing being built in South Africa

Crime

Organised crime is making South Africa the criminal capital of the world. Police are understaffed and underpaid, and corruption is a major problem. After 1997 the Government targeted crime as the number one problem. Some success is being seen in reductions of car hi-jackings, car thefts and business robberies. But there are still high levels of poverty and deprivation. The Jacob Zuma case in 2006 also highlighted the problem of rape in South Africa.

Employment

Affirmative action (positive discrimination for blacks and non-whites) has made inroads for non-whites in the civil service. Private companies are keen to promote blacks but there are acute shortages of skills. Whites are concerned about discrimination and the status of some jobs. Job creation targets under GEAR have been missed by a wide margin. Black Economic Empowerment has seen an increase in middle-class blacks, with around 2 million people earning more than 150,000 rand a year. Unemployment, however, is still around 30%.

Land

Redistribution has been slow because of the attempt to pay white farmers market value for their land. Government grants for blacks to buy this land are too low. Attacks on white farmers are becoming a major problem.

Black middle class

In 2006, the University of Cape Town produced a report which looked at the effect of black spending in the South African economy. The report claimed that the number of black middle-class people (defined as those earning at least 154,000 rand a year) was around 2 million of the 45 million population, and that this group was growing by 50% a year. The report stated that this group was now responsible for 23% of total consumer power in South Africa and that its impact was increasing rapidly. The end of Apartheid in 1994 had an enormous impact on access to jobs, finance, credit, homes and education. Companies were now trying to cash in on this boom by moving into townships which were once no-go areas, where three-quarters of this black middle class still live. Woolworths was hoping to open 10 stores in the townships.

Possible questions on social and economic issues

◆ To what extent are there social and economic problems in South Africa?

◆ Assess the effectiveness of government policies in South Africa to reduce social and economic inequalities.

◆ There has been real social and economic progress in South Africa since the ending of Apartheid. Discuss.

Questions and Answers

SAQ 2 Assess the effectiveness of government policies in South Africa to reduce social and economic inequalities. *(15 marks)*

Here you should analyse arguments for and against the view that the South African government's policies to reduce social and economic inequalities are working.

Answer to SAQ 2

After Apartheid ended in 1994, the Government was faced with huge problems in the social and economic areas of life. Non-whites in general, but blacks especially, lived in conditions that were far removed from those the majority of whites had. In the social areas of housing, education, crime and health, and in the economic areas of income, jobs and land, the differences between whites and non-whites were great.

The Government elected in 1994 under Nelson Mandela and the ANC introduced a number of policies to improve social and economic conditions for non-whites. The Reconstruction and Development Programme (RDP) was introduced in 1994. It set targets to be achieved by the Government in all these areas. It soon became clear the targets were far too ambitious and the Government shut down RDP in 1996 and replaced it with the Growth, Employment and Reconstruction programme (GEAR). This set more realistic targets as the Government began to realise the size of the task to be undertaken.

Through RDP and GEAR, the Government hoped to improve both social and economic conditions by increasing the number of people employed in the economy, and at the same time beginning a public works building programme to lift as many people out of poverty as possible. New houses, schools, hospitals and clinics would be built by the Government, employing as many blacks as possible in these areas. Many of these projects were done through contracts given to private companies, which were expected to have a positive employment policy towards non-whites. The Government itself also used affirmative action when hiring people into government posts, such as the civil service and council jobs. After 2003, the Government introduced Black Economic Empowerment (BEE) as it wanted to encourage black businesses rather that just rely on white companies having positive hiring policies towards blacks.

I will look at each of the social and economic areas to see if the government policies have reduced the inequalities that were present when Apartheid ended.

Questions and *Answers* continued ➤

Answer to SAQ 2 continued

In housing, the Government has managed to build 1.8 million new homes, installed electricity into 3.4 million homes and improve water and sanitation access for many millions of South Africans. However, there are still many people living in shacks, with no electricity or sanitation, and housing in big cities like Johannesburg has become a problem as more people move there looking for work. Many people still do not pay their rent, electricity or water charges, and companies installing meters are finding it hard going in some townships. There have even been some boycotts in townships.

In education, there has been an increase in the number of children attending school, in the numbers getting their school leaving certificate, and in the numbers going on to further education, especially girls. The curriculum was improved to cater more for non-white students, and the number of trained teachers has also gone up. However, poverty levels still prevent many children from going to school, and conditions of schools in the townships are still well below those of the more affluent white areas. Some blacks see little point in staying on at school as the prospects of getting a job after leaving are still poor.

Levels of crime are still high in many areas and there is a direct link between poverty and crime. Violent crime in the townships is a major area of concern, and levels of robbery and burglary are also high. The Government has targeted crime as a major priority, but police morale is low and corruption is a problem. The issue of rape has also been highlighted.

There has been a big improvement in the general health of the population. The Government is continuing to increase access to free health care services for more of the population, infant mortality rates are improving and rates of malnutrition are decreasing. Immunisation schemes are also getting to more of the population, especially in the rural areas. However, some people still have to go without medical care due to poverty, and HIV/Aids is becoming more of a problem each year.

Employment rates are improving, though only slowly, as more government public works schemes are introduced and as more blacks leave school with better qualifications. Affirmative action programmes are also improving the prospects of many non-whites and the Black Economic Empowerment policies are encouraging more black businesses to flourish. However, unemployment is still around 30% in the black community and some people argue the BEE has simply exchanged a white elite for a black one. The gap between black middle classes and ordinary blacks is increasing.

Land redistribution has improved in recent years with more black farmers getting land to work on. Some land has been bought from white farmers, at market prices, and the Government has also given some of its land as well. However, with 55% of blacks looking to farm some of their own land, the rate of transfer has been slow.

In conclusion, it can be seen that the Government's policies have greatly improved social and economic conditions for many people, given the huge gulf that existed after the collapse of apartheid. However, there are still many challenges for the Government to overcome, particularly in poverty, crime, health and land redistribution.

STUDY THEME 3B: THE PEOPLE'S REPUBLIC OF CHINA

What You Should Know

SQA:

The Chinese political system: the role and powers of the Chinese government at national, regional and local levels.

Political issues: participation and representation. The role of the Chinese Communist Party and the extent of political opposition. Political trends.

Social and economic issues: the nature and extent of social and economic inequalities; demands for change; the effectiveness of government responses and the consequences for different groups.

This topic can be split into two main sections:

1   Chinese Politics
2   Social and Economic Issues in China.

1 Chinese Politics

The main issues covered in this section are:

◆   The Chinese political system

◆   Organisation of the Communist Party of China

◆   Political opposition

◆   Human rights in China

In 1949, the Communist Party of China (CPC) took over the country and introduced a political system based on the communist ideas of Marxist–Leninism, but with a Chinese touch. China is a one-party state, and all aspects of the lives of individuals are controlled by the state. The structure of the Government is laid out in the Constitution, which has been revised several times. The Constitution also lays down those 'freedoms' individual citizens can enjoy, but in practice the CPC imposes limits on these freedoms.

Figure 7.1 The Chinese flag outside a Government building in Tiananmen Square, Beijing

The Chinese political system

The CPC dominates every aspect of the structure of government in China. Its organisation is very similar to the organisation of the Government. Every major post is filled by members of the CPC and they decide who gets all the important jobs in government. Over the years the CPC has been good at removing all elements of opposition and it maintains a strong grip on politics. The table below shows the main parts of the Government structure.

Table 7.1 The Government of China

Executive Branch	Legislative Branch	Judicial Branch
President, Hu Jintao	National People's Congress 2,979 members	Supreme People's Court
Vice-President, Zeng Quinhong		Judges appointed by National People's Congress
Both elected in 2003 by the National People's Congress for five years	Elected by municipal, regional and provincial People's Congresses for five-year terms	

Organisation of the Communist Party of China

General Secretary
The highest ranking official in the CPC, currently Hu Jintao

Standing Committee
Has around 9 members, who are the leaders of the CPC for all of China

Politburo
A group of around 25 who oversee the running of the CPC and whose places are more or less permanent

Central Committee
A group of around 300, which contains the leading figures of party, state and army

National Congress of the CPC
Meets every five years and rubber-stamps decisions taken by higher bodies.

Provincial Party Congress
Runs the CPC in each of the 23 provinces of the country, 5 autonomous regions and 4 municipalities

District organisation
Each province is split into districts which each have their level of the CPC

City and town party organisation
Cities and towns also have their levels of the CPC

Party sections in the workplace
The CPC maintains organised sections in every workplace in China

Party members
There are around 63 million members out of around 1.3 billion people

In theory, the party members at the bottom elect people into positions above, but in practice the leaders at the top make all the decisions. The CPC structure mirrors the Government of China and in this way the CPC has absolute control over political decision making in China. Even though some economic reforms have been introduced, the CPC has retained its political power.

Political opposition

There are some other parties in China called 'democratic parties', but they are very much under the control of the CPC. There have also been some moves to contest elections in small towns and villages, but the party still has effective control over government appointments. Censorship, including internet censorship, is used routinely by the state to control political speech and information. The Government suppresses protests and demonstrations (as in the Tiananmen Square protests of 1989), as well as organisations it considers to be a threat to its political control. Increasingly, however, social problems have become more frequently seen in the media, and exposés of corruption and inefficiency at lower levels are more common. The CPC tries to clamp down on reporters from time to time, but the CPC finds it hard to totally suppress such information. It has even been forced to change its policies in response to public outrage, especially after protests on single issues, largely tolerated by the CPC. Political concerns are seen now over the growing gap between rich and poor and the concern over growing corruption among the leadership and officials.

Human rights in China

China has often come under criticism because of its poor record of human rights. This involves not just the denial of political rights as described above, but also concerns other areas of life in China. China argues that human rights also include economic standards of living, health and education, and that rises in the standard of living indicate improvements in human rights. There are a number of points to be made about China's record on human rights:

◆ The Chinese Democracy Movement has been largely suppressed and many dissidents have been 'disciplined', arrested or even killed. Falun Gong, a spiritual movement incorporating Buddist and Taoist principles and healing techniques, became popular in China and, since 1999, the Chinese Government has tried to lessen its impact with various means of suppression.

◆ There are contested elections at local level but contestants must be approved by the CPC.

◆ The CPC does not allow free speech, free press, or organised protests or demonstrations of a political kind.

◆ There are allegations of lengthy detentions without trial (up to 3 months), torture, mistreatment of prisoners, public humiliation; and conditions in the *laogai* (forced labour camps) are very harsh.

◆ The Government's One Child Policy in China (see page 110) leads to forced abortions and sterilisation; many children are abandoned or babies killed by injection before birth.

◆ China's policy in Tibet and other parts of the country has seen accusations of genocide, attempts to eliminate cultures, and torture and death for dissidents.

THE PEOPLE'S REPUBLIC OF CHINA

Possible questions on Chinese Politics

◆ To what extent is there political opposition to the Chinese Communist Party?

◆ China's record on human rights has been poor and shows no sign of improving. Discuss.

◆ Assess the consequences of China's move towards a market economy on political freedom in the country.

Questions and Answers

SAQ 1 To what extent is there political opposition to the Chinese Communist Party. *(15 marks)*

Here you should analyse the control the CPC has of political matters in China, and what opposition there is to that control.

Answer to SAQ 1

The Communist Party of China (CPC) came to power in China in 1949 and started to build a system that would guarantee it could control all aspects of politics. The structure of the party was mirrored by the structure of the Government, and the CPC ensured that only party members could be elected to positions of power in the country. The leaders of the CPC are the leaders of China, and all decisions taken by the Government are first taken by the CPC.

The National Peoples' Congress of the CPC monitors everything the Government does. The President of the country, Hu Jintao, is also the General Secretary of the CPC. The leading members of the government are all members of the Politburo, which is one of the leading bodies in the CPC. At every level of government all the way down to the villages, the CPC controls appointments to decision making positions. Recently, there has been an increase in 'village democracy', but the CPC keeps a careful eye on who is elected to ensure they are acceptable.

There are around eight 'democratic' parties in Chinese politics, but these parties are all under the control of the CPC. Any political opinions or complaints procedures are strictly controlled by the CPC. The press and TV are all censored by the Government and the internet is now subject to strict laws. There is a Chinese Democracy Party, but many of its leading members are either in jail in China or in exile in the USA.

The political dissidents in China, such as the members of the Chinese Democracy Party, have been handled in such a way by the CPC that they do not appear to be a major problem to the Government. The Government sends them into exile if they are well known in the West, for example Wei Jingsheng, Fang Lizhi and Wang Dan. Less well-known dissidents are identified by the Government and given severe jail sentences. Finally, the government tries to address the greivances of the supporters of these movements to isolate the leaders and diffuse the situation. One thing that has helped the Government do this is the successful way it has moved from a communist to a market economy, bringing

Questions and Answers continued ➤

Answer to SAQ 1 continued

prosperity to many in the country. Most protests in China now are single-issue demonstrations, which are tolerated to a degree by the Government.

The CPC also ensures that any organised political group is banned. The Government has even conducted a campaign against the Falun Gong movement, as a spiritual meditation sect that has a large following in China. Some estimates have put it as high as 70 million. The Government is concerned that any organised group like this could be a focus of protest or demonstration against the CPC so it has burned books, blocked access to internet sources about the topic; there have also been allegations of torture and violence against Falun Gong's members.

In local areas, especially in the villages in rural China, there has been a move towards encouraging more local 'democracy'. There have been some 'contested' elections, though all the candidates are still subject to approval by the local CPC. One major problem has been the corruption of local party officials, who regularly use government money for their own benefit.

In conclusion, it can be seen that the CPC has a very firm grip of politics in China and any dissidence is severely dealt with. The increasing prosperity brought about by the move to a market economy has lessened the demands for reform in the country. People seem more concerned about improving their standard of living and not so concerned about political freedoms.

SAQ 2   China's record on human rights has been poor and shows no sign of improving. Discuss.   *(15 marks)*

Here you should analyse the policies of the Chinese Government on human rights, and look at arguments for and against China having a good record.

Answer to SAQ 2

Since the setting up of the Communist Government in 1949, the Communist Party of China (CPC) has tried to control the rights and freedoms of the people. Political rights and freedoms have been very strictly controlled and, until recently, the Government also closely monitored social and economic conditions. In recent years, however, the CPC has introduced economic reforms, which have moved China towards a market economy; this has had an impact on political, social and economic conditions in China.

In politics, the CPC is still the dominant force as far as decision making at a high level is concerned. Their candidates are the only ones allowed to take office at national and provincial levels. There are some 'democratic' parties, but they are under the control of the CPC. The China Democracy Party is banned and its leaders are in prison or exile. The press and TV are also controlled effectively by the Government, which is also trying to control the use of the internet. There have been campaigns against the Falun Gong movement, which is seen by the CPC as a threat to its control. Dissidents are severely dealt with through 'Re-education through labour' programmes and prison camps. There has been, however, a

Questions and *Answers* continued

Answer to SAQ 2 continued

move towards secret ballot elections in villages and townships, though these elected officials have clashed with the un-elected party officials.

The Chinese court system is still far from fair. The judges still take advice from the party officials, evidence is still admitted which has been gained through torture, and the police themselves have the power to send people to prison without a trial. The death penalty is still common for a range of offences and Amnesty International have claimed around 40 people a week are sentenced to death. Since 1996, however, with the passing of the Criminal Procedure Law, it has been accepted that there should be an effective defence lawyer, though the state often by-passes legal procedures, especially in cases of dissent.

Social conditions for people in China vary according to whether you are urban or rural citizens. There is no doubt that urban citizens, especially around the coastal areas, have seen improvements in their conditions with the move to a market economy. Housing has improved, with many citizens now able to buy their own homes. Movement around the country has increased with the relaxation of the Hukou and the Danwei. The introduction of private businesses has seen an increase in the middle classes in China. This has resulted in the average annual wage for urban people rising to around $1,028 in 2003, though rural people still only earn on average $317. Social conditions in the rural areas are still poor as there has been little sign of companies setting up in these areas.

The One Child Policy was also a huge infringement of human rights. The CPC introduced this policy to stop the growth of China's population and it has certainly meant that China is able to feed its people using its own resources. The policy meant couples had to wait until the Government told them when they could have their child and there were large penalties for those who did not follow it. In practice, however, ethnic minorities were not subject to the policy and many couples had two children spaced out over a number of years. The Government has also relaxed the policy, where the parents are only children themselves to combat the one-to-four problem of the elderly grandparents.

In conclusion, there is evidence to show that the Government in China maintains strict control over people in political matters, such as voting, elections and the basic freedoms seen in a democracy. In the economic and social areas, however, the CPC has been prepared to allow more freedoms than it has in the past in its move towards a market economy. People in urban areas are in a much better position to take advantage of these freedoms compared with people in the rural areas.

2 Social and Economic Issues in China

The main issues covered in this section are:

◆ Social and economic conditions in China

◆ Economic reforms

◆ Agriculture

- ◆ The Hukou
- ◆ China's wealth gap
- ◆ Social issues

Social and economic conditions in China

In 1949, when the communists took over China, they began to take all private property into state ownership. Farms were collectivised and businesses were taken under the control of State Owned Enterprises (SOEs). The Government began a series of Five-Year Plans which initially emphasised heavy industry to speed up China's industrialisation. The Great Leap Forward under Mao Zedong, and the Cultural Revolution which followed, were a disaster for the economy. In the late 1970s, Deng Xiaoping introduced economic reforms which were to bring about a huge change in China's economy. He introduced the Responsibility System that allowed farmers to produce food for private sale and he started Special Economic Zones (SEZs) to increase foreign investment in China's economy. With the ending of the communes, many farmers were forced to look for work in the cities. China's economy boomed in the 1980s and 1990s, but along with this came inflation and corruption. Workers, who had been used to the 'iron rice bowl' of guaranteed jobs, housing and benefits for life, were encouraged to start small private businesses. By the end of the 1990s, China had the fastest-growing economy in the world, but it also had the burden of running the SOEs, which were an increasing drain on the economy. There was also a marked difference in wealth between the urban and rural areas. China joined the World Trade Organisation in 2001 and this resulted in a big increase in foreign investment. It has also meant that China has had to open up areas that were previously well protected, such as banking and telecommunications. China is moving rapidly to a market economy, which will mean that Chinese consumers should get access to a wider range of goods at lower prices. The downside, however, is that the state-owned industries and the family-run farms are unlikely to be able to stand up to this competition.

Economic reforms

The Chinese Government has made quite a number of changes in recent years to the way the economy is run. In the early days of CPC control, the state-owned, state-run socialist economy was enforced by the CPC. When it became clear that it was impossible for China to prosper under this system, the CPC introduced a number of moves towards a more market-orientated economy:

- ◆ In 1993, one of the 'Four Cardinal Principles' was renounced – that meant that state ownership of all enterprises was dropped.
- ◆ In 1993 the Government opened up the grain market to competition, though increased prices led to some partial controls.
- ◆ Special Economic Zones were introduced to encourage foreign investment, and these have been very successful.
- ◆ Managers in enterprises were given greater freedom to take decisions on economic grounds and not just follow the Government's directives.
- ◆ Encouragement was given to private companies to set up, particularly in rural areas where unemployment was high.
- ◆ Joint ventures with foreign companies were encouraged, with companies like McDonalds or Coca Cola going into China.

Figure 7.2 A busy city street in the Chinese city of Shanghai

Challenges facing China in the economy

These reforms have seen a huge rise in the value of the Chinese economy, with growth rates around 10% in 2005, making China the world's sixth largest economy. This has brought with it, however, a number of challenges that the Government and people of China will have to face:

◆ The large SOEs did not participate in the growth achieved and are struggling to pay wages and pensions to their workers.

◆ Some 50–100 million surplus rural workers are not employed full-time and subsist on part-time work in villages and cities – migrant workers.

◆ The Government is struggling to reduce corruption and stop other economic crimes.

◆ It is also struggling to collect revenues and taxes from provinces, businesses and individuals – there is an increasing 'black' economy.

◆ Continued rapid economic growth is endangered by the threats to the environment from pollution, soil erosion and the fall in the water table.

◆ The rapid economic growth itself may lead to an overheating of the economy leading to higher inflation and major problems.

◆ Recently there have been signs of a labour shortage (due to the One Child Policy) and this has driven wages up in some areas.

Agriculture

In the early days of the CPC, farming was organised under the commune system, where Chinese farmers worked land given to them by the state, under the control of the state. This proved to be very inefficient and the household Responsibility System was introduced. This meant farmers were likely to get more money the more they grew. This was like the development of a market economy in agriculture. There are over 300 million Chinese farmers, just over half the workforce, and they have succeeded in making China self-sufficient in food production. However, there are only a few successful farmers and many have been forced by poverty to leave their land to look for work in the more prosperous urban areas.

The Hukou

The Hukou is a residency permit that was introduced by the Government to identify a person as officially a resident of a particular area. People needed this registration to get jobs, benefits, schooling and medical care. With large numbers of farmers unable to make a living in the countryside and moving to other areas to look for work, the system has largely broken down. There are an estimated 150 million Chinese living outside their officially designated area. Reforming the residency system has become a very controversial area for the Government. On the one hand, the economic reforms have encouraged migration from the interior to the coastal cities, and officials have turned a blind eye to Hukou transgressions, though some are still subject to poor treatment. On the other hand, there is a fear that this massive influx of people to the coast will put too big a strain on government services and cause more damage to the rural economy. In 2005, the Government announced plans to scrap the Hukou in 11 of the 23 provinces, though they might still not be implemented once city governments realise the strain that a fresh influx of migrants might put on local resources.

China's wealth gap

The move to a market economy in the cities has meant that there has been a huge increase in the number of private companies in some areas. In Wenzhou, a coastal city in central China, 99% of firms are privately owned.

Many people have rejected the farming life of their predecessors to take advantage of this free market. People who have started their own businesses are doing very well indeed. Even those who have not gone into business can get very well paid jobs. But not everyone is getting rich – those without education or opportunity are finding it tough to compete. They work for very low wages, often with no job security, and live in very poor conditions. Those left in the rural areas are even worse off. People say the schools are bad, there are very few doctors, and hardly any clinics or hospitals, local Communist Party officials are invariably corrupt, and often abuse their power for personal gain. Many farmers are losing their land to property developers as the cities move to the countryside. In China, agricultural land is owned communally. In theory each village owns the land around it. Each family holds its bit of land on a long-term lease. Farmland used to be almost worthless. But as China's cities expand it is now in high demand. Corrupt party officials often sell the land from under the feet of the villagers, who see none of the money paid for the land.

Social issues

You could be asked a question about the effects that economic reforms have had on the social conditions faced by the Chinese people. We have looked at the economic effects above; now we will look at a number of social issues.

Health care

In the 1960s and 1970s, China concentrated on helping poor rural people by employing 'barefoot doctors', who had basic medical skills and who travelled around the villages tending to basic medical needs. Each family paid a fixed amount into the commune funds and this paid for these doctors. With the collapse of the commune system and the introduction of the Responsibility System, many of these barefoot doctors stopped working and the Government was not prepared to finance the system properly. Today the old system, providing near-universal access to basic health care, has been dismantled, as the Government tries to spread the cost of providing health care to more than one billion people. The Government's answer has been to open up health care to private practice. Village doctors need to make a profit, however, but making money is not easy when your patients are too poor to afford medical services. A World Health Organisation survey, measuring the equality of medical treatment, placed China 187th out of 191 countries. Healthcare providers, like hospitals in the more affluent cities, have to make money and they do this by providing excessive services to those who can pay, and little to those who cannot. As a result, poor people do without and rich people are charged for many services they don't really need. Since 1980, government spending dropped from 36% of all healthcare expenditure to 17%, while patients' out-of-pocket spending rocketed up from 20% to 59%. One girl had 108 tests for appendicitis including a test for Aids. Back-handers to doctors to get operations done are common.

One World Bank study found 20% of China's poor blamed healthcare costs for their financial problems. The country's healthcare crisis reflects its biggest problems – fighting corruption, and bridging the ever-increasing divide between the rich and the poor, the city and the countryside.

One Child Policy

In 1979, Deng Xiaoping began what is called the One Child Policy in China. He was worried that over-population might be a stumbling block to economic development and so he began this initiative. It is not a legal policy, but an encouragement for families, especially in urban areas, to restrict their family size. It is widely seen in the West as an infringement of human rights in China. People in rural areas and members of ethnic minorities did not have to follow the policy as rigidly. Rural families could have a second child if the first was female, for instance. Additional children result in fines, or more frequently the families are required to pay economic penalties. The children who are in a one-child family pay less than the children in other families. Wealthy families are finding ways of by-passing this policy now.

This policy has had a number of effects on China's population. There is a high reported proportion of male births in China compared with other countries. This is due to under-reporting of female births, the illegal practice of sex-selective abortion and child abandonment or killing, which is regarded as a major crime. Boys are preferred by families as they are seen as more useful on farms and more capable of looking after parents later in life.

The policy has also had implications for social life in China. The 'One-Two-Four' problem, where one child has two parents and four grandparents, could create major problems if that one child has to look after elderly relatives. If personal savings, pensions or state welfare should fail, those elderly relatives will rely on one child to help them. The 'Little Emperor' effect where parents over-indulge their only child could cause problems, though no case studies have been done on this.

Figure 7.3 An early poster for China's One Child Policy

Housing and homelessness

With the coming of the market economy and the relaxation of both the Hukou (work permit) and the Danwei (work unit), there were a lot fewer controls on where Chinese citizens could live and work. It has been estimated that as many as 150 million migrant workers have moved from the countryside to the cities in search of a better life. When they do arrive in the cities, they are often discriminated against in terms of housing and education for their children. They can usually only find temporary employment in factories or on building sites. As the cities begin to sprawl into the countryside, many poor rural families are forced out of their homes to make way for the new middle-class suburbs that many of the richer urban workers can now afford. The gap between the rich urban workers and the poorer rural peasants is increasing all the time, and the improvements in access to TV, cars, better houses and better paid jobs all attract more people to the cities on a daily basis.

Possible questions on social and economic issues in China

◆ To what extent has the Chinese Government moved towards a market economy in recent years?

◆ Critically examine the effects of a move towards a market economy in China on the population.

Questions and Answers

SAQ 3 Critically examine the effects of a move towards a market economy in China on the population.   *(15 marks)*

Here you should analyse economic reforms introduced by the Chinese government and the effects of these reforms on the people.

Answer to SAQ 3

The Communist Party of China (CPC) adopted a socialist type policy for the economy when it took over the running of the country in 1949. This meant that all businesses and enterprises, all land, all factories, shops and offices, were owned and run by the state. There were very large State Owned Enterprises (SOEs) which controlled coal, steel, shipbuilding and heavy engineering. Smaller medium sized SOEs also operated in other smaller areas and all the land was owned by the state and farmed in communes. The state would issue a Five Year Plan, which would outline how each of the businesses would develop and by what methods. The Hukou, or residency permit, officially identified a person as belonging to a particular area and that person was given housing, a job, education and government services, through the Hukou. The Danwei, or work unit, was also used to control the movement of workers.

By the late 1970s, the Chinese economy was not producing enough to support its increasing population and the CPC introduced a number of reforms known as 'Socialism with Chinese characteristics'. The first Chinese economic reforms involved implementing the contract Responsibility System in agriculture, by which farmers were able to keep

Questions and Answers continued ➤

Questions *and* Answers *continued*

Answer to SAQ 3 continued

surplus from individual plots of land rather than farming only for the collective. This was followed by the establishment of township and village enterprises, which were industries owned by townships and villages. An open door policy was introduced by which China began to allow international trade and foreign direct investment. In the 1980s the Government introduced market institutions to move from a state-controlled economy to a price-driven market economy. More recently, the Government has focused on industrial reform, closing many of the old SOEs and bringing in a social security system.

These changes have had a major impact on the lives of people inside China. With the introduction of private businesses, some people have had the opportunity to start up their own companies. China now has many millionaires, and the richest 20% of urban households account for around 50% of the consumption in the country. Coastal areas like Beijing, Shanghai and Shenzen have seen many foreign companies come to invest in the Special Economic Zones set up and this has improved the wages in these areas tremendously. Urban workers earned around $1,000 a year in 2003, which is a big improvement on previous years. Housing in these areas is much better and many people own their homes now, with house prices rising quickly as a result of demand.

The attraction of jobs in the urban areas, however, has seen a massive migration of poorer people from the rural areas into the coastal cities. Not everyone has been able to share in the prosperity. Poverty in the urban areas has increased, with the gap between rich and poor widening. The poorest 20% of households account for only 5% of consumption. The closure of many of the old SOEs has seen increasing unemployment for many. The state has not yet developed a good social security system, though it is working on this, and people who do not have a job largely have to look after themselves.

In the rural areas, the situation is even worse. Rural workers earn only around $300 a year, compared with the $1,000 earned by urban workers. In the rural areas there are a lot of problems. The schools are bad, there are very few doctors and hardly any clinics or hospitals, and local communist party officials are often corrupt and abuse their power for personal gain. About 400 million Chinese still live on around $2 a day. The One Child Policy has also brought a lot of problems to the rapidly ageing Chinese population. As a result, as many as 150 million workers have left the countryside to look for work in the urban areas. They are often discriminated against when they arrive in the cities.

In conclusion, the economic reforms introduced in recent years have given many Chinese people the freedom to improve their living standards greatly, particularly in the well-off coastal cities. However, the gap between rich and poor, urban and rural, and those who believe in a capitalist future or those who believe in communist ideals, is something the Chinese Government is struggling to control.

STUDY THEME 3C: THE UNITED STATES OF AMERICA

What You Should Know

SQA:

The USA political system: the role and powers of the USA government at federal, state and local levels.

Political issues: participation and representation; immigration. Political parties and support from different groups. Political trends.

Social and economic issues: (case study: ethnic minorities) the nature and extent of social and economic inequalities; demands for change; the effectiveness of government responses and the consequences for different groups.

This topic can be split into two main sections:
1   American Politics
2   Social and Economic Issues in the USA

1 American Politics

The main issues covered in this section are:

♦   The USA political system
♦   The role and powers of the President
♦   Limits on the President's powers
♦   The powers of Congress
♦   The powers of the Vice-President
♦   The Supreme Court
♦   State and local government
♦   Participation and representation
♦   Minorities and politics
♦   Political parties
♦   Immigration

The USA political system

With American Independence in 1776, the 'Founding Fathers' laid down how the country would be run in a document called the **Constitution**. This outlined the rules for the political system and also listed the rights that each American citizen would have. Key features about the political system of the USA are written down in the Constitution.

Separation of powers

Most political systems are made up of three branches of government. Firstly, there is the **executive branch**. This is known as the Government and is responsible for executing or carrying out the policies of the governing party. Secondly, there is the **legislative branch**. This is the part of the system that legislates or passes the laws that govern the country. Many legislative branches consist of two assemblies sometimes both elected by the people. Thirdly, there is the **judicial branch**. This consists of the court system in the country, which ensures everything is done legally and according to the rules. In the USA, the executive branch is the President and his or her Government. The legislative branch is Congress and the judicial branch is the Supreme Court. Each of the three branches of government has to be entirely separate from each other. No person can be in more than one branch at any given time. The Constitution also laid down what the duties of each of the branches were.

Federalism

The USA is made up of 50 states and the Constitution outlined what the rights or powers of the national or Federal Government were and what each of the states could have power over. The Federal Government looked after matters that affected the USA as a whole, such as defence and foreign policy. The states were allowed to make their own laws on matters that were considered to be more local, such as law and order, education and transport. Each of the governments in the states closely mirrors the Federal Government of the whole country.

Duties of the branches of the US Government

The Constitution clearly lays down what each of the branches of the US Government can do. It also lists a number of checks and balances on each of the branches. This was to ensure that no one branch of the Government could dominate the others. We will look at the powers of each of the branches and what checks there are on their powers.

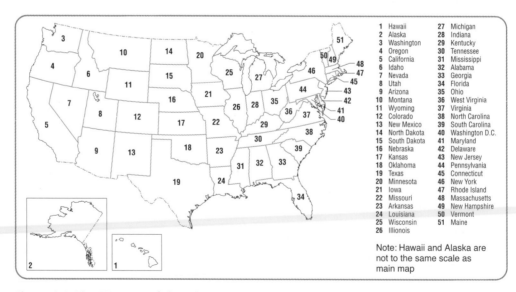

1	Hawaii	27	Michigan
2	Alaska	28	Indiana
3	Washington	29	Kentucky
4	Oregon	30	Tennessee
5	California	31	Mississippi
6	Idaho	32	Alabama
7	Nevada	33	Georgia
8	Utah	34	Florida
9	Arizona	35	Ohio
10	Montana	36	West Virginia
11	Wyoming	37	Virginia
12	Colorado	38	North Carolina
13	New Mexico	39	South Carolina
14	North Dakota	40	Washington D.C.
15	South Dakota	41	Maryland
16	Nebraska	42	Delaware
17	Kansas	43	New Jersey
18	Oklahoma	44	Pennsylvania
19	Texas	45	Connecticut
20	Minnesota	46	New York
21	Iowa	47	Rhode Island
22	Missouri	48	Massachusetts
23	Arkansas	49	New Hampshire
24	Louisiana	50	Vermont
25	Wisconsin	51	Maine
26	Illionois		

Note: Hawaii and Alaska are not to the same scale as main map

Figure 8.1 The 50 states of the USA

The Executive Branch (President and Vice-President)

This is the branch of the Government that decides what the policies of the Government are. The President and Vice-President are directly elected for a fixed term of four years. No President can serve more than two terms in office (eight years).

The Legislative Branch (Congress)

This is the branch of the Government that passes the laws (legislation). The US Congress is made up of two houses: the Senate and the House of Representatives. The Senate has 100 members, two from each state, who are elected for a term of six years. This gives equal weighting to all states, regardless of their population size. The House of Representatives has 435 members, each elected for a term of two years. They are allocated to each state in terms of population. Large states like California have many representatives (sometimes called Congressmen), while small states like Nevada have few.

The Judiciary (Supreme Court)

There are nine Justices on the Supreme Court, each appointed by the President. They are judges who can decide if any decisions made by the President or Congress come within the rules laid down by the Constitution. They can declare a law or a decision unconstitutional, which means it is not allowed. They are like the independent guardians of the Constitution.

The role and powers of the President

The office of the President of the United States is the most powerful office in the democratic world. The President has a number of powers:

◆ He or she is commander-in-chief of the armed forces and the various state militia.

◆ He or she is the chief diplomat for the USA, can appoint ambassadors and make treaties with foreign powers (subject to Senate approval).

◆ He or she can appoint many people to important offices within the administration or on various commissions.

◆ He or she can recommend Justices to the Supreme Court and judges to the lower courts.

◆ As Chief Executive, he or she ensures that the laws are carried out (through some 3 million civil servants).

◆ As Chief Legislator, he or she can recommend a legislative programme to Congress and use persuasion, patronage and personal pressure on Congressmen to support bills he or she wants passed.

It is no wonder many people argue that the President is indeed the most powerful person in the world. However, the separation of powers and the checks and balances built into the American political system mean that there are several important limitations on the power of the President.

Limits on the President's powers

◆ **Powers of Congress**. The separation of powers means that the Constitution has given Congress the power to:

 – declare war to allow the President to command forces

 – reject or delay laws put forward by the President

 – decide what funds to allocate for Presidential proposals

– overturn the Presidential veto by a two-thirds majority

– (through the Senate) confirm Presidential appointments and ratify treaties

– (through the Senate) impeach the President and remove him by two-thirds majority.

◆ **Term of office**. No American President can serve more than two terms in office. At the end of his term he or she may find it difficult to get support for policies – 'lame-duck' President.

◆ **Government bureaucracy**. Departments like the Defence Department and the Department of State are often at odds with each other and this makes it difficult for the President to follow a particular policy. There may also be direct criticism from the White House staff or the Cabinet and it could prove difficult for the President to sack them. There may also be difficulty with the President's own party who may expect some patronage in return for supporting him.

◆ **Character of the man (or woman)**. Image is such a crucial feature of the post and it is important that the President has the 'charisma' needed to persuade people to follow him or her. Some US Presidents have been very influential people who find it easy to get things done. Others have not had that same kind of attraction.

◆ **Composition of Congress**. The President may find the job much more difficult task if Congress is controlled by the other party. Bill Clinton found this to be the case in the late 1990s when the Republicans held both the Senate and House of Representatives.

◆ **The Supreme Court**. Although the President appoints Justices to the Supreme Court he or she can not dismiss them, and they may declare any of the President's actions are 'unconstitutional' as they see fit.

The powers of the Vice-President

The powers of the Vice-President (VP) depend very much on what the President decides to give in the way of responsibilities. The VP may have originally been an important rival of the President and the two may have 'done a deal' to get the VP's supporters to swing behind the President in exchange for a 'meaningful' role in government. Against this, the two may not get on, or the VP may simply have been there to secure the votes from a particular region of the country. This could mean the VP takes a minor role. The VP does have several main functions:

◆ to carry out any tasks required by the President

◆ to act as Chairman of the Senate during debates

◆ to replace the President or stand in for him or her when required.

The most important role is as a replacement for the President. If the president is out of the country, or incapacitated by illness, then the VP can stand in for him or her. If the President is impeached out of office or is assassinated, then the VP is immediately sworn into office.

The powers of Congress

Both Houses have equal powers when it comes to passing legislation. The US Congress does have a fair number of powers, but it has to operate these powers in co-operation with the Executive branch. The numerical basis of the structure of the House of Representatives means that the more populous states can influence decisions. This is offset by the fact that the Senate has an equal number of members from each state and so is more representative of the geographical areas. The main powers of Congress are:

◆ Money for the Executive can only be provided by the Appropriations Bills passed by Congress.

◆ Declarations of war must come from Congress.

◆ The Senate can 'advise and consent' on treaties entered into by the President.

◆ The Senate can 'advise and consent' on a wide range of appointments made by the President including Supreme Court Justices and Cabinet members.

◆ The Senate can set up a Senate Committee to investigate any issue.

◆ The Senate has the power to impeach the President.

The Supreme Court

The Supreme Court is the highest legal authority in the land. Its nine Justices are there to determine what the Constitution may be at any given time on any major issue. A 200-year-old document needs clarification, interpretation and application to contemporary social and political problems. The President, the Executive and the Legislature accept its decisions, even though it has no real means of enforcing them.

State and local government

Each of the 50 states has its own government that is based on the federal system. The Governor is elected to run the state in the same way the President runs the country. For example, Arnold Schwarzenegger was elected as Governor of California in 2003. Each state has its own Senate and House of Representatives and there is a State Supreme Court to give decisions on legal matters. The powers of the state are clearly laid down in the Constitution and allow the state to pass its own laws on areas such as law and order, education, transport and local taxation. This means that the law can vary from state to state, with different age limits for certain things and different laws on gun control. Each state is divided up into counties, which have their own mayors, councils, elected sheriffs, judges, and a whole host of other elected posts. The USA probably elects more people than any other democracy. The mayorship of a large city like New York or Los Angeles is an important position with a lot of power. In many cities, where minorities have tended to concentrate, the mayor is either black or Hispanic. This is true in cities like Washington DC (60% black), Detroit (82% black) and Philadelphia (43% black) who have black mayors, and cities like Los Angeles (46% Hispanic), Miami (66% Hispanic) and San Jose (30% Hispanic), who all have Hispanic mayors.

Figure 8.2 Arnold Schwarzenegger, being elected as Governor of California in 2003

Participation and representation

The federal system of the USA means that when you look at participation and representation you have to look at the different levels of government there are. You also have to remember that in the USA before you can vote in any elections you have to register to vote. The tables below show us what kind of participation there is in the different levels and in the different groups, and what kind of representation the various groups have.

Registration

This used to be a problem for blacks as they often had to go to a specific place to register and there could be intimidation from extremist white groups such as the Ku Klux Klan to stop them from registering. The Government introduced a number of measures to try to improve rates of registration (see below).

The table below shows rates of registration for the various groups.

Table 8.1 Registration for voting

Year	Whites	Blacks	Hispanics	Asians
1992	70%	64%	35%	NA
1996	68%	63%	36%	NA
2000	70%	64%	35%	31%
2004	68%	64%	34%	35%

Turnout

It can clearly be seen that blacks and especially Hispanics do not register in the same numbers that whites do. This is bound to be reflected in the representation figures. Registration is not the only problem, however, as you still have to persuade people to turn out to vote after they have registered. The table below shows rates of turnout at recent elections.

Table 8.2 Turnout for voting

Year	Whites	Blacks	Hispanics	Asians
1992	64%	54%	27%	NA
1996	56%	51%	27%	NA
2000	60%	54%	27%	25%
2004	60%	56%	28%	30%

Attempts to improve participation

As a result of the continuing poor registration and turnout figures for blacks and Hispanics in recent years, there have been a number of attempts to improve participation.

◆ Majority–minority districts were created which drew the boundaries in such a way as to give minorities a better chance of representation.

◆ Motor–Voter Laws were passed to improve registration, allowing people to register to vote when they applied for driving licences.

◆ Various groups have campaigned to encourage minority participation, e.g. 'Operation Big Vote' in 2000 and the Unity 04 campaign.

- George Bush has appointed an all-time-high number of ethnic minority people into his Cabinet – e.g. Colin Powell and Condoleeza Rice.
- The parties are choosing more minority candidates in areas where there is a significant minority vote – especially the Democrats.

Representation

We will now look at the effects the pattern of registration and turnout has on the representatives elected at the various levels, starting with the Federal Government.

The Presidency

All of the Presidents of the US until this point (2006) have been white males. This is not too surprising as whites make up 70% of the total population and males have tended to dominate politics in the USA, as in most other countries. Jesse Jackson, a black politician, did try to win the Democrat Party's nomination in the 1984 and 1988 elections but was unsuccessful.

Congress

The Senate is made up of two senators from each state, giving a total of 100. In the current Congress (elected in 2004), there is only one black Senator, Barack Obama (D) from Illinois, two Hispanic Senators, Ken Salazar (D) from Colorado and Melquiades Martinez (R) from Florida, and two Asian Senators, Daniel Akaka (D) and Daniel Inouye (D), both from Hawaii.

In the House of Representatives, where there are 435 members; there has been an increase in the number of representatives from minorities in recent years. There are now 42 blacks (all of whom are Democrats), 24 Hispanics (5 Republicans and 19 Democrats), 4 Asians (3 Democrats and 1 Republican) and 1 Native American (D). It can clearly be seen that, given the percentage of the population that the minority groups make up (30%), they are all under-represented at the federal level. In the Senate alone, there should be around 12 Hispanic and 12 black Senators if population ratios were taken into account.

Women are also under-represented at the federal level. There are 14 women in the Senate out of 100 (5 Republicans and 9 Democrats) and there are 68 women in the House of Representatives out of 435 (23 Republicans and 45 Democrats). This again clearly shows that women are under-represented compared with their percentage of the total population.

State Governors

There have been very few examples of black or Hispanic Governors in the 50 States. Douglas Wilder served briefly as the Governor of Virginia from 1990 to 1994, but at the present time there are no black or Hispanic Governors in any of the 50 States and there are only seven women Governors.

Minorities and politics

A popular question topic that could be in the exam is the issue of whether political progress has been made in relation to minorities. The arguments for and against this are outlined below.

Figure 8.3 Senator Barack Obama

Key Points

Political progress has been made

◆ Levels of registration for blacks especially have increased in recent years.

◆ Turnout at elections at all levels has also increased – much bigger Hispanic turnouts in 2000 and 2004.

◆ There is an increase in the number of elected officials at federal level – black Senator; 42 blacks and 24 Hispanics in House of Representatives.

◆ There is increased representation for blacks and Hispanics at local level – e.g. the number of mayors in large cities.

◆ The black and Hispanic Caucuses in Congress have become very influential as they have built up seniority in many committees.

◆ There are an increased number of appointed officials in Bush Cabinet.

Political progress has been poor

◆ Registration levels, especially for Hispanics, still lag well behind those of whites.

◆ Turnout levels, again especially for Hispanics, are still poorer.

◆ Hispanic turnout in 2004 was much better, but 75% of this vote is in only two states – Texas and California – and most black voters are in southern states.

◆ The number of elected officials at federal level is still well below that expected, given the population ratios – there should be 12 black and 12 Hispanic Senators.

◆ Though there has been an improvement in the number of elected officials at the state and local level, whites still account for 96% of officials.

◆ Apathy amongst blacks and Hispanics is still a problem – some groups, like the Nation of Islam, even argue against participation.

Political parties

There are two main political parties in the USA, the Democrats and the Republicans. You should not make the mistake of trying to compare these two parties to the main parties in the UK. Broadly speaking, however, the Democrats are more likely to get their support from the poorer classes, women and the racial minorities. In the 2004 Presidential election, John Kerry, the Democrat candidate, got around 90% of the black vote and around 55% of the Hispanic vote, but still lost. The Republicans are more likely to be supported by middle-class whites.

Immigration

The American Dream was the magnet that attracted many different nationalities and races to America. Early immigration was mainly from Europe and this lasted until around 1970. From 1970 to the 1990s, immigration swung away from Europe with Asian and Hispanic immigrants seeking this Dream. In the 1990s, half of all legal immigrants were Asian and a quarter were Hispanic. The 1986 Immigration Reform and Control Act (IRCA) offered legal status to illegal immigrants who came in before 1982, but illegal immigration still proved to be a problem. Job competition, particularly after the recession in the early 1990s, allowed angry whites and blacks who were unemployed to blame illegal immigrants for taking their jobs. The fact that Hispanics did not seem to be willing to assimilate into the US population and culture, particularly in language, also unsettled whites and blacks. It has also led to demands for 'English only' laws in many states, including California.

Tighter controls on the border with Mexico have been introduced, tighter visa controls have also been investigated, and the 1986 IRCA also made it illegal to hire illegal aliens, with fines for employers who did.

In November 1994, Californians voted 59% to 41% for Proposition 187 in favour of denying over 2 million illegal immigrants access to the state's welfare, public health and education services, with whites, blacks and Asians voting for and Hispanics voting against. This was immediately challenged in the courts.

Key Points

Arguments for immigration
- The USA was founded on immigration and it would be a mistake to close the door – immigrants bring a lot to the economy and culture.
- In Texas and California especially, immigrants are vital for the economies of these areas – businesses use their cheap labour.
- In due course, immigrants have higher wage levels and less dependence on welfare benefits than native-born Americans – they are a net asset.
- Many immigrants are political refugees from China, Korea, Central and South America – they need a 'haven' to escape from persecution.
- States like California have agreed to educate and house the children of illegal immigrants – this will help them to integrate into US society.

Arguments against immigration
- Many immigrants are uneducated and unskilled and are seen as a drain on the health, welfare and education systems.
- Immigration is a major issue in California and Texas – Proposition 187 passed by people in state vote – evidence of opposition to immigration.
- Areas populated by different ethnic groups often experience tension and antagonism – newcomers are often harassed.
- Before 9/11 it was an economic issue now it is one more to do with security, hence the tightening of regulations and laws.

Possible questions on American politics
- To what extent can the powers of the President of the USA be limited?
- Critically examine the work of Congress in the USA.
- To what extent have minorities made political progress in the USA?
- Assess the effectiveness of attempts to improve representation and participation in the USA.
- Immigration continues to be a good thing for the USA. Discuss.

Questions and Answers

SAQ 1   To what extent can the powers of the President of the USA be limited?

(15 marks)

Here you should analyse the powers of the US President and outline the limits on those powers.

Answer to SAQ 1

In the US political system, the Constitution lays down the rules that mean there is a separation of powers. The Executive Branch (President), is entirely separate from the Legislative Branch (Congress), and both of these branches are closely monitored by the Judicial Branch (The Supreme Court). The Constitution also lays down the powers of each of the branches and the checks and balances that are in place to ensure that no branch of the Government can become too powerful.

The President has a number of powers that could be argued make him the most powerful elected person in the democratic world. Firstly, the President is the Commander-in-Chief of the US armed forces. If the USA has to go to war, as in Afghanistan and Iraq in recent years, the President is able to command a large number of troops and equipment and can successfully prosecute a war. However, before he can do this, the President must get the agreement of the Senate since only the Senate can declare war. The Senate must also agree to allocate funds for this war.

Secondly, the President is the Chief Diplomat for the USA. This means that he is the main spokesperson for the country. Given that the USA is very important in many areas of the world, this gives the President tremendous influence on the world stage. It could be argued that the President has become the 'leader of the western world' and that the USA through its attack on world terrorism sets the agenda for the rest of the countries. However, the Constitution states that the Senate has to approve all appointments and treaties, although, in this area, the President's power is quite strong. He does still have to ask Congress for the money for all these things.

Thirdly, the President appoints the members of the Government and controls the civil service that runs the day to day affairs of the country. He can decide who he wants in the various departments of the Government. For example, George Bush appointed Colin Powell as Secretary of State and later replaced him with Condoleeza Rice. However, all of these appointments have to be agreed to by the Senate, and Congress has the power to carry out investigations into the activities of the Government, as in the investigations of the camp at Guantanamo Bay.

Fourth, the President is the Chief Legislator in that he can put forward a legislative programme and suggest proposals for a Budget to fund this. Every Bill that is passed by Congress also has to go to the President, who can veto any proposals he does not like. However, Congress has to pass his laws and his budget, and Congress can overturn his veto by a two-thirds majority in both houses.

Questions and Answers continued ➤

Questions and Answers continued

Answer to SAQ 1 continued

Finally, the President has some authority in the Judicial Branch in that he is the one who chooses the Justices for the Supreme Court. He can choose judges who have the same political views as he does and so may be able to influence their decisions. However, the Senate must approve his appointments, and some Presidents may not get to appoint any Justices during their term of office.

In conclusion, the President of the USA has many powers that may make him the most powerful elected official in the world, but there are many checks and balances built into the US system which restrict these powers to a certain extent.

2 Social and Economic Issues in the USA

The main issues covered in this section are:

◆ Distribution of ethnic minorities

◆ Social and economic inequalities of ethnic minorities

◆ Government policies – affirmative action

Distribution of ethnic minorities

The population of the USA is made up of many different groups, but the main groups are shown in the table below.

Table 8.3 Ethnic groups in the USA

Group	Number	Percentage
White	200 million	70%
Black	37 million	12%
Hispanic	39 million	13%
Asian	12 million	4%
American Indian	3 million	1%
Total	291 million	100%

A majority of blacks (59%) live in the central cities (ghettoes) while only 28% of whites do. 49% of whites live in the suburban areas while only 27% of blacks do. Blacks find it difficult to get out of the inner cities.

American Indians

Most American Indians live in the west or south-west states in or near reservations. Their average income is lower than the American average but it is increasing in those areas where casinos have opened.

Asians

Over 14 groups make up this category with Chinese, Filipino, Japanese, Asian Indians and Koreans the largest. Some concentrate into tight groups in the major cities, though Asians are perhaps the most integrated group in middle-class white areas.

Hispanics

This is the fastest-growing group in US society and it became the largest minority group in the early 2000s. The three main subgroups are Mexicans (60%), Puerto Ricans (12%) and Cubans (5%). Mexicans are heavily concentrated in the west and south-west with 9 million in California alone. Puerto Ricans are concentrated in the north-east (70%), with over one-third in New York. Cubans live mostly in the south, with 70% in Florida and especially in Miami. Mexicans come to get jobs to improve their poor standard of living. Many, possibly as high as 10 million, are illegal immigrants. Because of their special status, Puerto Ricans can come when they wish in search of the American Dream. Cubans are mostly refugees from communist Cuba, though many of the 'boat people' in the 1990s have been returned.

African Americans (blacks)

The majority of the black population (52%) is concentrated in the south, with 78% of them living in metropolitan areas and 22% living in rural areas. Around 18% of blacks live in the industrial areas of the north-east, being heavily concentrated in the major cities of New York, Philadelphia, Newark and Washington DC. Around 19% of blacks live in the Mid-West again in heavy concentrations in the cities like Detroit, Chicago, Gary and St Louis. Over 9% of blacks live in the west, with California accounting for 77% of all blacks in the west, again in heavy concentrations in big cities like Los Angeles and San Francisco.

Blacks living in the 'Old South' are the descendants of slaves brought to America. After the Second World War, many blacks were attracted to the cities of the industrial north and west. As these traditional industries went into decline in the 1970s and 1980s, this trend went into reverse and the black population in the south began to rise marginally.

Population growth

The US population is growing as a result of both childbirth and immigration. The rates of childbirth are different for the main racial groups, with the Hispanic group having the highest rates, and the whites the lowest. Whites already feel their political control over certain areas slipping as blacks and Hispanics become majorities. Blacks also feel their position slipping as Hispanic communities grow. By 2050, the white group will only just be the majority, and the USA may well soon be a whole country of minority groups. Many

Figure 8.4 Illegal immigrants trying to cross the Mexico–US border in 2006

people think that the best way to stop Hispanics growing as quickly is to control immigration, and return illegal immigrants who are already there.

Social and economic inequalities of ethnic minorities

There are a number of points to be made about the economic and social conditions of blacks and Hispanics before looking into these areas in more detail. First, conditions have improved within the black and Hispanic communities in recent years. Second, this improvement has not been equally distributed: middle-class blacks and Hispanics are much better off than blacks in the ghettoes and Hispanics in the barrios. Third, blacks and Hispanics still continue to suffer more disadvantage than whites, with blacks probably worse off than Hispanics.

Blacks

Since the Second World War, there are a number of figures that show blacks are much better off now than they were before the civil rights movement in the 1960s and the adoption of affirmative action. Over 60% of blacks rose into middle-class incomes, where the figure before the Second World War was 5%. Blacks living in the suburbs grew in the 1980s from 5.4 million to 8.2 million. Blacks who are high-school graduates increased from 51% in 1980 to 85% in 1993. However, this has seen a sharp divergence within the black community.

The two largest groups in the black class structure are a lower class dominated by female-headed families and a middle class composed of families headed by a husband and wife.

Hispanics

The Hispanic underclass live in the 'barrio', which is their ghetto. The statistics show that, compared with whites, more Hispanics are poor, unemployed and at a disadvantage in education and health. Cities like Los Angeles are occupied by the Hispanic underclass, yet they do not suffer as badly as the black community. By 2004, nearly 22% of the Hispanic community was in poverty, with 42% of Hispanic children being in poverty. Puerto Ricans are the poorest group, with Cubans much less so. The economic recession of the 1990s and the influx of new immigrants in recent years accounted for the growth of poverty in the Hispanic community, though increasing numbers of Hispanics are becoming 'middle class'.

Hispanics are able to integrate more easily than blacks and most middle-class Hispanics live in white suburbs. Mixed marriages are also more common, which suggests the Hispanic culture is more readily acceptable to the dominant white one.

Cuban stay-on rates at school are closer to the white rates, though Mexicans tend to leave school early. Mexicans have embraced the enterprise culture of the American Dream and many leave school early to find work in some enterprise owned by family or friends.

Family life is still important to Hispanics. Births to unmarried mothers and traditional families are close to those of the whites, for those Hispanics who have made it to the middle class. The Cubans had fewest births to unmarried mothers, though Mexicans and Puerto Ricans figures were far higher.

Asians and Pacific Islanders (API)

Asian immigrants are the ones who come to America determined to do well. They work long hours in tough areas to accumulate capital. They develop old run-down areas of the cities, like Koreatown in LA, into areas of economic activity. The statistics show that Asian Americans are equal to or better than whites in terms of their economic or social conditions. Asians have more incomes above $50,000 than whites. Around 40% of Asians complete college, almost twice as many as whites. The number of births to unmarried mothers is lower than for whites. However, these figures disguise the fact that, while Japanese and Koreans have successfully integrated into white America, refugees from Cambodia, Vietnam and Laos have not been doing well. Many speak little English, their children drop out into gang life, and Filipinos, in particular, do mundane jobs and fall behind the rest.

Following SQA guidelines, we will consider the following issues of inequality between groups:

◆ employment

◆ poverty

◆ education

◆ health

◆ housing

◆ crime and the law.

Employment

Black unemployment rates are between two and three times those of whites. The rate is even higher for young blacks. In 2004, 13.3% of blacks were unemployed, 8.9% Hispanics, 6.1% of whites, and only 6.3% of Asians. White median incomes in 2004 were $47,450, while black median incomes were $30,170, Hispanics were $35,929 and Asians were $56,161.

The figures show that, compared with whites, blacks suffer from higher unemployment, and are paid lower wages, no matter their educational levels. At all levels of jobs there is a marked difference in incomes between whites and blacks, with black professionals earning only 62% of the income of white professionals. The Glass Ceiling Commission set up in 1991 reported that the top executives in most big corporations continue to be white males.

Poverty

Poor Americans can get financial help through the various welfare programmes that were introduced to help the poor and minority groups. In the early 1990s, 10% of whites were on welfare, while 33% of blacks were. Only 3% of white parents applied for AFDC (Aid to Families with Dependent Children), while 14% of black parents got AFDC. In 2004, the poverty rate for blacks was 25.6%, compared with 22% for Hispanics, 10.3% for whites and 11.8% for Asians. In 2002, the percentages of people receiving Benefits were as follows:

◆ Food Stamps: 18.5% of blacks, 5.5% of whites, 12.2% of Hispanics and 3.5% of Asians.

◆ Medicaid: 35.6% of blacks, 16.9% of whites, 35.8% of Hispanics and 18.6% of Asians.

◆ Public housing: 13.4% of blacks, 2.5% of whites, 5.8% of Hispanics and 3.3% of Asians.

A high proportion of blacks are living in a poverty trap. Most poor people do not have the necessary qualifications or role models to escape from the cycle of poverty. The lack of economic opportunity makes it difficult for most young people to find ways out. Being born into a poor background, with parents who are unemployed, being taught in schools with limited resources, having limited job opportunities and suffering negative peer pressure leads many blacks into a life of poverty that repeats down through the generations.

Education

Educational achievement is closely linked to employment and income in the USA. In 2004, more than 24% of blacks do not have a high school diploma compared to 18% of whites, 44% of Hispanics and 15% of Asians. Only 13% of blacks have a college degree, whereas 25% of whites do, compared to 10% of Hispanics and 45% of Asians. The shortage of teachers in inner city schools is twice the national average. In the 21st century, the unskilled jobs in the local mill or car factory are no longer there and for many in the ghetto, street crime is the best way of making money. Even those blacks who get a degree are more than twice as likely to be unemployed. This must be due to discrimination.

Health

The figures show that the health of blacks is worse than that of whites. In 2002, blacks could expect to live for 72.3 years compared with 77.7 for whites. Life expectancy figures for blacks also decreased between 1985 and 1995. The number of people without health insurance in 2004 was 19.7% for blacks compared with 11.3% for whites, 16.8% for Asians and a very high 32.7% for Hispanics. Access to work often means access to health insurance and since blacks are less likely to work they are more likely to be uninsured. Gang membership, drugs and the lifestyle in the ghetto all add to the problem. Homicide is the main cause of death for black males aged 15 to 24. The number of uninsured people is increasing, and blacks and Hispanics make up the bulk of this. Childbirth figures show infant mortality is 16.5 per 1,000 in the black community and only 6.8 per 1,000 for whites.

Housing

There is a large amount of residential segregation in America. In 1968 the Kerner Commission warned that America was dividing into two societies: one largely black and poor, located in the central cities; and one predominantly white and affluent, located in the suburbs. Residential segregation is extreme because blacks found it hard to get mortgages, black families who did move were intimidated, and urban policies in the 1970s concentrated blacks in vast schemes – the projects. Segregation is at its highest in the cities of the north-east. In 2003, 47.6% of blacks owned their home, compared with 72.2% of whites and 46.3% of Hispanics. Most rented accommodation is in the inner cities which affects more blacks.

Figure 8.5 A poor inner-city area in Chicago, USA

Family life

Traditional family life in America is still strong despite the trend away from the two-parent nuclear family in general. In 1995, while 82% of white families were still like this, only 47%

of black families were. The importance of female-headed families in the black community can be seen in the fact that in 1995 only 14% of white families were like this, but 46% of black families were. This has a significant consequence of welfare dependency in the black community. The family has lost the respect of many children in the black community, with the gang becoming the 'real' family as it is permanent, trustworthy and demands respect. Female gangs are becoming a growing feature of US society. In 1997, the Million Woman March in Philadelphia was organised by ordinary women fed up with crime unemployment, teen pregnancy and other social problems.

Crime

Crime is a major part of life in the USA and is a particular problem in the ghetto. In 1992, there were more black men in prison than in college. One out of every four black men will go to prison in his lifetime. Black people are 8.5 times more likely to go to prison than white people. The reason most crime is in the inner city is because many convicted offenders committed crimes near where they lived. In 1995, figures suggested the most likely victim of a violent crime would be a young black male. In 1995, 49% of all murder victims were black. Street violence exploded during the 1980s with increases in drug abuse, particularly crack cocaine, and gang violence spread throughout the ghettoes.

Government policies – affirmative action

Affirmative action is a term used to describe those measures taken by the Government to eliminate discrimination against minority groups in jobs, education and promotion opportunities. The programmes cover the two main areas of education and employment, with the aim of opening up opportunities to the American Dream. Blacks and Hispanics tended to be concentrated in the low-paid, low-skilled jobs, even if they had a college education.

History of affirmative action

The Government first tried to stop the discriminatory practices of many southern states by passing the Civil Rights Act in 1964, the Voting Rights Act 1965 and the Education Act 1965. These civil rights laws made it illegal to discriminate against a person on the grounds of race. This was followed by the increases in the Welfare Benefits system in the late 1960s to alleviate the poverty found increasingly in the minority groups. The Poverty Programmes – Food Stamps, Aid to Families with Dependent Children (AFDC), Medicare and Medicaid, Unemployment Benefit, and the free School Lunch Programme – were all improved. This was not really a solution to the problem, however, and affirmative action was pushed forward.

The Nixon administration in the late 1960s, followed by Presidents Ford, and Carter in the 1970s, passed legislation which extended the scope of affirmative action programmes, and the Supreme Court passed decisions under the Civil Rights Act which supported this.

Affirmative action in employment

There were a number of things done to improve opportunities in employment. Job adverts were placed in places likely to be seen by a wider range of people. Firms were given targets to achieve in terms of their workers' profiles that corresponded with the profile in the district. Government contracts would only be given to those firms operating progressive employment policies. A number of case studies showed how bad the problem could be. The Alabama State Police in 1970 did not have any black troopers, and in 1987 the San Francisco Fire Department was ordered to increase the number of officers from ethnic minority backgrounds. Trade unions were also notoriously bad in discriminating against minorities.

Affirmative action in education

A number of different programmes were tried to improve educational opportunities for minorities. The Outreach Programme helped by giving extra tuition to minority students. There were programmes designed to help minority students take up places in science, engineering and maths courses. Then there was busing, which involved transporting children to schools outside their area. This was introduced to achieve better integration in schools and improve the quality of schools in poor areas. The resentment caused by busing and the expense associated with it put into question its usefulness.

Opposition to busing came from whites and blacks, because of loss of parental involvement, time taken in travelling to schools, increasing white flight (whites moving away from non-white areas), and the break-up of community life. There was an increasing body of opinion that argued busing had outlived its usefulness. It was also argued that busing encouraged parents to pull out of the state system and go private. In 1995, a Supreme Court ruling effectively ended compulsory busing.

How successful is affirmative action?

There has certainly been a rise in the black middle class, from 1% in 1940, to 39% in 1970, 47% in 1990 and around 60% in 2004. Some people argue, however, that the black middle class has been held back by Affirmative Action Programmes (AAPs) as blacks were encouraged to become public employees or to work with large corporations, rather than become entrepreneurs. Asians and Hispanics increased their middle class at a quicker rate because of higher involvement in their own businesses. White middle class stands at 74% in 1990, so blacks still lag behind. For the poor blacks, AAPs have done nothing, and the gap between middle class and poor blacks has widened. Black students in college rose to 11% in 1990, but with the ending of affirmative action in the University of California and the Hopwood Case in Texas in 1995 there has been a dramatic fall in the number of ethnic minority students in these states.

Key Points

Arguments in favour of affirmative action

◆ Social and economic inequalities still exist and affirmative action (AA) is the best way of tackling them.

◆ Without AA programmes, progress for minorities is likely to be slow.

◆ AA programmes show that the Government is committed to improving the position of minority groups.

◆ AA attempts to redress the effects of past discrimination against non-whites.

◆ AA would provide positive role models for minorities in the future.

Opposition to affirmative action

Reagan and Bush had both been against AA, and the decisions of their Supreme Court in the 1990s reflected this. Clinton tried to reverse this, but the electorate was becoming increasingly conservative. In the recession of the early 1990s, many whites feared unemployment and AAPs were thought to be unfair to them. The mood of white middle America swung against AAPs and in 1996 the Republican Party made sweeping gains at both federal and state level. Although Clinton won the presidency, only 39% of white males voted Democrat while 49% voted Republican. In California, voters passed Proposition 187 in 1994, which denied the families of illegal immigrants free state medical help or free education. Pete Wilson, the Republican Governor, was re-elected in 1994 on an anti-immigration, anti-affirmative action programme. In 1996, the voters of California also passed Proposition 209, which called for the ending of all affirmative action programmes. This has been challenged in the courts, but could well pass the final test of the Supreme Court. There are many other states awaiting this decision with interest. There appears to be a swing away from affirmative action.

Key Points

Arguments against affirmative action

- AA is opposed by many non-whites as they feel it is demeaning.
- AA alienates a lot of whites as they feel they are being discriminated against.
- Some people see AA as tokenism and argue it does nothing to help minorities as many would have succeeded anyway.
- AA is expensive to taxpayers who think too much money is already being taken from them.
- It is seen as causing unemployment amongst whites.
- It is electorally unpopular with both whites and non-whites.

Possible questions on social and economic issues in the USA

- To what extent have ethnic minorities in the USA made social and economic progress in recent years?
- Affirmative action is the best way of improving the social and economic position of ethnic minorities in the USA. Discuss.

Questions and Answers

SAQ 2 To what extent have ethnic minorities in the USA made social and economic progress in recent years? *(15 marks)*

Here you should analyse the social and economic progress made by ethnic minorities, providing as many examples of progress made as you can and the limits on that progress.

Questions and *Answers* continued ➢

Questions and Answers

Answer to SAQ 2

There are a number of social areas where we can see that ethnic minorities have made gains in recent years. In housing, the number of blacks and Hispanics who have been able to move into what used to be white middle-class areas has increased. Around 60% of blacks and Hispanics could now be considered to be middle class and are able to afford the more expensive housing in the suburbs. However, there has been an increase in the number of 'vanilla' suburbs and there is still a large black and Hispanic underclass that remains tied to the ghetto and the barrio.

In education, black and Hispanic drop-out rates are improving, with more ethnic minorities achieving high-school diplomas. The number of minorities who achieve a degree at college is also increasing, with Asian rates among the highest. However, blacks and Hispanics still lag well behind whites in both of those areas and many young people in the minority communities are still detached from a positive learning experience. Inner-city schools still have difficulty in attracting good teachers, and the facilities are still poor.

With the increase in the black and Hispanic middle class, family structure, particularly in the black community, has improved. Male role models are more in evidence, and conditions in these homes have provided a positive family experience for many people. However, poor black families tend to have larger numbers of female-dominated single-parent family structures, and poor Hispanic families tend to have more children to look after.

Middle-class families who have moved out of the poorer inner city areas have also found that the problem of crime does not affect them as much. Policing is better and there are fewer gang and drug problems in the suburbs. This has had a positive effect on many young people from the ethnic minority groups. However, in the poorer areas, gangs and drugs are still a major worry and the role models many young people see are the gangsters and drug dealers.

There are also a number of economic areas where ethnic minorities have seen some progress in recent years. In employment, improved education and the affirmative action programmes have seen increasing numbers of blacks and Hispanics going into better jobs. This can be seen in the increased number of middle-class blacks and Hispanics. These better jobs have brought better incomes for an increasing number of people. However, black and Hispanic unemployment figures are still greater than whites, and average wages are also lower. Promotion prospects for minorities are still not as good as whites. There is also the problem of the blacks and Hispanics remaining in the poorer areas whose job prospects are very poor.

Although the black and Hispanic middle class have undoubtedly benefitted from better incomes, poverty levels in the underclass are still high. When you look at the welfare system, in all categories, such as Food Stamps, Medicaid, and public housing, blacks and Hispanics still have very high levels compared with whites.

In conclusion, it can be seen that there has been some social and economic progress for blacks and Hispanics, particularly the middle class. However, there are still large numbers of blacks and Hispanics trapped in the underclass.

Questions and *Answers* continued ➤

Questions *and* Answers *continued*

SAQ 3   Affirmative action is the best way of improving the social and economic position of ethnic minorities in the USA. Discuss.   *(15 marks)*

Here you should analyse evidence for and against the view that affirmative action has improved the social and economic position of ethnic minorities.

Answer to SAQ 3

Affirmative action (AA) was introduced in the USA to give ethnic minorities a helping hand in terms of improving their standard of living. It is positive discrimination in favour of ethnic minorities, as it was believed that things were stacked against them. AA covered two main areas: education, where busing was introduced to achieve a better social mix in schools; and employment, where employers were encouraged to hire more people from the minorities.

It was argued that, since many social and economic inequalities still existed in US society, AA was the only effective way of dealing with these inequalities. By forcing schools to become more integrated, it was felt that minorities would have a better chance to improve their standard of living, through improved education standards. However, busing proved to be very unpopular with both communities and was expensive to operate. Whites did not like forced integration and blacks felt they were not able to take part in school life that took place some distance away. Black students also felt out of place in the white schools.

It was also argued that giving employers incentives, like government contracts, would see an increase in the number of minorities hired in the workplace. Higher education standards would give more minorities the qualifications needed to get into the workplace. This was proved to be correct in that the number of blacks and Hispanics who can now claim to be middle class has increased in recent years. However, many of these people would probably have improved their status anyway, and many non-whites see AA as being demeaning to them because it could be argued they only got the job because of AA and not because they deserved it. A number of employers also took on a token number of blacks in lowly positions to make it look as though they had complied with AA.

AA was also a way of the Government showing its commitment to improving the position of the ethnic minorities. It hoped its attempts would redress the balance after years of prejudice and discrimination. Without AA, it argued, progress would be extremely slow. However, many whites then argued that AA was discrimination against them. Some whites lost places in colleges and were refused jobs because of their colour. A number of court cases were put through the Supreme Court and it had to make a number of decisions about AA. Republican Presidents like Reagan and Bush have also backed off AA as it is unpopular among white voters, and indeed among some blacks and Hispanics.

In conclusion, it can be seen that there are arguments both for and against affirmative action as a way of improving the position of blacks and Hispanics in the USA.

STUDY THEME 3D: THE EUROPEAN UNION

What You Should Know

SQA:

Aims, growth and achievement of the European Union (EU). The main institutions and their influence within the Union.

Co-operation and conflict with reference to political, social and economic issues: constitutional arrangements; enlargement; the single market and single currency; regional and social policy.

Case study of the Common Agricultural Policy and the Common Fisheries Policy.

This topic can be split into three main sections:

1   The Organisation and Structure of the European Union
2   Co-operation and Conflict within the EU
3   The Common Agricultural Policy and the Common Fisheries Policy.

1 The Organisation and Structure of the European Union

Figure 9.1 Current and possible future members of the European Union

Structure of the EU

The European Union has a number of different bodies. Each has its own functions and is elected or appointed in its own way.

The European Parliament

The European Parliament (formerly European Parliamentary Assembly) is the parliamentary body of the European Union (EU), directly elected by EU citizens once every five years. Together with the Council of Ministers, it composes the legislative branch of the institutions of the EU. It meets in two locations: Strasbourg and Brussels.

The European Parliament cannot initiate legislation, but it can amend or veto it in many policy areas. In certain other policy areas, it has the right only to be consulted. Parliament also supervises the European Commission; it must approve all appointments to the Commission, and can dismiss it with a vote of censure. It also has the right to control the EU budget.

The European Parliament represents around 450 million citizens of the European Union. Its members are known as Members of the European Parliament (MEPs). Since 2004, there have been 732 MEPs. (It was agreed that the maximum number of MEPs should be fixed at 750, with a minimum threshold of six per member state and no member state being allocated more than 96 seats.) Elections occur once in every five years, on the basis of universal adult suffrage. There is not a uniform voting system for the election of MEPs, although all member states must use a type of proportional representation (PR). The UK uses the Party List system, with Scotland being a single constituency electing seven MEPs.

Figure 9.2 The European Parliament in Strasbourg

The Council of Ministers

The Council of Ministers contains Ministers of the governments of the EU. Along with the European Parliament, the Council of Ministers forms the legislative part of the EU. The Council has a President and a Secretary-General. The President of the Council is a Minister of the state currently holding the Presidency of the European Union. Each country takes it in turn to hold the Presidency for six months. The UK had the Presidency in the second half of

2005. The main job of the Presidency is organising and chairing meetings, though working out compromises to solve any difficulties is also common. The Council of Ministers performs a number of functions:

- **Legislation**. the Council passes EU Law on the recommendations of the European Commission and the European Parliament.
- **Approval of the EU budget**. The Council and the Parliament must agree on the budget.
- **Foreign and defence policy**. While each member state is free to develop its own foreign and defence policy, the Council seeks to achieve a common foreign and defence policy for the member states.
- **Economic policy**. The Council also seeks to achieve a common economic policy for the member states.
- **Justice**. The Council seeks to co-ordinate the justice system of the member states, especially in areas such as terrorism.

The Council is a single body, but is in practice divided into several different councils that meet in Brussels, each dealing with a different area. Each council is attended by a different minister. For example, meetings of the Council in its Agriculture and Fisheries body are attended by the agriculture ministers of each member state. There are currently nine bodies.

The Council votes either by unanimity or by qualified majority voting. The voting system used for a given decision depends on the policy area to which that decision belongs; according to the founding treaties, some subjects require a unanimous vote, while others require only a qualified majority. Even in those areas that require a qualified majority, the Council is required to try to reach a unanimous decision where possible.

Countries of the EU hold different numbers of votes in the Council. The number of votes held by each country is based indirectly on the size of the country's population, but smaller countries are granted a greater number of votes than their population would strictly merit. This concept is aimed at balancing the voices of larger countries with those of smaller countries.

Large countries like the UK, Germany and France have 29 votes while smaller countries like Ireland and Denmark have 7.

The European Commission

The European Commission is the executive body of the European Union. Alongside the European Parliament and the Council of Ministers, it is one of the three main institutions governing the Union. Its main roles are to propose and implement legislation, and to act as 'guardian of the treaties which provide the legal basis for the EU'. The Commission consists of 25 Commissioners, one from each member state of the EU, supported by an administrative body of several thousand European civil servants divided into departments called the Directorate-General. The term 'the Commission' is generally used to refer both to the administrative body in its entirety, and to the team of Commissioners who lead it.

Unlike the Council of Ministers, the Commission is intended to be a body independent of member states. Commissioners are therefore not permitted to take instructions from the Government of the country that appointed them, but are supposed to represent the interests of the citizens of the EU as a whole.

The Commission is headed by a President (currently Jose Manuel Durao Barroso from Portugal). Its headquarters are located in Brussels.

A European Constitution

The Treaty establishing a Constitution for Europe (TCE), commonly referred to as the European Constitution, is an international treaty intended to create a Constitution for the European Union. It was signed in 2004 by representatives of the member states of the EU but was subject to ratification by all member states, which has not yet happened. Its main aims were to replace the overlapping set of existing treaties that comprise the Union's current constitution, to codify uniform human rights and democratic principles throughout the EU, and to streamline decision making in what is now a 25-member organisation.

The TCE was signed by representatives of the member states in 2004 and was in the process of ratification by the member states until, in 2005, French and Dutch voters rejected the treaty in referenda. The failure of the Constitution to win popular support in these countries caused other countries to postpone or halt their ratification procedures, and the Constitution now has a highly uncertain future. Had it been ratified, the treaty would have come into force in 2006.

It is claimed the Constitution would have improved the working of the EU in a number of ways:

◆ It would have simplified a lot of the jargon and decision making.

◆ It would have created an EU Foreign Minister co-ordinating policy.

◆ It would have taken more decisions through qualified majority voting.

◆ It would have created a permanent President instead of six-month rotas.

◆ It would have increased the power of the European Parliament.

◆ It would have reduced the size of the Commission.

◆ It would have reduced the power of veto in the Council of Ministers.

Points of contention

Several countries and people did not like the new Constitution for a number of reasons:

◆ Opponents argued that the document was very long and too complex.

◆ Increased qualified majority voting means the loss of individual power.

◆ Critics claim more European laws would reduce national laws further.

◆ Eurosceptics argue it is yet another step towards European statehood.

◆ By not reducing the Commission's powers the Constitution is still undemocratic.

Possible questions on the organisation and structure of the EU

◆ Critically examine the decision making process of the EU.

◆ To what extent are the interests of Europe put before the interests of individual countries when decisions are made in the EU?

2 Co-operation and Conflict within the EU

Main policies

As the changing name of the European Union (from European Economic Community to European Community to European Union) suggests, it has changed over time from a primarily economic union to an increasingly political one. This is highlighted by the increasing number of policy areas that fall within EU's sphere. Political power has tended to shift upwards from the member states to the EU. Some member states have a tradition of strong regional government. This has led to an increased focus on regional policy and the European Regions. A Committee of the Regions was established as part of the Treaty of Maastricht.

EU policy areas cover three main types of co-operation.

◆ Autonomous decision making: member states have granted the European Commission the power to issue decisions in certain areas such as competiton law and state aid control.

◆ Harmonisation: member state laws are harmonised through the EU legislative process, which involves the European Commission, European Parliament and Council of Ministers. As a result of this, European Union law is increasingly present in the systems of the member states.

◆ Co-operation: member states, meeting as the Council of Ministers, agree to co-operate and co-ordinate their domestic policies.

The tension between EU and national government is something that has been seen throughout the development of the European Union.

The Treaty of Maastricht 1992, which established the European Union, divided EU policies into three main areas, called pillars.

The three pillars:

1. The first or 'Community' pillar concerns economic, social and environmental policies.

2. The second or 'Common Foreign and Security Policy' (CFSP) pillar concerns foreign policy and military matters.

3. The third or 'Police and Judicial Co-operation on Criminal Matters' (PJCC) pillar concerns co-operation in the fight against crime. This pillar was originally named 'Justice and Home Affairs'.

The idea of European control is very strong in the first pillar dealing with social and economic matters, while the second and third pillars are much more controlled by the individual governments at Council of Ministers level.

Single market

Many of the policies of the EU are focused on the development and maintenance of an effective single market. Efforts have been made to create harmonised standards designed to bring economic benefits through creating larger, more efficient markets. There are some internal policies for member states such as free trade, the euro, competition law, the Common Agricultural Policy (CAP) and the Common Fisheries Policy (CFP). There are also external policies, such as customs tariffs, that affect non-members.

The Common Foreign and Security Policy

The Common Foreign and Security Policy or CFSP was established as the second of the three pillars of the European Union in the Maastricht Treaty of 1992 and further defined and broadened in the Amsterdam Treaty of 1997.

The CFSP sees NATO as responsible for territorial defence of Europe and 'peace-making' while since 1999 the European Union is responsible for implementation missions, i.e. peace-keeping, policing of treaties, etc. A common foreign policy is a future objective, but this has some way to go before being realised. A common security policy is another objective, including the creation of a 60,000-member European Rapid Reaction Force for peace-keeping purposes and a common policy on asylum and immigration.

Enlargement

The European Union's 25 member states had approximately 460 million inhabitants in 2004. The European Union's member states combined represent the world's largest economy by gross domestic product (GDP). Countries have been joining regularly since the EU started and there are even more countries looking to join in the future. Romania and Bulgaria will join in 2007, and Turkey also wants to join. In order to join the European Union, a state has to fulfill certain economic and political conditions: basically it must have a secular, democratic government, rule of law and corresponding freedoms and institutions. According to the EU Treaty, each current member state and also the European Parliament have to agree to any enlargement of the membership. There are a number of arguments both for and against the enlargement of the EU.

Key Points

Arguments for enlargement

◆ Greater co-operation will improve the chances of peace and security.

◆ The internal market will grow to include many more customers.

◆ The living standards in the new member countries will be a lot better.

◆ Workers from the new countries can be a source of cheap skilled labour.

◆ Problems like crime and illegal immigration can be tackled more easily.

Key Points continued ➣

Key Points continued

Arguments against enlargement

- Cheap labour might cause unemployment in some richer countries.
- Companies might move to the Eastern European countries.
- Migrants might put a strain on housing and benefits.
- Subsidies to the new countries might have to be very large.
- With over 25 members, decision making might become very difficult.
- Money might have to be diverted from existing countries to the new ones.

The euro – a single european currency

The **euro** is the official currency of the EU and is the single currency for over 300 million Europeans in the following twelve European Union member states: Austria, Belgium, Finland, France, Germany, Greece, Ireland, Italy, Luxembourg, the Netherlands, Portugal and Spain; these are collectively also known as the Eurozone.

The euro was launched as physical coins and bank notes in 2002. All EU member states are eligible to join if they comply with certain monetary requirements, and the eventual use of the euro is mandatory for all new EU members.

The euro is managed and administered by the Frankfurt-based European Central Bank (ECB). As an independent central bank, the ECB has sole authority to set monetary policy.

Figure 9.3 Euro bank notes and coins: a common currency in most EU countries

Denmark, Sweden and the UK are the only old EU states outside the Eurozone. The ten new countries who joined in 2004 are required to join the euro when conditions allow. There are a number of arguments for and against the euro:

Key Points

For the euro

◆ If all countries are tied to the euro, exchange rates will be more stable.

◆ The euro will also allow interest rates to be kept at low levels.

◆ Businesses and consumers will not have to pay conversion fees.

◆ Prices should be easier to see across countries and be kept at low levels.

Against the euro

◆ Euro-sceptics argue that it is a step towards European Union superstate.

◆ The UK's inability to set its own interest rates will be bad for the country's economy.

◆ A common currency goes against the principle of a country not interfering in affairs of another.

◆ In Denmark and Sweden, referenda were held in which people voted against joining.

Regional policy

European regional policy is a policy that allocates more than a third of the budget of the European Union to the reduction of the gaps in development among the regions. The Union seeks to use the policy to help lagging regions to catch up, restructure declining industrial regions, diversify the economies of rural areas with declining agriculture, and revitalise declining neighbourhoods in the cities. There are four Structural Funds to help in these areas.

◆ **The European Regional Development Fund** (ERDF) finances infrastructure, job-creating investment, local development projects and aid for small firms.

◆ **The European Social Fund** (ESF) promotes the return of the unemployed and disadvantaged groups to the workforce, mainly by financing training measures and systems of recruitment assistance.

◆ **The Financial Instrument for Fisheries Guidance** (FIFG) helps adapt and modernise the fishing industry.

◆ **The Guidance Section of the European Agricultural Guidance and Guarantee Fund** (EAGGF-Guidance) finances rural development measures and provides aid for farmers, mainly in regions lagging behind in their development.

Possible questions on co-operation and conflict within the EU

◆ To what extent are there disagreements within the EU over enlargement?

◆ Critically examine the EU's policy towards a single currency.

◆ Assess the effectiveness of the EU's single market in improving living standards.

Questions and Answers

SAQ 2   To what extent are there disagreements within the EU over enlargement.

(15 marks)

Here you should analyse the advantages and disadvantages of increased membership of the EU.

Answer to SAQ 2

The European Union started out after the Second World War as an organisation of six countries who decided to co-operate with each other in improving their industries and businesses. They were so successful at this that many other countries decided to join, until the total reached 25 in 2006, with more lined up to join. The original countries obviously benefited from the EU both in terms of economic and social improvements, but there is now doubt about the continued improvement of all member countries. There are a number of arguments for and against the continued enlargement of the EU.

Those who claim that enlargement can only bring more benefits put forward a number of arguments. Firstly, they argue that bringing in more countries to co-operate with each other on a wide range of issues can only improve the chances of continuing peace and security. In particular, involving Eastern European former communist states can only bring more stability to those regions. The threat of world terrorism can be better tackled if as many countries as possible are involved in co-operating with each other.

Secondly, the living conditions in the new member states are more likely to improve if those countries have the help of the richer European countries, such as Germany, France and the UK, especially since the cost of including these new countries is low.

Thirdly, the businesses and industries of the members of the EU will have many millions of new customers for their products. Not only will the people of these countries get access to a far greater choice of consumer goods, but the companies in the EU will have the chance to make greater profits.

Fourthly, businesses and industries in the existing member countries will have a source of cheap and often skilled labour, as workers will be able to move around the EU, following work. Finally, member countries will be able to better tackle the problems of international crime and illegal immigration, as there will be greater co-operation between members and fewer problems of access to files and so on.

There are, however, those who claim that further enlargement of the EU can only bring problems. Firstly, the wider availability of cheap labour will mean more unemployment in richer countries. Workers in many of the new member countries are willing to work for a lot less than those in countries like Germany, France and the UK. Companies might also move from places like the UK to Eastern European countries that have recently joined.

Questions and *Answers* continued ➤

Answer to SAQ 2 continued

Secondly, any increase in migration from some poorer countries to the West may put a huge burden on jobs and social security benefits in richer countries. Some of these richer countries are still trying to deal with problems caused by their own unemployment without an influx of new migrants.

Thirdly, the poor economies of many of these new members are likely to need a lot of support when they first join. This would put a strain on the already stretched budgets of the EU, particularly the CAP, as many new members have large farming communities.

Fourthly, the decision making process in the EU is already complicated enough, without increasing membership to 25 countries. With more decisions made by qualified majority voting and less use of the veto, existing members could find themselves outvoted by the new poorer members, who may not have the same interests in mind.

Finally, money might have to be diverted from the existing members to the new states and this would cause problems with many people in existing countries. There are those in the UK, for example, who think that far too much is already being spent on the CAP, without a large increase in member countries who need it.

In conclusion, there are many arguments for and against the enlargement of the EU, though it seems that those in favour of enlargement are winning the fight as the number of member countries continues to increase.

3 The Common Agricultural Policy and the Common Fisheries Policy

Common Agricultural Policy

The Common Agricultural Policy (CAP) is a system of European Union agricultural subsidies which represents about 44% of the EU's budget. These subsidies work by guaranteeing a minimum price to farmers and by direct payment of a subsidy for crops planted. This provides some economic certainty for EU farmers and production of a certain quantity of agricultural goods. Reforms of the system are currently underway including a phased transfer of subsidy to land stewardship rather than specific crop production from 2005 to 2012. Detailed implementation of the scheme varies in different member countries of the EU. There are a number of arguments for and against the CAP:

Key Points

Arguments for the CAP

◆ It will increase agricultural productivity.

◆ It will provide guaranteed sources of food supplies.

Key Points *continued* ➤

Key Points *continued*

◆ It will provide farmers with a fair standard of living.

◆ It will ensure reasonable prices to consumers.

◆ It will reduce rural unemployment.

Criticisms of the CAP

◆ The CAP accounts for almost half of the EU budget.

◆ It creates a huge oversupply of certain agricultural products (food mountains).

◆ The CAP causes artificially high food prices throughout the EU.

◆ Some countries like France, Spain and Portugal receive a lot of money.

◆ Enlargement after 2004 will mean even more money will be needed.

Reform of the CAP

For many years it was argued that the CAP had to be reformed, though this has been difficult, as countries like France are determined to keep the CAP in its present form. However, in recent years there has been a greater willingness to accept some kind of change.

In 2003, EU farm ministers agreed to a major reform of the CAP, based on almost entirely stopping subsidies for a particular crop. The new arrangements are based on a single farm payment.

The expansion of the EU in 2004 increased the number of farmers from 7 million to 11 million, increased the agricultural land area by 30% and crop production by 10–20%. The 2004 entrants into the EU have immediate access to price support measures. However, direct payments will be phased in over ten years. EU states agreed in 2002 that agricultural expenditure up to 2013 should not increase in real terms. This will require a cut in subsidies to the original states of around 5% to finance payments to the new members. Romania and Bulgaria may join in 2007, which would increase the required cut to 8%. The overall EU and national budgets for subsidy have been capped. This will prevent growth in the total bill to the taxpayer.

As of 2006, the EU has decided on some reforms of sugar subsidies. The guaranteed price of sugar is to be cut by 36%, with European production projected to fall sharply as a result of this. According to the EU, this is the first serious reform of sugar under the CAP for 40 years.

The Common Fisheries Policy (CFP)

The Common Fisheries Policy (CFP) is the fisheries policy of the European Union. It sets quotas for member states which stipulate *how much of each type of fish each country is allowed to catch*. In 2004 it had a budget of €931 million, approximately 0.75% of the EU budget. The policy has been criticised both by scientists concerned about dwindling fish stocks, and by fishermen, who say it is threatening their livelihoods.

Fishing is an important economic activity within the EU. It contributes generally less than 1% to gross national product, but employs 260,000 fishermen catching 8 million tonnes of fish in 1995. The EU fleet has 97,000 vessels of varying sizes. Fish farming produced a further 1 million tonnes of fish and shellfish and employed another 85,000 people. Fishing represents no more than 10% of local employment in any region of the EU, but it is often in areas where other

Figure 9.4 The Common Fisheries Policy sets strict guidelines on how much fish, and which types of fish, EU countries are allowed to take from the sea

employment opportunities are limited. For this reason, community funds have been made available to fishing as a means of encouraging regional development.

Fish stocks risk over-fishing unless catches are controlled. The CFP sets quotas for how much of each species can be caught. Each country is given a quota based upon the total available and their traditional share of the catch (Total Allowable Catch, TAC). This has been a source of contention among states who joined the EU after the system had been set up and so did not have a historical catch share. Each vessel is allocated an individual quota for regulated species. Catches and landings must be recorded. Regulations are made about the kind of fishing gear which may be used. Areas may be closed from fishing to allow stocks to recover.

Key Points

Advantages of the Common Fisheries Policy

◆ It protects the fish stocks through regulating the amount of fish caught.

◆ It helps the fishing industry to regulate equipment used to catch fish.

◆ It maintains a common market in fish products matching supply and demand.

◆ It manages fishing for the benefit of fishing communities and customers.

◆ It sets up fisheries agreements for the international community.

Criticisms of the Common Fisheries Policy

◆ Quotas and bans have had a huge effect on some fishing communities.

◆ Countries like Spain, Portugal Greece and France have blocked major reforms.

◆ The countries above have also been less efficient in enforcing quotas.

◆ The Scottish fishing industry has been particularly badly hit.

◆ Enlargement of the EU since 2004 will also have a major impact.

Reform of the CFP

There was a wide-ranging review of the CFP in 1992. It was concluded that there had been over-investment in vessels, over-fishing and that numbers of fish landed were decreasing. The review identified a need to improve compliance with the regulations. This led to a tightening of regulations and better monitoring of individual vessels.

In 1995, it was decided that, although fishing could be managed by reducing the fleet size, available fish vary from year to year too much to make this sensible. So a permit system was introduced stating where and when boats are allowed to fish. Scientific studies were commissioned to better determine available stocks and guide the allocation of permits.

Another review was carried out in 2002 that introduced more reform. The reform was necessary as several fish stocks had fallen below levels at which their recovery would be threatened without the introduction of protective measures. New rules on conservation and the sustainable exploitation of fisheries resources came into force on 1 January 2003. In particular, they aimed to achieve a reduction in the fishing effort with a view to sustainable management. Other measures also encouraged the reduction of the fishing fleet, including decommissioning vessels if appropriate.

Possible questions on the Common Agricultural Policy and the Common Fisheries Policy

◆ Critically examine the arguments for and against the Common Agricultural Policy.

◆ To what extent does the CFP meet the needs of European citizens?

Questions and Answers

SAQ 3 Critically examine the arguments for and against the Common Agricultural Policy. *(15 marks)*

Here you should outline the advantages of the Common Agricultural Policy (CAP) and compare them with the disadvantages.

Answer to SAQ 3

When the European Union was originally set up, one of the cornerstones of its organisation was the Common Agricultural Policy (CAP). The six original member states all strongly intervened in their agricultural sectors, in particular with regard to what was produced, maintaining prices for goods and how farming was organised. They were determined to continue to support agriculture, though this support went against the other ideas of free trade in particular. They decided that supporting the agriculture sector was far too important to leave to the chance of free trade, so they set up the CAP to control and organise farming. Farmers were guaranteed a price for their product and they received extra money for growing certain crops. This system has operated largely untouched since the 1960s, though there are many who think it is well past time to reform the CAP.

***Questions* and *Answers* continued ➤**

Questions *and* **Answers** *continued*

Answer to SAQ 3 continued

Those who support the CAP put forward a number of arguments in its favour. Firstly, by supporting farmers in the production of food, the EU is making sure that there is enough food for all of the people in EU countries. Farmers know what prices they are going to get and are able to plan long term to improve their productivity.

Secondly, by giving subsidies to farmers for growing certain crops, the EU is also able to ensure the basic staple foods of EU citizens are in plentiful supply.

Thirdly, as farmers know they have a stable income each year, they are willing and able to stay in farming as their standard of living is such that it encourages people to stay in the industry. Cheap foreign imports are kept out by price controls and this keeps EU farmers in work. A large number of people in some EU countries are employed in farming, and in some regions this is the only available employment.

Fourthly, as the EU is able to control and regulate prices, the consumer knows that the prices of farming products will be stable. There will be no major rises or falls in the price of products each year depending on the harvests.

There are those who think the CAP does not bring many advantages to the people of the EU and they put forward a number of arguments against the CAP. Firstly, considering that the CAP accounts for almost half of the total budget of the EU, some argue that the benefits of supplies of food and greater agricultural employment are not worth the huge amount being spent.

Secondly, the fact that the CAP intervenes to buy up 'surplus' food creates a huge quantity of food in storage. Consumers cannot get access to this surplus as it would mean the price of products would fall due to the greater supply of food in the market and farmers would not get their guaranteed price.

Thirdly, by controlling the supply of food on the market in the way it does, the CAP keeps prices artificially high. Consumers have to pay more than they would normally under free market conditions. They are in effect paying twice for the food in the shape of higher prices and in the taxes they pay to subsidise the CAP.

Fourthly, countries like France, Spain and Portugal have large farming sectors and it is in their interests to keep the CAP working as it does. They receive large amounts of support from the CAP, and many other countries such as Britain, which do not have many people working in farming, think the CAP should be reformed.

Finally, with the enlargement of 2004 and future countries joining, even more money will have to be spent subsidising the farming industries in the new countries. Many of these countries have large and poor farming sectors and they will expect help from the EU to improve standards.

In conclusion, there are arguments both for and against the operation of the CAP, though in recent years the calls for reform of the CAP have increased.

Chapter 10

STUDY THEME 3E: THE POLITICS OF DEVELOPMENT IN AFRICA (EXCEPT THE REPUBLIC OF SOUTH AFRICA)

What You Should Know

SQA:

Health and health care issues; access to education, food and safe water. The links between health, education, food and development.

Economic, political and social factors affecting development.

The respective roles of African governments, African Union, the European Union, Non-Governmental Organisations, the United Kingdom and the United Nations in promoting development.

This topic can be split into three main sections:

1. Conditions in Africa
2. Economic, Political and Social Factors Affecting Development
3. The Role of Organisations in Promoting Development.

1 Conditions in Africa

Background

Before you can study the issues surrounding development in Africa, you must be able to understand how conditions in African countries are measured to allow comparisons to be made between them and countries like our own. This section contains information you will need to explain the background to the questions you will be asked in the exam.

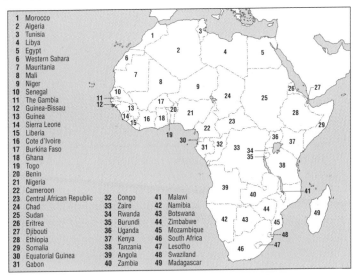

1	Morocco
2	Algeria
3	Tunisia
4	Libya
5	Egypt
6	Western Sahara
7	Mauritania
8	Mali
9	Niger
10	Senegal
11	The Gambia
12	Guinea-Bissau
13	Guinea
14	Sierra Leone
15	Liberia
16	Cote d'Ivoire
17	Burkina Faso
18	Ghana
19	Togo
20	Benin
21	Nigeria
22	Cameroon
23	Central African Republic
24	Chad
25	Sudan
26	Eritrea
27	Djibouti
28	Ethiopia
29	Somalia
30	Equatorial Guinea
31	Gabon

32	Congo
33	Zaire
34	Rwanda
35	Burundi
36	Uganda
37	Kenya
38	Tanzania
39	Angola
40	Zambia

41	Malawi
42	Namibia
43	Botswana
44	Zimbabwe
45	Mozambique
46	South Africa
47	Lesotho
48	Swaziland
49	Madagascar

Figure 10.1 The countries of Africa

There are a number of different indicators of conditions in African countries that cover the main areas of development – namely, health, education and food. For health, we can look at figures indicating birth rates, infant mortality, life expectancy and incidences of particular illnesses like malaria, HIV/Aids and diarrhoea. For education we can look at figures indicating attendance at school, literacy rates and qualified teachers. We will also look at the links between education and economic conditions such as GDP per capita. For food, we can look at indicators of calorie intake, malnutrition, access to safe water, and so on. We will take each of these three main areas in turn and examine the main issues surrounding them and the links between each of them and Development in Africa.

Health and health care issues

We start by looking at some facts and figures that show us what health conditions are like in some African countries compared with the UK:

Table 10.1 Health conditions in African countries compared with UK

Country	Population (millions)	Infant mortality 1,000 births	Under 5 mortality rate	Life expectancy	Annual number of deaths of children under 5
UK	60	5	6	79	4,000
Cameroon	16	87	149	46	84,000
DR Congo	53	129	205	44	572,000
Ethiopia	69	110	166	48	509,000
Ghana	20	68	112	57	76,000
Kenya	32	79	120	48	159,000
Malawi	11	110	175	40	96,000
Mozambique	19	104	152	42	117,000
Nigeria	136	101	197	43	1,049,000
Rwanda	8	118	203	44	74,000
Somalia	10	133	225	47	81,000
Sudan	34	63	91	57	106,000
Tanzania	36	78	126	46	177,000
Uganda	26	80	138	48	195,000

Source: UNICEF 2004 figures

UNICEF tells us that more than 10 million children under five years of age die every year of preventable diseases or malnutrition, nearly half of them in the first weeks of life. In some developing countries, the toll is so harsh that more than one in five children die before they reach their fifth birthday. Many of those who do survive are unable to grow and develop to their full potential. Most deaths result from five causes, or a combination of them:

◆ acute respiratory infections (ARI)   ◆ malaria

◆ diarrhoea   ◆ malnutrition.

◆ measles

Poverty and the failure to ensure universal access to basic social services are to blame. Complications related to pregnancy and childbirth kill more than half a million women each year – more than one every minute – and injure and disable many more.

HIV/Aids

HIV/Aids has become one of the biggest problems facing people in Africa in recent years. By the end of 2002, 42 million people were living with HIV/Aids, including almost 12 million young people aged between 15 and 24 and more than 3 million children under the age of 15. For the first time since the start of the epidemic, half the number of people living with HIV/Aids were women and girls. In 2002 alone, Aids killed more than 2.5 million adults and 610,000 children. By 2010, the cumulative toll is expected to rise to 45 million.

Malaria

Malaria is a serious disease that is spread through mosquito bites. UNICEF reports that, each year, there are 300 million to 500 million cases of malaria throughout the world and about 1 million child deaths. In areas where malaria is common, it can be the leading cause of death and of poor growth among young children.

Diarrhoea

UNICEF reports that Diarrhoea kills over 1 million children every year through dehydration and malnutrition. Children are more likely than adults to die from diarrhoea because they become dehydrated more quickly. About one in every 200 children who contract diarrhoea will die from it.

Education

Again we will look at the facts comparing the UK with some of the developing African countries in the table below:

Table 10.2 Education facts for African countries compared with UK

Country	Primary school enrolment, 2004 (%)	Adult literacy, 2004 (%)
UK	100	NA
Cameroon	75	68
DR Congo	52	65
Ethiopia	31	42
Ghana	61	54
Kenya	78	74
Malawi	76	64
Mozambique	60	46
Nigeria	62	67
Rwanda	75	64
Somalia	11	NA
Sudan	53	59
Tanzania	82	69
Uganda	79	69

A good education is regarded as the best way out of poverty for a lot of people, especially for girls and women. Of the 121 million children in the world who are not in school 65 million are girls. In Sub-Saharan Africa, 24 million girls were out of school in 2002. World wide, 83% of all girls out of school live in Sub-Saharan Africa, South Asia, East Asia or the Pacific. Two-thirds of the world's 875 million illiterate adults are women. It is particularly important to improve the education of girls, as a better-educated woman is likely to remain unmarried for longer, and have fewer children. Her children will be more likely to survive, and be better nourished and be better educated. An educated woman is also likely to be better paid in the workplace, to be better able to protect herself against HIV/Aids and to assume a more active role in life.

Figure 10.2 A classroom in a primary school in Malawi

Food and food shortages

According to the Food and Agriculture Organisation (FAO) there are more than 850 million people each day who cannot get enough food to meet their minimum energy needs. Around 200 million children under 5 suffer from malnutrition. According to some estimates, malnutrition is an important factor among the nearly 13 million children under 5 who die every year from preventable diseases and infections, such as measles, diarrhoea, malaria and pneumonia, or from some combination of these. Almost one-quarter (198 million) of the undernourished are in Sub-Saharan Africa, which is also the region with the highest proportion of its population undernourished.

Malnutrition is one of the prime causes of low-birth-weight babies and poor growth. Low-birth-weight babies who survive are likely to suffer growth retardation and illness throughout their childhood, adolescence and into adulthood, and growth-retarded adult women are likely to carry on the vicious cycle of malnutrition by giving birth to low-birth-weight babies. Some 30 million infants are born each year in developing countries with impaired growth caused by poor nutrition in the womb.

Malnutrition in the form of deficiencies of essential vitamins and minerals continues to cause severe illness or death in millions of people worldwide, a high proportion of whom are in African countries. More than 3.5 billion people are affected by iron deficiency, 2 billion are at risk of iodine deficiency and 200 million pre-school children are affected by insufficient vitamin A. All of these deficiencies can lead to severe illness.

Malnutrition can result in productivity and economic losses, as adults afflicted by nutritional and related disorders are unable to work. It can lead to education losses, as children are too weakened or sickly to attend school or to learn properly. It can also mean healthcare costs of caring for those suffering from nutrition-related illnesses and costs to society of caring for those who are disabled and, in some circumstances, their families as well.

Reasons for food shortages
The FAO has estimated that the world should be able to produce more than enough for all of the people that live on the planet, but it is clear that this is not happening. We will look at the main reasons put forward to explain why so many people are starving to death today.

Conflict
Armed conflict affects people's right to food by destroying crops, food stocks, livestock and farm equipment. FAO has calculated that since the early 1970s war has cost $4,300 million a year – enough to pull 330 million people from the ranks of the undernourished. In Rwanda in 1995, war displaced three out of four farmers and cut the harvest in half.

Free trade
Free trade both benefits and challenges the right to food. If rich countries stopped subsidies to their farmers, poor countries' farm products would become more competitive. These countries could then produce a greater share of their own food and earn more from exports. But until markets change, countries that rely on cheap food imports may actually be worse off.

Women's role in farming
Women's contributions to food production and food security would be far greater if they enjoyed equal access to essential resources and services. In many societies, tradition and laws bar women from owning land. Without land to serve as collateral, women are also cut off from access to credit. And without credit, they often cannot buy essential inputs – such as seeds, tools and fertiliser– or invest in irrigation and land improvements. A recent FAO survey found that female farmers receive only 5% of all agricultural extension services worldwide.

Environmental factors
FAO projections show increasing pressure on the environment from a variety of food production trends. By 2030, crop production in the developing countries is projected to be 70% higher than in 1995–97. About 80% of this increase will continue to come from intensified crop production, for example, higher-yielding varieties and higher cropping intensities. The rest will come from further expansion of arable land. Arable land in the developing countries is projected to increase by 12%, most of it in South America and Sub-Saharan Africa, with an unknown but probably considerable part coming from deforestation. Increased use of fertilisers will lead to more widespread nitrate contamination of water resources. Intensive livestock production will cause ammonia damage to ecosystems. As large-scale commercial farming operations increase, they could displace small-scale livestock farmers, thus making rural poverty and food insecurity worse.

Water scarcity

Limited water resources are already a constraint to development in large parts of the world, such as North Africa. As development and population growth continue, this problem is increasing, as are tensions between water users. Agriculture usually faces strong competition from the municipal and industrial sectors, which are able to pay more for water. Government agricultural policy must address water allocation because of its implications for the economy and food security. Different regions have very different water problems. Sub-Saharan Africa extracts less than 2% of available water for all uses and needs to make significant investments in irrigation so that farmers can increase their productivity. North Africa uses 59.7% of available water, and some countries are already exploiting water resources fully.

HIV/Aids

HIV/Aids increases present and future food insecurity through its impact on households' ability to produce food, because of labour shortages and loss of knowledge about farming methods. It also affects households' ability to buy food, because of impoverishment due to the loss of productive family members and of assets. Communities find it harder to produce and buy food, as the epidemic reaches every home, and neighbours become too overburdened to help each other with food, loans or a hand in the fields.

Countries find it harder to import food, as HIV/Aids reduces GDP growth per capita by an estimated 1% annually in Africa. Rural communities also bear a higher burden of the cost of HIV/Aids as many urban dwellers and migrant labourers return to their villages when they become sick. At the same time, household expenditures rise to meet medical bills and funeral expenses and, while the number of productive family members declines, the number of dependants grows.

Malnutrition

Hunger, which afflicts one in five of the developing world's people, is a major factor itself in food shortages. Without proper intervention, under-nutrition, and the death and disease it causes, are repeated with each generation. The hungry suffer in silence and often many of them show no outward sign of the severity of their hunger. Chronic hunger increases susceptibility to disease and leaves people feeling weak and lethargic, reducing their ability to work. This is reflected in economies and contributes to a devastating cycle of household hunger and poverty. Vitamin and mineral deficiencies in children lead to stunted growth, blindness and compromised mental development. Iron-deficiency anaemia contributes to 20% of maternal deaths in Africa and Asia.

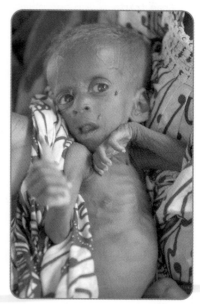

Figure 10.3 An African child suffering from malnutrition

Possible questions on conditions in Africa

◆ To what extent are education and health the most important factors that affect development?

◆ Critically examine the reasons for food shortages in Africa.

Questions and Answers

SAQ 1   Critically examine the reasons for food shortages in Africa.   *(15 marks)*

Here you should analyse the different reasons for food shortages in Africa, providing as many examples as you can.

Answer to SAQ 1

According to the Food and Agriculture Organisation (FAO) there are more than 850 million people each day who cannot get enough food to meet their needs. Worldwide, about 200 million children under the age of 5 suffer from malnutrition. Malnutrition is also thought to be an important factor in the deaths of about 13 million children under 5 every year from preventable diseases and infections, such as measles, diarrhoea, malaria and pneumonia. Almost one-quarter (198 million) of the undernourished are in Sub-Saharan Africa, which also has the highest proportion of its population undernourished.

There are a number of reasons put forward to explain why food shortages cause so many problems in Africa. In many African countries at the present time, there are conflicts going on. In Darfur in Sudan, in Somalia, and in Burundi, for example, conflicts have caused many people to escape their homes and become refugees. This has placed a large burden on the areas they have moved to, which may not have enough food for all these extra people. The conflict itself has meant that large areas of land are covered in landmines, and farmers are unable to go and tend to their crops. The infrastructure of many conflict areas, such as roads and bridges, has also been destroyed by the fighting.

Another reason for food shortages in African countries is to do with the conditions of trade that exist. Many African farmers have been forced to grow cash crops, such as cotton, coffee, tea and tobacco. Their countries are in massive debt to Western banks and governments and they have been persuaded to grow these crops to sell to the West to pay off these debts. This has meant that they do not grow basic foodstuffs to sell to locals, and imported food is very costly. Many rich countries also have subsidies and tariffs that protect their own farmers in producing crops such as maize and sugar, which means that African farmers can't compete fairly with rich farmers abroad.

The position of women in many African countries also contributes to food shortages. Women do not tend to own much of the land, but they tend to do a lot of the farming. As they do not have any land as collateral, they find it hard to get loans from the bank and this means they do not get access to funds to buy seeds, fertilisers or tools. They also find it hard to invest in irrigation schemes or other improvements to the land, and so the yield of crops does not really increase.

Questions and *Answers* continued ➢

Questions *and* Answers *continued*

Answer to SAQ 1 continued

There are a number of environmental factors that lead to food shortages. More and more land is being turned over to crop production and this inevitably leads in many African countries to deforestation. This adds to the already poor water supplies and can lead in some cases to desertification. The number of fertilisers being used is also on the increase and this could lead to water contamination. Large-scale livestock farming is also increasing, leading to increases in ammonia damage to ecosystems and also to the demise of the small-scale farmer who cannot compete with the bigger businesses. The increasing problems of water scarcity will also add to the difficulties faced by African farmers.

The increasing problem of HIV/Aids in many African countries also adds to food shortages. Death and disability caused by Aids lead to labour shortages, and families are unable to pay for food if some members are unable to work. Countries also find they have to import more food to cater for the victims of Aids, and the food supply is even lower than normal as there are more dependants and fewer workers.

Malnutrition and hunger themselves are major factors in contributing to food shortages. One in five of the people in the world's developing countries suffer from hunger and they are unable to work effectively in farming. Hunger also leads to deficiencies in vitamins, proteins and minerals needed to keep healthy, and leads to increases in diseases, weakness and lethargy, again affecting the ability to work.

In conclusion, there are many factors that lead to food shortages and in many African countries they combine to form the basis of the very difficult conditions that large numbers of Africans find themselves in.

2 Economic, Political and Social Factors Affecting Development

We will explain the main factors that affect development in African countries, and the main policies that have been put forward to solve some of these problems.

Economic factors

There are a number of economic factors that affect development in the areas of health, education and food. Some of these factors affect one area more than another but they have an impact on all three.

World Trade

The rich developed countries in the world have supported the idea of free trade with the less developed countries. They do not want to support import quotas or taxes or export subsidies as they believe that companies should be allowed to get on with business without the interference of government regulations. This has benefited the rich countries as they have had the money to be able to buy resources they need from poor countries, resources such as raw materials and food that they cannot grow themselves.

The total value of world trade has increased from around $200 million in 1952 to over $6,000 million in 2002. But many poor countries have been left behind as the rich countries have subsidised agriculture and blocked access to their own markets. The growth in world trade has been unevenly spread. Some developing countries – often in Asia – have increased growth by producing more manufactured goods. But others – often in Africa – have fallen further behind.

World Trade Organisation

The World Trade Organisation (WTO) is an international body that tries to promote free trade among countries by getting them to abolish subsidies and tariffs. Set up in 1995 and based in Geneva, its members include most of the rich countries of the world such as the USA, Britain, France, Germany, Japan. It sets the rules for trading in the world and now has around 150 members. It has been heavily criticised for its role in relation to the trade issues concerning African countries. In particular, it is seen as a club for the rich countries who have not opened up their markets to the developing countries of the world, by removing subsidies. In Doha in 2001, a new trade round of the WTO, designed to open up the global economy and make conditions better for poor countries, was launched. After the WTO meeting in Hong Kong in 2005, it also agreed to end farm export subsidies by 2013. However, there was little progress on key issues such as tariffs for agricultural produce and liberalising trade in manufactured goods.

Cash crops

Many poor countries depend on a single primary export such as wood, coffee, copper or cotton, sometimes called cash crops. Burundi gets 73% of its income from coffee, and Zambia gets 70% of its income from copper. But prices for such commodities have been declining. Prices of manufactured goods have, in contrast, risen in relative terms.

Subsidies

Huge agricultural subsidies by Western countries to their small farm populations through the CAP far outweigh the aid given to developing countries. The rich countries have repeatedly pledged to reduce the size of their farm supports. So far the amount of such subsidies has changed little in 20 years, while the amount of aid has declined. Often, food surpluses from the EU are sent to African countries, which reduces local prices and makes it hard for local farmers to survive.

Poverty

Globally, the proportion of people in poverty has declined, but as the population grows the actual number of poor people is still rising. Declining poverty in Asia suggests the benefits of trade have trickled down to the poorest. But poverty is expected to rise in Africa, where trade is weak and factors such as war, HIV and debt also play a part.

Debt

With the independence of many African countries after the Second World War, and the setting up of new governments in these countries, organisations like the World Bank and the International Monetary Fund lent large sums of money to these new regimes. Much of that money was spent on massive programmes to build dams and highways. Many of the governments that were lent this money were dictatorships or kleptocracies (corrupt governments) and a lot of the money was spent on the armed forces to keep dictators in power, or the money simply disappeared into private bank accounts. The debts owed by many African countries grew to the point where many could not afford to even pay the interest, never mind the debt itself.

Many people argue there should be 'debt relief' given to poor African countries. The Jubilee Debt Campaign, formed after the Jubilee 2000 Campaign in the UK, argues that the unpayable debt of poor countries should be cancelled.

Political factors

There are a number of political factors that affect development in Africa. Many of these are the result of the ending of years of colonial rule, with African countries being given independence, but not being ready to govern themselves. Wars and civil strife have been common in Africa and this has greatly affected development. In many countries, such as Uganda, the army took over the country, and much of the aid was spent on the armed forces. In some others, such as Rwanda, a single group ruled, and corruption and inefficiency were common. In the Democratic Republic of the Congo (DRC) more than 3 million people have died since 1998 in that conflict alone. Another difficulty has been the incidence of bad government in some African countries.

War in Africa

In early 2004, the British Prime Minister, Tony Blair, established the **Commission for Africa**. The seventeen members of the Commission, including Bob Geldof, and nine from Africa, published their report 'Our Common Interest' on 11 March 2005. The report argued that the prevention of conflict in Africa was one of the most important things that had to be done to improve the chances of progress in the continent. The effects of conflict were so devastating that conflict had to be tackled as a priority.

Figure 10.4 Millions of people have fled their homes during the war in the Darfur region of Sudan, which began in 2003

Government in Africa

When the police can't be trusted to be fair, it becomes difficult for people to run their businesses honestly. Without taxes being paid from businesses there will be less money spent on things like health, education and transport. Health clinics run out of medicines, schools have no teachers and farmers find it difficult to sell their crops because roads flood when it rains.

Source: Commission for Africa, 'Our Common Interest', 2005

The failure of African governments to deliver key services to their people has significantly affected their development.

Social factors

We already looked at the main issues in health, education and food in the first section. Here we look at the main proposals for tackling these.

Tackling health issues in Africa

The Commission for Africa puts forward a number of ways it thinks health issues can be tackled:

◆ Preventable diseases must be eliminated through paying for low-cost treatments such as Vitamin A pills or treating nets around beds with insecticide to prevent bites from malaria-carrying mosquitoes.

◆ An extra million health workers need to be trained during the next ten years. The money paid to health workers should be increased.

◆ Africa needs a supply of medicines at a cost it can afford. Drug companies put most of their effort in to developing treatments for the diseases of rich countries, where they will earn more money. They should have incentives to focus also on the diseases which affect Africa.

◆ Rich nations should help pay for the removal of fees for basic health care until African governments can meet these costs themselves.

◆ The way donors give aid needs to be changed. Rather than focusing on specific diseases donors need to look at all the problems together. They need to work with Africans, supporting the healthcare services developed by African governments.

◆ Clean water is another way in which health can be improved. The decline in aid for water and toilet facilities should be reversed, so that the Water Action Plan, which the world's eight richest countries agreed in 2003, can be implemented.

◆ Progress can be made in the fight against HIV and Aids. African governments need to take bold steps which take into account cultural factors and the power relationships between men, women and young people. Rich countries need to agree a common approach and to make more aid available. An extra $10 billion a year needs to be provided.

◆ The Commission also looks at ways the most vulnerable people can be helped. In rich countries there are welfare state systems designed to prevent people who are ill, old, disabled or looking after children from falling into poverty. This is sometimes called social protection. Some people in the past have thought that social protection was something which African countries couldn't afford, but the Commission disagrees. It says that it's money well spent.

Tackling education issues in Africa

The Commission for Africa has identified a number of areas of progress but has also identified things still needing to be done:

◆ The number of children in primary schools in Africa is increasing overall. In Uganda, parents used to have to pay fees to send their children to school, now primary school is free.

◆ There has been a dramatic increase in the number of children attending primary school, to nearly 90% of both boys and girls. Now the challenge is to ensure that they all get a good education and have opportunities to go on to secondary school.

◆ But more can be done. The Commission says that an estimated $7–$8 billion a year extra is needed to fund education in Africa properly. This money is needed to provide free basic education, get more teachers in the classrooms, more girls into school and to ensure that what is taught is suitable for African needs.

◆ Donors need to support African governments to develop education services at all levels, from primary to secondary and higher education, and adult learning as well.

Tackling food shortages

Earlier in this chapter the reasons for food shortages given by the FAO were outlined. They were:

◆ Conflict

◆ Free trade

◆ Women's role in farming

◆ Environmental factors

◆ Water scarcity

◆ HIV/Aids

◆ Malnutrition

Each of these has to be dealt with if food insecurity is to be tackled. The Commission for Africa outlined specific ways to tackle the problems:

◆ Agriculture in Africa was developed mainly to export a narrow range of basic goods to rich countries rather than growing crops for domestic consumption. This legacy remains and African countries should be encouraged to develop other aspects of agriculture.

◆ The trade barriers put up by rich countries against imports from Africa are absolutely unacceptable. They are out-of-date, environmentally destructive and ethically in-defensible. 'They must be scrapped,' the Commission's report states.

◆ Dependence on agricultural exports also means that Africa is vulnerable to changes in world prices. For example, between 1980 and 2000, the price of sugar fell by 77%, the price of cocoa fell by 71% and the price of coffee fell by 64%. Diversity would help African countries.

Figure 10.5 A farmer irrigating the land in Bouake, Ivory Coast

◆ Farming will be helped if more land can be irrigated so that the soil is less dry and if roads and warehouses can be improved so that farmers can get more of their crops to market.

◆ Farming can also be improved if poor people, especially women, are given legal rights to the land they are cultivating.

◆ Some countries in eastern and southern Africa have been successfully developing new types of crop, such as cut flowers and fresh vegetables, which are sold to rich countries.

◆ The Commission also suggests that countries could produce much more food for selling to other African countries, particularly those which are regularly short of food. This would have two benefits: it would help economies grow and it would also help prevent crisis situations when food can't be found.

◆ Climate change is a major concern. It seems that northern and southern Africa are likely to get drier while tropical parts of Africa are likely to get wetter. There is more risk of floods like those in Mozambique in 2000 which left half a million people homeless. The Commission says that climate change is a worldwide issue which must be tackled by the whole world working together.

Possible questions on the economic, political and social factors affecting development

◆ Critically examine the economic factors that affect development in Africa.

◆ Assess the importance of trade as a major influence on development in Africa.

◆ To what extent is conflict a factor in preventing development?

◆ Assess the effectiveness of African governments in promoting development.

◆ To what extent is health the most important factor in development?

◆ Education is the most important factor for development in Africa. Discuss.

◆ Critically examine the role of food aid in providing food security.

Questions and Answers

SAQ 2   Critically examine the economic factors that affect development in Africa.

(15 marks)

Here you should provide as many arguments as you can to show that economic factors are promoting development in Africa, and also outline any arguments that show economic factors are hindering development.

Answer to SAQ 2

For many years, trade between the countries of the world has been important in making countries rich. It has been organised on the basis of free trade. This, in theory, has allowed countries to specialise in what they are good at producing, sell it to the rest of the world, and in return buy other goods and services they can't make. For years, the UK has sold manufactured goods made in its factories to many countries around the world, and in return it has bought a lot of the food it cannot grow. African countries want to see their economies grow. They want to trade with the rest of the world and increase their wealth, as has happened with countries in Asia in recent years. However, there are a number of problems and difficulties with this idea in practice in relation to African countries.

African countries should be able to make a success of exporting a number of food products to the rest of the world. They can produce sugar and cotton, for example, and are able to compete with any other countries. However, the EU has used subsidies to help European farmers produce cheap beet sugar, and the US has used subsidies to help its cotton farmers. This not only protects these farmers from African competition, but it reduces world prices for these products. This has effectively excluded African farmers from these world markets.

The idea of free trade should mean that African farmers can sell their produce anywhere in the world. Even if EU and US farmers have their incomes protected, the Africans should still be able to sell in other areas. However, not only have these rich countries used subsidies to protect their own farmers, but they have also erected trade barriers to African produce by taxing African goods when they enter these markets. This makes African produce a lot more expensive and few people buy their products.

The World Trade Organisation (WTO) has been set up to oversee the rules for trade around the world. It is committed to free trade and is supposed to enforce free trade rules on its members. However, despite the fact that many poorer African countries have complained about the unfairness of subsidies and trade barriers, the WTO has been very slow to implement its own rules.

The countries in Africa could start by improving trade between themselves and within their own countries. There are no trade barriers in this area and they could perhaps build up their own businesses and industries before taking on the richer countries. However, within many African countries there are barriers just the same. A large number of road blocks prevent the free movement of goods and services in countries like Nigeria. Tolls, or bribes,

Questions and *Answers continued* ➤

Questions and **Answers** continued

Answer to SAQ 2 continued

have to be paid to move goods around the country. The paperwork involved in many countries concerning bureaucratic and customs rules means it can take as long as 30 days to export something from Ethiopia, for example.

The poverty in many African countries, linked to the problems in health, education and food insecurity, also mean that many people are unable to play their full part in the economic development of African countries. The governments of these countries are struggling to manage the basic systems that add to the development of a country. HIV/Aids is a major problem in many African countries, leaving many people unable to work. Basic education levels are poor and many people do not have the skills or qualifications needed in the economic sector. Health levels are such that again many people are unable to play their part.

Finally, there is evidence that some African countries can succeed in organising and developing their economies. Many agricultural products come from Africa, such as tea, cotton, tobacco, coffee, sugar and so on. These are sometimes referred to as 'cash crops'. However, many of these countries have run up huge sums in debt to rich countries. Instead of being able to use any money they do get from trade, these countries have to pay off their debt. It has been argued that wiping out the debt of African countries would not only benefit them, but would also benefit the rich countries through better trade opportunities.

In conclusion, there are many arguments to say that African countries should be able to make a success of their economies through the system of free trade organised in the world. However, there are even more arguments to say that the economic conditions attached to these trade rules mean that African countries will find it hard to improve their economic position, unless major changes are made to the way trade is organised.

3 The Role of Organisations in Promoting Development

Introduction

There are a number of ways that aid can be given to the countries and people of the developing world. Governments in rich countries can decide to spend money to help people in poor countries. They can do this either on their own – **bilateral aid** – or they can do this as members of organisations such as the European Union or the United Nations – **multilateral aid** – where all the countries' money is pooled together and spent in a way that the organisations decide. Voluntary organisations and charities, such as Save the Children and Oxfam, can also raise money from individuals and use this money to help those most in need. These groups are often referred to as **Non-governmental organisations** (NGOs) as they are not directly part of governments' response to situations in developing countries. We will look at various organisations and the ways they try to help poor countries to develop, particularly those in Africa.

African Governments

The independence of many African countries after colonial rule left many of them unprepared for government. This resulted in poor government through the army taking control, through one-party dictatorships and through the dominance of one group in many countries. Each of these situations often resulted in lack of freedom for the people, corruption and inefficiency and lack of progress due to bad government. You should be able to discuss some examples of countries which have suffered from bad government, and what can happen as a result of bad government. You should also be able to outline the ways in which governments must change to promote development in Africa.

The African Union

The African Union (AU) was founded in 2002 as the successor to the Organisation of African Unity, and it has 53 members. The purpose of the organisation is to help secure Africa's democracy, human rights and a sustainable economy, especially by bringing an end to intra-African conflict and creating an effective common market.

The AU faces many challenges, including *health issues* such as combating malaria and the HIV/Aids epidemic, *political issues* such as confronting undemocratic regimes and mediating in the many civil wars ; *economic issues* such as improving the standard of living of millions of poor, uneducated Africans; *ecological issues* such as dealing with recurring famines, desertification and lack of ecological sustainability.

In dealing with conflict in Africa, The AU's first military intervention in a member state was the May 2003 deployment of a peace-keeping force of soldiers from South Africa, Ethiopia and Mozambique to Burundi to oversee the implementation of the various agreements after the war there. Around 7,000 AU troops are also deployed in Sudan for peace-keeping in the Darfur conflict.

Conflict is not the only issue that the AU will have to deal with. It has committed itself to developing the economy of Africa with the introduction of a single currency, a single bank and a single market. Some countries have already gone down this road through the New Partnership for Africa's Development (NEPAD), formulated in 2001. This programme is likely to take a very long time, however.

The European Union

The EU is involved in helping out in humanitarian crises around the world. This includes help in trouble spots, where wars have caused problems to the local populations, and also help in disasters such as earthquakes, hurricanes, floods or drought. The EU's relief operations are handled by ECHO, which is the humanitarian aid office. The EU knows that ECHO itself cannot mobilise the resources needed to help in crises, so its job is to provide the funds for relief, while relying on humanitarian partners – non-governmental organisations (NGOs), the UN specialised agencies and the international Red Cross – to deliver the food and equipment and carry out the emergency programmes. In recent years, about two-thirds of the EU's relief effort has been channelled to NGOs with about 20% going to UN agencies and 10% to the International Committee of the Red Cross.

The EU's humanitarian assistance comes in three main types: emergency aid, food aid and aid for refugees who have fled conflict areas and for people displaced within a country or region at war. Disaster relief and humanitarian assistance are short term, but the EU has an 'exit strategy' whereby it does not come out of an area until it is satisfied that people can cope or that longer-term development aid is in place. EU operations are under way in Liberia, Burundi, the Democratic Republic of Congo, Sierra Leone and Darfur in western Sudan, while measures are being taken to tackle the severe food shortages affecting several southern African countries.

In 2000, the EU reached the Cotonou Agreement with over 70 African, Caribbean and Pacific (ACP) countries, which governed trade between these countries and the EU. The deal requires those ACP countries enjoying special trading status with the European Union to respect human rights and democratic principles. In return, the EU is expected to provide 20 billion euros ($18.85 billion) over seven years to ACP countries provided they uphold basic principles of good governance. The new deal also provides for a progressive removal of restrictive trade barriers over the next 15 years to 2015. Some people are worried that EU farmers may go out of business if low-cost goods come in from Africa, but others argue that African countries can only be helped if taxes and subsidies are abolished.

Non-governmental organisations (NGOs)

As the term suggests, NGOs are organisations that do not come under the control of the Government, but are run by volunteers and ordinary members of the public. They tend to raise their own money through voluntary and private sources, though in recent years the UK Government and others have used NGOs to carry out development work for them.

There are a large number of NGOs in the UK. Some, like Oxfam and Save the Children, are well known and cover many aspects of development in Africa. Others, like Concern, which is based in Ireland, but has offices in Scotland, and Water Aid UK, concentrate on a particular aspect of development. They are able to formulate their policies and priorities independently of governments. They were often the first agencies to become involved in emergencies in the past. However, they have become a lot more involved in long-term sustainable development in recent years.

NGOs tend to work in co-operation with overseas partners and they are keen to see the involvement of local community groups, church groups and local NGOs where the projects are run and organised by local people themselves.

Oxfam

Oxfam GB is a development, relief and campaigning organisation that works with others to find lasting solutions to poverty and suffering around the world. It was set up during the Second World War to help war refugees and displaced people, but continued after the war as an international charity to help people suffering from wars or other causes. Oxfam's goal is a world where everybody is 'Secure, Skilled, Equal, Safe, Healthy and Heard'. It attempts to help people do this in a number of ways.

- **Emergencies**. The Oxfam storehouse has a lot of equipment ready to be sent quickly to places around the world. Oxfam is helping 650,000 people in Darfur, Sudan, by providing water tanks, sanitation facilities and essential daily items.

- **Development**. Oxfam tries to involve local people by helping to provide expertise, training and funding so local people can find the best possible way to improve their situation. Oxfam is showing Ethiopian farmers how to grow more crops per acre.

◆ **Campaigning**. Oxfam is campaigning to set a global agenda that is fair to the world's poorest people. It is currently looking at fair trade, reducing the arms trade and improving children's education. It was heavily involved in the Make Poverty History campaign in 2005.

Save the Children UK

Save the Children 'fights for children in the UK and around the world who suffer from poverty, disease, injustice and violence'. Save the Children, like Oxfam, works to relieve the problems caused in short-term emergencies and also looks at development work, particularly associated with children. Emergencies have natural and/or human causes. Examples include war, refugee crises, famine, drought and floods. Some happen suddenly, but many others – such as famine and war – build up over time and can be predicted. Many crises are 'chronic' in that they last for many years and a state of crisis becomes the norm. 'Children are particularly vulnerable in emergencies because they are physically weaker than adults and risk being separated from their families. Emergencies blight childhood, a crucial time for developing and learning'.

◆ **Emergencies**. Save the Children is currently working in the Ivory Coast and the Democratic Republic of the Congo to help children overcome problems caused by years of war. It is also working to overcome a food crisis in Ethiopia and Kenya caused by years of drought. A similar crisis is happening in southern Africa, in Malawi and Mozambique, where food shortages are being addressed.

◆ **Development**. Save the Children is actively involved in development work in health, education, HIV/Aids and relieving poverty. It aims to help provide access to affordable good-quality health services in countries like Zambia, which has recently introduced free health care in rural areas. It works in countries like Mozambique to improve access to schools for all children.

Key Points

Advantages of NGOs

◆ NGOs often go to places that governments won't or can't go to, e.g. Darfur.

◆ They respond very quickly in emergency situations, supplying livestock and food, e.g. in southern Africa and north-east food crises.

◆ The UN increasingly relies on NGOs to help it carry out its programmes – World Food Programme, WHO, FAO.

◆ NGOs are good at small-scale projects involving local people in decisions – they work in partnership with local communities.

◆ NGOs can focus attention on problem areas and force governments to help – as in Mozambique.

Key Points continued ➤

Key Points *continued*

Criticisms of NGOs

◆ There are a lot of NGOs all competing for funds and resources – over 100 NGOs in the UK are involved in African countries.

◆ Some NGOs may help in certain areas but they do not have the resources to tackle problems over a wide area – e.g. widespread famine in north-east Africa.

◆ NGOs are unaccountable and undemocratic and may have their own agendas.

◆ Short-term solutions in emergencies may be tackled, but the NGOs do not have the structure or resources to tackle long-term development needs.

◆ Many NGOs get money from governments and are therefore subject to guidelines and rules over how that is spent.

The UK Government

The Department for International Development (DFID) is the part of the UK Government that manages Britain's aid to poor countries and works to get rid of extreme poverty. It has two headquarters, one in London and the other in East Kilbride. The DFID describes international development as efforts, by developed and developing countries, to bring people out of poverty and so reduce how much their country relies on overseas aid. The DFID thinks a number of things can be done to help, such as settling conflicts, increasing trade and improving health and education.

Spending

The DFID says the UK is committed to the United Nations target of spending 0.7% of gross national income on aid. But the UK is currently spending only 0.3% of gross national income. The DFID does say, however, that the UK is the fifth largest donor in the world, after the United States, Japan, Germany and France, and that Britain has raised its spending on aid to more than £3 billion a year – a 52% increase from 1997. Just over half of the UK's aid money goes directly to developing countries. This is known as bilateral aid. The rest is channelled through international organisations, such as the European Union, the World Bank, the International Monetary Fund and the United Nations. This is known as multilateral aid. Countries in Africa get about 46% of all the UK's aid, which amounts to £589 million. The DFID channels the money it uses for development aid in a number of ways:

◆ **International financial institutions**. The World Bank and the International Monetary Fund get some money from the UK and they lend it to developing countries to reduce poverty.

◆ **The United Nations**. The UN agencies receive money which they use in their various fields to help the poor.

◆ **The European Union**. Member states give money to the EU which helps developing countries.

◆ **Voluntary organisations**. Groups like Oxfam and Save the Children receive money to support development and humanitarian work in poor countries.

◆ **Directly to developing countries**. Governments in poor countries get money under strict conditions to help reduce poverty.

Emergency aid

The DFID is also involved in helping countries when disasters or emergencies occur, such as earthquakes, flooding, hurricanes or conflict. To improve the effectiveness of emergency help, it often channels funds and expertise through organisations such as the UN, International Red Cross and other international agencies. It has supported the World Food Programme, for example, in different parts of the world.

Tied aid

In April 2001 the UK Government 'untied' all of its aid. This means that the UK does not grant aid on the basis that the countries receiving it must use the goods and services that the UK specifies. The DFID is committed to achieving the UN Millennium Development Goals.

The United Nations

When the United Nations was set up after the Second World War, it established a number of agencies to help it organise how to improve the living standards of people around the world, which is one of its main aims. While each of the agencies has different responsibilities, their work is obviously interlinked. We will look at some of the main UN agencies. In 2000 the UN adopted eight Millennium Development Goals (MDGs) to be achieved by the year 2015. These goals aimed to meet the needs of the world's poorest people.

Millennium Development Goals (MDGs)

1. Halve Extreme Poverty and Hunger

    Reduce by half the number of people living on less than $1 a day.

    Reduce by half the proportion of people who suffer from hunger.

2. Achieve Universal Primary School Education

    Ensure that all boys and girls complete a full course of primary schooling.

3. Empower Women and Promote Equality Between Women and Men

    Eliminate gender disparity in primary and secondary education preferably by 2005 and at all levels by 2015.

4. Reduce Under-Five Mortality

    Reduce by two-thirds the under five mortality rate.

5. Reduce Maternal Mortality

    Reduce by three-quarters the maternal mortality rate.

6. Reverse the Spread of Diseases Especially HIV/Aids and Malaria

    Halt and begin to reverse the spread of Aids and the incidence of malaria and other diseases.

7. Ensure Environmental Sustainability

    Integrate the principles of sustainable development into country policies and programmes; reverse loss of environmental resources.

    Reduce by half the proportion of people without sustainable access to safe drinking water.

    Achieve significant improvement in lives of at least 100 million slum dwellers, by 2020.

8. Create a Global Partnership For Development with Targets for Aid, Trade and Debt Relief

    Develop a better trading system for countries and reduce the debt problems.

The Food and Agricultural Organisation (FAO)

With its headquarters in Rome, the FAO is a specialised agency of the UN that works to raise levels of nutrition and standards of living; to improve the production, processing, marketing and distribution of food and agricultural products; to promote rural development; and, by these means, to eliminate hunger. In the last 40 years, the proportion of hungry people in the world has fallen, but the FAO estimates there are still around 800 million people in the developing countries who suffer from hunger, so it still has a lot of work to do.

The **World Food Programme (WFP)** is an agency of the UN organised by the FAO which distributes food to support development projects, to long-term refugees and displaced persons, and as emergency food assistance in situations of natural and man-made disasters. Development projects now make up less than 20% of WFP programmes, as emergency and long-term refugee situations result in increasing demands for WFP programmes and resources. The WFP operates exclusively on donations of commodities and money. In 2000, 3.5 million tonnes of food aid was distributed to 80 countries by the WFP at a cost of $1.7 billion. In 2006, the WFP was involved in humanitarian disasters in East Africa, where Ethiopia, Somalia and Kenya were suffering from a long drought. It is involved in West Africa, where Niger also suffered from drought. It is also involved in southern Africa, which suffers from a deadly combination of HIV/Aids, food insecurity and a weakened capacity for governments to deliver basic social services: the Triple Threat.

United Nations Childrens Fund (UNICEF)

As the name suggests, this UN agency was set up specifically to help the lives of children around the world. It too is concerned about the effects of hunger, but it is also involved in other aspects of the development of children. UNICEF has five main priorities:

Girls' inequality

Educating girls yields many social benefits for the current generation and those to come. An educated girl tends to marry later and have fewer children. The children she does have will be more likely to survive, they will be better nourished and better educated.

Immunisation of children

Every year, more than 2 million children die from diseases that could have been prevented by inexpensive vaccines. Immunisation is essential to save children's lives. It is also an affordable means of protecting whole communities and it reduces poverty.

Figure 10.6 UNICEF workers organising an immunisation programme in Niger

Protecting vulnerable children

Every day millions of children are exploited, abused, or are victims of violence. Bought and sold like commodities, children are forced to be soldiers, prostitutes, sweatshop workers or servants. This results in children who are uneducated, unhealthy and impoverished. UNICEF works with individuals, civic groups, governments and the private sector to help create protective environments for them.

HIV/Aids

Today, more than half of all new HIV infections strike people under the age of 25. Girls are hit harder and younger than boys. Infant and child death rates have risen sharply, and 14 million children are now orphans because of the disease. UNICEF works closely with young people on preventing new infections.

Early childhood

Every year, 132 million infants are born but nearly 11 million die before age 5 and tens of millions more are left with physical and/or mental disabilities or learning impairment because they and their carers lack the basic conditions needed for young children to survive.

The World Health Organisation (WHO)

The WHO is the UN agency which is responsible for improving the general health and well-being of the world's population. Its major task is to combat disease, especially key infectious diseases. As well as co-ordinating international efforts to monitor outbreaks of infectious disease such as SARS, malaria and Aids, it also has programmes to combat such diseases by developing and distributing vaccines. After years of fighting smallpox, WHO declared in 1979 that the disease had been eradicated – the first disease in history to be completely eliminated by man. WHO is nearing success in developing vaccines against malaria and schistosomiasis and aims to eradicate polio within the next few years.

World Health Day

World Health Day is celebrated every year on 7 April and each year concentrates on a different issue of world health that the WHO thinks needs to be tackled. In 2005 the theme was the health of mothers and children. In 2006, it was on the importance of health workers in the fight for better health.

Africa Malaria Day

Each year on 25 April the WHO also helps to highlight the issues caused by malaria. About 80% of all malaria deaths occur in Africa south of the Sahara, and the great majority in children under 5. A new class of drugs based on a plant called artemisinin is nearly 95% effective in dealing with malaria and WHO wants to see a much greater use of this in Africa.

Emergencies

The WHO is also quick to become involved in emergencies and disasters as they happen. At the moment it is helping to tackle health problems caused by the situation in the Horn of Africa, namely Ethiopia, Kenya, Somalia and Sudan, by strengthening health services and intervening in areas of poor nutrition.

United Nations Education, Scientific and Cultural Organisation (UNESCO)

UNESCO was set up at the same time as the other UN agencies and it has the responsibility of promoting co-operation among the UN members in the fields of education, science, culture and communications. Of these, education is the one most relevant to the SQA syllabus. Like the other UN agencies, UNESCO is committed to all the MDGs, though there are some that apply more to this particular agency:

- Halve the proportion of people living in extreme poverty in developing countries by 2015.
- Achieve universal primary education in all countries by 2015.
- Eliminate gender disparity in primary and secondary education by 2005.
- Help countries implement a national strategy for sustainable development by 2005 to reverse current trends in the loss of environmental resources by 2015.

UNESCO is particularly concerned that, in spite of all the commitments made by governments under international instruments for providing education for all, especially free and compulsory quality basic education, millions of children still remain deprived of educational opportunities, many of them because of poverty. Today, 862 million of the world's citizens are illiterate, according to the UNESCO Institute for Statistics. Moreover, one in five children between the ages of 6 and 11 in developing countries – about 115 million – are not in school; 56% of these children are girls.

Possible questions on organisations in promoting development in Africa

There is some overlap here with the previous section on economic, political and social factors that affect development. There could be exam questions asking about the response of the various organisations to a particular development area such as health, education or food insecurity.

- Critically examine the role of African governments in promoting development in Africa.
- To what extent does the British Government promote development in Africa?
- Critically examine the effectiveness of non-governmental organisations (NGOs) in responding to problems in Africa.
- Assess the effectiveness of one UN agency in responding to problems in African countries.

Questions and Answers

SAQ 3 Examine the effectiveness of non-governmental organisations (NGOs) in responding to problems in Africa. *(15 marks)*

Here you should provide as many arguments as you can to show that NGOs have responded well and also outline any criticisms of their response.

Answer to SAQ 3

There are many different NGOs operating in Africa. NGOs are organisations that do not come under the direct control of the Government of a country. They are made up of private individuals and organisations that want to help improve conditions for people in African countries. They get most of their money from donations and subscriptions from members of the public and private companies. Some of them, such as Oxfam or Save the Children, have been set up to help in specific areas. Others, such as Comic Relief or Make

Questions and Answers continued ➤

Questions and Answers

Answer to SAQ 3 continued

Poverty History, have been set up in response to particular issues in Africa. They all try to put pressure on governments and organisations like the UN and the European Union to do more to help, but most of them are heavily involved in Africa themselves.

There are arguments for and against the view that NGOs respond well to problems in African countries. NGOs often go into places that governments or organisations can't or won't go to. In Darfur in Sudan, for example, the UN and other governments pulled a lot of their people out as a result of the dangers associated with the ongoing war there. This meant that NGOs such as Oxfam were the only people helping in the region. However, the scale of the problems in Darfur means that NGOs, with their limited resources, can't really tackle what needs to be done in a meaningful way. The problems are just too big for them to solve.

NGOs are able to target specific problems in a country and they work directly with the people of that country on the ground. They are particularly keen to involve local people in their own decision making and aim to help provide small-scale sustainable development projects. The Scottish Catholic International Aid Fund is heavily involved in a number of countries, including Malawi, in improving health and education in local communities. However, some of these initiatives may not be maintained when the individual workers concerned leave to return home or when the sources of finance dry up. Some NGOs may be excluded from specific areas by a hostile or suspicious government in that country.

NGOs are usually the first to respond to disasters or emergencies. Many of them have equipment or resources waiting to be committed to an area and they don't have to go through the sometimes long and complicated procedures that governments and UN organisations have to. However, their long-term commitment to these emergencies often depends on their level of funding, and some of the smaller NGOs are limited in this respect.

NGOs are able to publicise situations and keep them in the public eye. Groups like Make Poverty History have been influential in keeping pressure on governments to respond to African problems, such as the G8 summit at Gleneagles. They may also persuade the public to keep up donations for a particular emergency, such as the food crisis in north-east Africa. However, some NGOs aims may not be in line with those of their own government and they may find it difficult to prompt governments into action. The efforts of NGOs may even be undermined by the policies of some governments towards that region.

Finally, NGOs increasingly work as operating agencies for governments and the UN. The governments and the UN provide the finance, and the NGO provides the people and the resources to provide certain types of help. The World Food Programme, for example, uses many different NGOs, including Oxfam, to distribute aid to poor countries. However, this makes the NGOs subject to the rules and conditions laid down by governments and the UN, and this may not entirely be in line with their own objectives.

In conclusion, there are arguments for and against the view that NGOs respond well to problems in African countries. In some ways they are able to tackle problems effectively, though they also have difficulties in responding to some problems.

STUDY THEME 3F: GLOBAL SECURITY

What You Should Know

SQA:

The organisation and role of the United Nations (UN): aims, membership, institutions, decision making procedures, reforms/changes. The role of the North Atlantic Treaty Organisation (NATO): international role, reforms/changes.

Origins and consequences of recent threats to peace and security, including international terrorism, demanding an international response.

International responses: the EU, NATO and the UN responses to recent threats to peace and security including international terrorism.

This topic can be split into three main sections:

1   Organisation and Role of the United Nations (UN)
2   Organisation and Role of the North Atlantic Treaty Organisation (NATO)
3   Threats to World Peace and Responses to Them

1 Organisation and Role of the United Nations

The main issues covered in this section are:

◆   Origins and aims of the UN

◆   Organisation and structure of the UN

◆   The peace-keeping role of the UN

◆   Challenges facing the UN

Figure 11.1 The UN flag

Origins and aims of the United Nations

With the end of the Second World War in Europe in 1945, many countries agreed that there had to be an organisation of countries of the world to prevent any such conflict becoming possible again. These countries met in 1945 and formed the United Nations. Membership has grown to include almost 200 countries and these countries have all agreed to accept the Charter of the UN and all the obligations associated with it. The UN has a number of purposes:

◆   To maintain international peace and security

◆   To develop friendly relations among nations

◆   To co-operate in solving international economic, social, cultural and humanitarian problems and in promoting respect for human rights and fundamental freedoms

◆   To be a centre for harmonising the actions of nations in attaining these ends.

Organisation and structure of the UN

The structure of the UN is built around six main bodies as shown below:

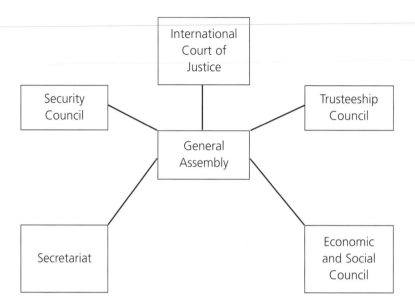

The General Assembly

All UN members are represented in the General Assembly and each has one vote. The Assembly holds regular sessions from mid-September to mid-December, although, for the rest of the year, special committees and bodies carry out much of the work. The General Assembly's main purposes are:

◆ To debate issues relating to the UN Charter

◆ To make proposals about international issues

◆ To consider the UN budget and how much each member should pay

◆ To elect the non-permanent Security Council members

◆ To supervise the work of the many UN agencies

◆ To admit new members

◆ To appoint the Secretary General.

Figure 11.2 A meeting of the UN General Assembly

The General Assembly makes decisions by a two-thirds majority on important matters such as admitting new members, and by simple majority on day-to-day issues. It has no power to enforce its decisions, and the Security Council can veto any nominee for Secretary General.

The Security Council

The Security Council is where the real power of the UN lies, and member states are expected to carry out its decisions. It has fifteen members, five of whom (China, France, Russia, the UK and the USA) are permanent members. The other ten are elected by the General Assembly for a two-year term and represent various areas of the world. The permanent members have the power of veto over decisions. In disputes between countries the Security Council can do a number of things:

- It can ask parties to reach agreement by peaceful means.
- It can mediate in disputes and suggest possible solutions.
- It can enforce economic or military sanctions.
- It can send in fact-finding missions to examine the problem.
- It can send in UN peace-keeping Forces to keep opposing forces apart.
- It can authorise coalitions of member states to use military action.

The Secretariat

The Secretariat is the civil service of the UN and it has a staff of around 20,000 drawn from many of the member states. They work at UN Headquarters in New York and offices all over the world. They carry out the day-to-day work of the UN. At its head is the Secretary General, currently Kofi Annan, who is appointed for a five-year term. He advises the Security Council on threats to world peace and security, but the ultimate power lies with the Security Council.

Other main bodies

The Economic and Social Council, the Trusteeship Council and the International Court of Justice are responsible for the social and economic work of the UN, the administration of territories preparing for self-government and settling legal disputes between member states. We will focus on the other bodies listed above who are responsible for global security.

The UN budget

The main source of funds is from the member states, whose contributions are assessed on their capacity to pay: rich countries pay more than poor countries. Countries are also assessed for the costs of peace-keeping operations. Japan and Germany have complained that they pay more than the UK, France, China or Russia, yet they cannot get permanent membership of the Security Council. The UN and all its agencies and funds spends around $10 billion each year. This is a relatively small sum compared with the wealth of the rich countries, yet the UN has faced a financial crisis in recent years. Many member states have not paid their full dues and the huge increase in peace-keeping duties since the beginning of the 1990s has seen the debt owed to the UN rise above $2 billion. There have been many demands for reform of the way the UN is financed.

The peace-keeping role of the UN

Peace-keeping reform under Kofi Annan

After the failure of the UN to prevent genocide in Rwanda in 1994 and the fall of Srebrenica in Bosnia in 1995, Kofi Annan commissioned an inquiry to look into practical and achievable prescriptions for future peace-keeping operations. **The Brahimi Report**, published in 2000, came up with a number of recommendations:

◆ Where preconditions for success did not exist, it would be best not to mount an operation – no action for its own sake.

◆ Greater numbers of well-equipped and well-trained troops.

◆ More support staff at Headquarters and stronger political, financial and material support from members of the Security Council.

Figure 11.3 UN peace-keepers in action in Lebanon, 2006

◆ More stringent standards for judging the performance of peace-keepers in the field and at Headquarters.

The General Assembly responded positively to these proposals and the new strategy was applied successfully in 2002 in East Timor and Sierra Leone. With the war in Iraq in 2003, however, there has been some criticism of the extent to which UN policies are shaped by the USA. In particular, there have been calls for countries like Japan, Germany, Brazil and India (the 'group of four') to be given permanent seats in the Security Council.

The role of the United Nations in securing world peace

Up until the 1980s, the split in the world caused by the Cold War meant that the power of veto was used regularly by the Americans against the Russians, and vice versa. The end of the Cold War in the early 1990s was seen by many as a golden opportunity for the UN to secure greater world peace than ever before. In 1992, the UN proposed its 'Agenda For Peace' which called for 'preventative diplomacy'. This meant the UN would be able to intervene in a dispute before it led to hostilities. A standby force could be quickly sent to trouble spots around the world. These proposals were heavily criticised, however, as the cost would be very high and the UN could become a judge and jury on matters of dispute.

The Peace Dividend after the Cold War also gave hope that the world would be a more peaceful place. It was underestimated, however, just how much the superpowers had kept the world in a degree of law and order. When the Cold War ended, the USA and the former Soviet Union's ability or interest in keeping tensions at bay declined. The UN was faced with a large increase in the number of tensions and conflicts around the world. Former Yugoslavia, Iraq, Chechnya, Somalia, Rwanda and Kosovo dominated the international stage.

Challenges facing the UN

Faced with the dramatic rise in conflicts and tensions that demand UN peace-keeping initiatives, the UN continues to face a number of challenges:

◆ The UN has to rely on the willingness of member countries to act – if they don't back the Security Council, the UN will fail.

◆ The increase in peace-keeping operations, and the interests of the USA and the UK in these, has led to other traditional supporters becoming reluctant to act.

◆ Since 9/11 the USA has become more involved in Afghanistan and Iraq – many believe it has used the UN to serve its own purposes.

- There have been difficulties in conducting operations under a unified command structure – language problems and unwillingness of some nations to accept other commands has led to chaos.

- Financing operations, getting forces to conflict areas, and then supplying them properly has been difficult. UN administration is slow.

- It has been almost impossible for the UN to deal effectively with internal conflicts as they are not viewed as being in the UN's mandate.

- The interests of the major nations seems important in deciding on action – compare Iraq with Rwanda.

- Indecision and failure to act quickly is seen by many as an indication that UN peace-keeping is poor – as seen in Bosnia, Rwanda and Somalia in the 1990s.

- The influence of the USA over the UN appears to be growing – particularly as seen by the developing world.

Possible questions on the organisation and role of the United Nations

- To what extent has the UN been successful in resolving conflict in recent years?

- Critically examine the view that the role of the UN in resolving conflict has changed dramatically in recent years.

- To what extent are the UN's proposed reforms likely to improve its response to conflicts around the world?

Questions and Answers

SAQ 1   To what extent has the UN been successful in resolving conflict in recent years? *(15 marks)*

Here you should provide as many examples as you can of the methods the UN has used to resolve conflict and analyse how successful they have been.

Answers to SAQ 1

The United Nations was set up after the Second World War and one of its key aims was to prevent conflict, if possible, and to resolve conflict if it could not be prevented. The Secretary General of the UN is one of the key people responsible for resolving conflict. He can advise the Security Council of threats to world peace and security, and he can recommend courses of action. However, the ultimate power rests with the Security Council.

There are a number of methods the UN can use to prevent or resolve conflict. The Secretary General can send in fact-finding missions or teams of negotiators or inspectors to a country or region that is having difficulties. They can report back to him and he can tell the Security Council what he thinks should be done. However, like all proposals put to the Security Council, it is sometimes difficult to get agreement, especially from the five permanent members, namely the USA, the UK, Russia, China and France. They can often use, or threaten to use, their power of veto to block any action they do not agree with. This was the case in getting agreement on what to do in Iraq.

Questions and **Answers** continued ➣

Questions *and* **Answers** *continued*

Answer to SAQ 1 continued

Another action the UN can take is to place economic or military sanctions on a country. Economic sanctions usually involve some kind of trade restrictions on a country, for example, the oil embargo on Iraq, while military sanctions can mean the ban of the sale of arms or equipment to a country, for example, the UN military sanctions on South Africa during Apartheid. However, countries who do have sanctions placed on them can often get around those sanctions, and some people argue that they can have a damaging effect on the people of a country, such as Iraq, while not really affecting what the leaders do.

The UN can also send in peace-keepers to a country to stop a conflict after it has happened, such as in Bosnia and Kosovo. UNPROFOR managed to keep the rival sides apart in the former Yugoslavia, and the UN has also been relatively successful in Afghanistan in keeping the peace. However, the UN has to persuade countries to send in troops and this has become more and more expensive in recent years. Some countries may also be unwilling to send troops on UN missions as they are worried about the adverse reaction this might have in their own country if troops are killed.

While the UN has been quite successful in maintaining peace in a number of areas when conflict has broken out, it has not been as successful in getting the sides to agree to a lasting peace. This has been the case in Africa with difficulties in Rwanda and Somalia and more recently in Sudan. The UN has also not been directly involved in the Iraq conflict, with some people arguing that the global power of the US has been too dominant here, though it has been involved in attempts to find a lasting peace. Once again it has been difficult to see a lasting solution in the near future.

In conclusion, the UN has been successful in a number of areas in both keeping the peace and finding a lasting solution. However, there are also some areas around the world where the UN has failed to achieve either.

2 Organisation and Role of the North Atlantic Treaty Organisation

The main issues covered in this section are:

- ◆ Origins and aims of NATO
- ◆ Organisation and structure of NATO
- ◆ The peace-keeping role of NATO
- ◆ Enlargement of NATO
- ◆ The changing role of NATO

Origins and aims of NATO

NATO was formed in 1949, as a defensive political and military alliance of Western democratic countries against the threat of Soviet Union communism. It was established under the North Atlantic Treaty (4 April 1949) by Belgium, Canada, Denmark, France, Great Britain, Iceland, Italy, Luxembourg, the Netherlands, Norway, Portugal and the United States. Greece and Turkey entered the alliance in 1952, West Germany (now Germany) entered in 1955, Spain joined in 1982.

The key aims of the NATO alliance are:

◆ to promote the common values of its members

◆ to develop economic and political co-operation

◆ to use member's armed forces for 'collective self-defence'.

Organisation and structure of NATO

The highest authority within NATO is the North Atlantic Council (NAC), which is composed of permanent delegates from all member countries and meets once a week. All decisions are taken collectively and a consensus reached before a decision is finalised. The Council is responsible for setting up other committees and planning groups which have delegated powers.

The Defence Planning Committee (DPC) is responsible for collective defence matters, though France is not represented because of its decision not to take part in military actions.

The Nuclear Planning Group (NPG) is responsible for dealing with all matters relating to NATO's nuclear weapons (France is not represented).

The Military Committee is made up of the Chiefs of Staff from all countries and is responsible for all military matters.

The Integrated Military Structure helps to co-ordinate logistics, standardisation of weapons and air defence arrangements.

The **Secretary General** is in charge of the administrative support for the work of the alliance, mostly at NATO Headquarters in Brussels. He is the voice and media focus of NATO.

The peace-keeping role of NATO

NATO after the Cold War

As the communist states of eastern Europe collapsed after 1990, the main reason for NATO, that is, the defence of Western countries against communist aggression, disappeared. Many argued that this meant there was a need for NATO to reconsider its position. Some countries, including France and Germany, argued for the disbandment of NATO and the creation of a new alliance less dependent on the USA. Others argued that the USA and its forces were crucial to the security of Europe. There was also the upsurge in nationalism in Europe and the potentially unstable governments in Eastern Europe. By the early 1990s, NATO forces were being deployed in Bosnia on behalf of the UN, Georgia was in civil war and there were attempts to overthrow the new democratic government in Russia. It was clear that NATO had to search for a new role.

Figure 11.4 NATO forces operating in Bosnia

The New Strategic Concept 1991

The New Strategic Concept was introduced to help NATO adapt to meet the new security threats in Europe. Its main focus was:

◆ to enable NATO to work with other international agencies and with non-member states

◆ to improve dialogue, reduce tension and foster closer ties with the former Soviet Union and former communist states in Eastern Europe through the Euro-Atlantic Partnership Council (EAPC).

Partnership For Peace 1994

This process was furthered in 1994 by the Partnership For Peace agreement which enabled participating countries to:

◆ discuss defence spending and military planning

◆ ensure democratic controls over defence spending

◆ contribute to peace-keeping operations under the authority of the UN and the Organisation for Security and Co-operation in Europe (OSCE)

◆ participate in defence planning, training and military maneouvres

◆ develop military forces which are better able to co-operate.

Many people feared this would be little more than a talking shop but this has proved to be incorrect, as the following show.

◆ All of the participating countries contributed to NATO involvement in Bosnia under the UN IFOR mission.

◆ Both NATO and Russian forces ended the Kosovo conflict and ended the presidency of Milosevic in Serbia.

◆ A number of former Soviet Republic and Warsaw Pact countries have gone on to join NATO.

◆ Russia has been involved in the NATO-Russia Permanent Joint Council since 1997; it discusses political and security matters and agrees on any joint actions.

Enlargement of NATO

With the collapse of communism in the early 1990s, the issue of enlargement had to be addressed. Some former communist countries expressed a desire to join NATO, now that they were democracies, but there were a number of concerns expressed about enlargement.

Key Points

Arguments for enlargement

◆ The more members NATO had, the less likely any aggressor would be to attack.

◆ There could be a greater sharing of the defence costs if there were greater numbers.

◆ There would be a better chance of dealing with world terrorism if NATO could rely on more support.

◆ There were still a number of dictators in the world who could threaten world peace.

◆ It was important that NATO appeared strong even in the face of Russian objections.

Key Points continued ➤

Key Points *continued*

Arguments against enlargement

- Reform in Russia might be undermined by encouraging the rise in nationalism in areas seeking independence.
- An arms race with Russia might result and, given the poor state of Russia's forces, increase the dangers of a nuclear conflict.
- Some of the countries interested in joining are not necessarily stable as they have volatile political situations.
- The richer countries may not want to subsidise the poorer countries.
- France and Germany in particular wanted a more streamlined alliance based on Europe, with less reliance on the USA.

Since Russia and NATO had reached an agreement where Russia did not want to join NATO, but was happy to co-operate with it, and, since Russia did not appear too concerned about former Soviet states joining, NATO enlargement went ahead.

1999 – Czech Republic, Hungary and Poland all joined the alliance.

2004 – seven further countries – Bulgaria, Estonia, Latvia, Lithuania, Romania, Slovakia and Slovenia – joined, bringing the total membership of NATO to 26 nations.

The changing role of NATO

With the world political landscape changing so rapidly, it was felt that a new way of organising NATO's forces had to be found to meet the new security challenges that lay ahead. In 1999, the Defence Capabilities Initiative was launched, which aimed to get forces more quickly to areas of concern and support them better in the field. The Prague Summit of 2002 also made several recommendations. This was an important meeting as it was the first time NATO had met since the terrorist attacks on the USA in 2001. As a result of that attack, NATO forces were in Afghanistan and tension was increasing with Iraq. The meeting agreed to a number of key measures aimed at ensuring that NATO had the tools it needed to meet 'grave new threats and profound security challenges of the 21st century'. The key measures were:

- A NATO Response Force, capable of being deployed quickly to any crisis area, was set up.
- A simplified command structure was put in place, with one operational – the strategic command for operations (Europe), and one functional – the strategic command for transformation (USA).
- Individual members made commitments to improve and modernise their military capabilities.
- An agreement was reached on a military concept for defence against terrorism and the five initiatives against nuclear, biological and chemical weapons.

Possible questions on the organisation and role of the North Atlantic Treaty Organisation

- Critically examine the arguments for and against expanding NATO membership.
- To what extent is there no longer any need for NATO?
- To what extent have there been changes in both the role and membership of NATO?

Questions *and* Answers

SAQ 2 Critically examine the arguments for and against expanding NATO membership.

(15 marks)

Here you should look at arguments for NATO expansion and also arguments against expansion and come up with a conclusion.

Answer to SAQ 2

The NATO alliance was set up in 1949 as a defensive alliance against the threat posed by the Soviet Union after the Second World War. Many Western democratic countries feared the spread of communism and thought they could best protect themselves by banding together. The original members included the UK, France, Germany, with other Western democratic countries and also the USA and Canada. Many of the European countries felt they could only stand up to the Soviet Union if the USA was tied into the alliance. By the end of the Cold War in the early 1990s, NATO had a membership of sixteen countries. With the collapse of communism, some Eastern European former communist states wanted to join NATO and, in 1995, Hungary, the Czech Republic and Poland joined. In 2005, another seven countries joined: Bulgaria, Estonia, Latvia, Lithuania, Romania, Slovakia and Slovenia. This brought the total membership of NATO to 26 nations.

Many people would argue that by including more countries, as it has, NATO has made itself into a huge block that will deter countries from attacking it. It successfully stopped the Soviet bloc from expanding during the Cold War, and now it covers a much bigger area in Europe. However, some of the new members are very young democracies and are not as stable as the more established members would like. Those countries close to Russia, such as the Baltic states, are vulnerable to pressure from Russia and this could be a concern.

It is also argued that there are more members now to share the costs of defence. If NATO needs to send peace-keeping troops to places like Iraq, for example, it should be able to rely on more countries to support the likes of the USA and the UK who have carried a lot of the burden recently. However, the richer countries in NATO may have to subsidise the poorer ones and there may be further difficulties in standardisation of ammunition and equipment, not to mention the increased language difficulties.

With NATO having seen off the threat of the Soviet Union and communism and with its expansion to 26 members, some people argue that the job of NATO has been made a lot easier. Russia has become a lot friendlier with NATO and is co-operating with it through the NATO-Russia Permanent Joint Council. However, there is still a chance that Russia could become unstable and once again threaten the Western democracies, and there are still many threats to the West, particularly in the form of dictators who support world terrorism, such as Saddam Hussein, and countries that support terrorism.

The enlarged NATO could be said to be in a better position to deal with threats to world peace. The missions in Afghanistan and Iraq carried out by NATO have improved the chances of world peace. However, with many more members, it may be more difficult to achieve a consensus, given that there are already divisions within NATO between the USA and the UK, who supported the invasion of Iraq, and France and Germany, who did not.

It can be seen that there are arguments both for and against the expansion of NATO.

3 Threats to World Peace and Responses to Them

The main issues covered in this section are:

◆ The UN and international peace and security

◆ NATO and international peace and security

◆ Case studies – Bosnia and Herzegovina, Kosovo, Iraq

In this last section, we will be looking at how both the UN and NATO have become involved in a number of different areas around the world. Since, in recent times, they have become very closely associated with each other, it is not necessary to highlight areas where first the UN has been involved and then where NATO has been involved. You should remember that some areas of conflict around the world can be used to show the involvement of both organisations.

The UN and International Peace and Security

There are a number of actions that the UN can take to maintain peace and security around the world.

◆ The Secretary General can use the power of mediation and preventative diplomacy (Agenda For Peace) to stop conflicts from beginning.

◆ The Security Council can send in fact-finding missions, inspectors, military observers, order cease-fires, no-fly zones and no-go areas.

◆ The UN can co-operate with NATO in asking them to patrol cease-fires, or supply forces for peace-keeping duties – as in Bosnia.

◆ The UN may also ask NATO to provide troops to enter a country and overthrow its leaders – as in Iraq.

◆ The UN can impose economic sanctions against a country – as in Serbia, Iraq.

◆ The UN can impose arms sanctions against a country – as in Iraq.

Successes of the UN

You could be asked to say if the UN has been successful in its attempts to maintain world peace and security. You could argue:

◆ The UN maintains many peace-keeping missions in countries, which prevents conflicts from getting worse – for example, in Bosnia, Liberia, Cyprus, etc.

◆ In countries where the UN has deployed sufficient troops and given them a strong mandate, there have been successes – for example, in East Timor, Liberia, Ivory Coast.

◆ In times when the members of the Security Council have all agreed to action, it too has been successful – for example, in Bosnia, Kosovo.

◆ When the UN has kept out former colonisers as peace-keepers and used troops from neighbouring countries there have been successes – for example, Australian troops in East Timor, African troops in African countries.

◆ When the UN has persuaded NATO to become involved and provide the troops and fire power it is able to get things done – for example, in Bosnia, Kosovo.

Failures of the UN

You could also be asked to say if the UN has had any failures in maintaining world peace and security. You could argue:

- The UN has been unable to prevent conflicts from breaking out all over the world – there are many examples of this.

- The UN has also failed to bring an end to many conflicts that it polices – there are still UN peace-keeping forces in many parts of the world.

- The UN has been slow to organise forces and send them in to conflict zones – for example, in Rwanda, Somalia.

- Members are often reluctant to commit troops as it can be expensive and costly in terms of deaths – for example Security Council members in Africa.

- The USA and the UK in particular seem to get involved only if their own national interests are bound up in that area – for example, Iraq, Afghanistan.

NATO and international peace and security

There are a number of actions that NATO can take to maintain peace and security around the world. Remember that in recent years NATO has become more involved outside Europe.

Case studies

You should know about several areas around the world where NATO and the UN have been involved in recent years, which will allow you to quote actual examples of their involvement. You should note any successes or failures on the part of NATO or the UN.

Bosnia and Herzegovina

The collapse of communism in the late 1980s and early 1990s had a major effect on Yugoslavia. The communists had managed to keep a number of countries together, but in 1991 both Croatia and Slovenia had proclaimed independence from Yugoslavia. The Serbian-dominated Yugoslav army had tried to crush the revolt in Croatia and Slovenia but the UN had managed to arrange a cease-fire between Croatia and the Serbs.

In Bosnia, however, a greater problem lay in the fact that the country was divided into three main groups: the Bosnian Serbs, who had close ties to Serbia; the Bosnian Croats, who had links to Croatia; and the Muslims,

Figure 11.5 The former Yugoslavia, with the new states and boundaries

who lived in ethnically mixed towns in Bosnia. The UN cease-fire did not hold and the UN sent in a peace-keeping force to Bosnia to keep the sides apart – UNPROFOR, the UN Protection Force, which consisted of 14,000 peace-keepers.

In 1992, the UN also agreed to economic and military sanctions against Serbia, which was accused of aiding the Bosnian Serbs in their policy of ethnic cleansing and other atrocities. The UN and European Union peace efforts failed, and heavy fighting broke out. The UN asked NATO to begin air patrols across Bosnia, and later NATO carried out air strikes against targets in Serbia. In 1995, a truce was signed by the Bosnian Serbs and the Bosnian Government, but this was broken when the Muslim safe areas in Srebrenica and Zepa were overrun by the Bosnian Serbs and many people were massacred. NATO planes and UN artillery responded by attacking Serb targets near Sarajevo and at this point the Bosnian Serbs asked Serbian leader Milosevic to negotiate for them.

Within three months of this action, the Dayton Agreement, brokered mainly by US President Bill Clinton, was signed which brought an end to the conflict.

Key Points

Bosnia and Herzegovina

- The UN's reluctance to use force against the Serbs led to protracted fighting and the attempt at ethnic cleansing.
- Threats of military action by the UN were met with attacks on UN safe areas by the Serbs.
- When NATO became involved and used force in 1994, the Serbs quickly came to the negotiating table.
- The USA was originally reluctant to get involved as Russia had been a traditional supporter of Serbia.
- NATO forces remain in the area to ensure the peace agreement.

Kosovo

Kosovo was considered for a long time to be a part of Serbia, even though the majority of its population are ethnic Albanians. When Yugoslavia began to break up in the early 1990s, the Kosovo Liberation Army (KLA) began a series of military attacks on Serbian targets inside Kosovo, and the Serbian security forces responded with a military repression of the population as a whole. NATO and the UN both expressed their concern at the escalating ethnic tension in the region. By 1998, more than 250,000 Kosovo Albanians had been driven from their homes, with some 50,000 living in the open as winter approached.

The UN Security Council passed a resolution in 1998, demanding a cease-fire. Serbian forces refused to follow the terms of the agreement and continued to use force to repress the Kosovo Albanians. In 1999, air strikes were launched against targets in Serbia and NATO sent in troops in the shape of the Kosovo Force (KFOR). KFOR's strength reached a peak of 50,000 men and women from 30 nations including all 19 NATO members, and they succeeded in creating a lasting peace for the region.

Key Points

Kosovo

- ◆ The UN repeatedly failed to stop the Serbs attacking the Kosovo Albanians.
- ◆ Once again NATO's involvement and willingness to act forced Serbia to climb down.
- ◆ NATO bombing, however, was not as accurate as was claimed.
- ◆ The atrocities in Kosovo were not as bad as was claimed.
- ◆ More than 800,000 civilians that had fled did return to their homes.
- ◆ The KLA was demilitarised and a new Kosovo police service set up.

Iraq

In 1990, Saddam Hussein's army invaded Kuwait, but was expelled by a US-led UN coalition force in 1991 (the First Gulf War). The UN Security Council then required Iraq to scrap all weapons of mass destruction and long-range missiles, and to allow UN verification inspections. The UN had also put tough economic sanctions on Iraq, including an oil embargo, which had harsh consequences for Iraqi civilians. In 1997, the UN started an 'Oil for Food Programme' to give some relief to civilians.

Despite great pressure from the UN, Saddam Hussein continued to defy UN resolutions, but the Security Council was divided over what action to take. The USA and the UK favoured military action, but Russia, France and China wanted diplomacy. In 1998, Clinton and Blair finally agreed to begin air attacks on Iraq, after UN inspectors had been given no co-operation. There was some doubt as to whether they could do this under existing UN resolutions. Some argued that the USA and the UK were putting national interests before the interests of the UN.

In 1999, the USA attempted to enforce a no-fly zone over parts of Iraq. Iraq continually refused to allow the return of inspectors and, in 2001, British planes bombed military sites in Iraq. On 11 September 2001, the attacks by Al Qaeda on New York focused US attention on world terrorism, and Iraq was identified as part of the 'Axis of Evil'.

In 2002, UN inspectors returned to Iraq and stated that Saddam was still refusing to co-operate and account for missing banned weapons of mass destruction. In March 2003, despite failing to get the UN to agree to a resolution sanctioning military action, the USA and the UK mounted an attack to topple Saddam Hussein. They argued their authority lay in past resolutions, the failure of Iraq to disarm and claims of evidence that said weapons of mass destruction were still in Iraq. The invading forces gained a quick military victory and ousted the Government of Saddam Hussein (Second Gulf War, 2003). An overwhelming majority of governments and world public opinion thought the USA and the UK had acted against international law. The US–UK occupation encountered increasing armed resistance in Iraq, and support for the war declined steadily in the invading countries. The UN eventually did become involved, but the bombing of its headquarters in Baghdad in 2003, when fifteen UN workers died, caused the UN to pull out and keep its distance. Since then, the USA and the UK have followed a timetable for introducing democracy into Iraq. A provisional government was elected in 2004 and a Constitution and a further democratic election were voted on in 2005. The UN has largely kept out of this process.

Key Points

Iraq

◆ The UN successfully managed to eject Saddam Hussein from Kuwait in 1991 with the co-operation of NATO – Operation Desert Storm. However, the UN Charter would not allow an invasion of Iraq.

◆ The UN attempted to enforce 'no-fly zones' in north and south Iraq to protect the Kurds and Marsh Arabs – US and UK planes.

◆ The UN introduced economic sanctions, including an oil embargo after 1991.

◆ UN weapons inspectors were sent into Iraq though they were frequently obstructed.

◆ The USA and UK-led invasion in 2003 ousted Saddam Hussein but it has split the UN in two – France and Germany were against invasion.

◆ The USA eventually agreed to let the UN participate in Iraq after the invasion – but only on a small level.

◆ The calls for US and UK troops to be withdrawn have increased as casualties rise.

Possible questions on threats to world peace and responses to them

◆ The importance of the UN in maintaining world security has declined in recent years. Discuss.

◆ To what extent has the influence of the USA on the UN become too important when dealing with threats to global security?

◆ Assess the effectiveness of the UN in containing the threat to world security in relation to either Bosnia or Iraq.

Questions and Answers

SAQ 3 The importance of the UN in maintaining world security has declined in recent years. Discuss. *(15 marks)*

Here you should look at the role of the UN in maintaining world security, and analyse arguments for and against the view that this role has declined.

Answer to SAQ 3

The UN was set up after the Second World War to try to improve the lives of people around the globe. One of the ways it was thought this could be achieved was in resolving conflict and so improving security. The UN has a number of methods available to achieve this aim, including fact-finding missions, negotiations, imposing sanctions and taking direct action such as sending in peace-keeping forces. There are a number of arguments put forward to suggest that the importance of the UN is still great, though there are others to suggest the UN has been declining in importance in recent years.

Questions and Answers continued ➢

Questions and Answers continued

Answer to SAQ 3 continued

The UN is still seen by many as the most important international body in the world. Its members include almost all of the countries in the world and it is still looked to by many to give a lead in international affairs. It has been heavily involved in many conflict areas around the world, including a number of ongoing problem areas in Africa, such as Rwanda, Somalia, Sudan, Ivory Coast and Burundi. It is also still involved in the former Yugoslavia, in Bosnia and Kosovo. It is conducting peace-keeping operations in Afghanistan. It is involved in East Timor, and in India and Pakistan. However, increasingly, a number of countries, especially the USA, are willing to act outside the UN framework, in areas such as Iraq, if they don't think the UN is likely to back up their intentions.

Some would argue that the UN has evolved to meet the needs of the world in response to the threats posed by international terrorism. The UN has been willing to adopt sanctions against countries and leaders deemed to be a threat to world security, such as in Iraq and in Libya. It has set up bodies to look into counter-terrorism and has indicated its willingness to monitor situations and verify claims made by countries suspected of breaking international rules, for example, in the case of Iran and its nuclear capability.

However, the UN has had to rely increasingly on the military might of countries such as the USA, and their willingness to act on behalf of the UN. As this has become a much more expensive undertaking in recent years, there has been some reluctance of countries to commit resources to the cause of the UN.

The UN has also been criticised for taking too long to intervene in disputes. In Darfur, Sudan, for example, the UN took so long to respond to this crisis that some people have argued it is too late to prevent the humanitarian disaster that has happened, and, as a result, too late to halt the conflict that is now well established. However, without the support of the main countries of the UN Security Council, such as the USA and the UK, it is unlikely that the massive funds needed to help in this conflict would be forthcoming.

In conclusion, the UN is still seen as having a major role to play in preventing and resolving conflict in the world. It has probably come to depend a lot more on countries like the USA, however, to perform this role adequately, and the role it plays now is very different from the one it played twenty years ago, before the threat of international terrorism was such a big problem.

PAPER 2 – THE DECISION MAKING EXERCISE

Paper 2 is split into two parts: the first part consists of a number of evaluating questions worth 10 marks in total; the second part is a Report, based on given sources, worth 20 marks, giving a total of 30 marks for Paper 2. The time you are given to tackle both of these parts is 1 hour and 15 minutes. The DME is based on the Social Issues section of Paper 1.

Evaluating Questions

You will have to answer four or five short questions which are entirely based on the sources you will be given. You will be told which sources the answer must come from and the answer you give will be very brief and to the point. You must not bring in any background knowledge to the answers you give here. There are various types of evaluating question the exam board can ask:

Detect exaggeration …
You will be asked to identify a statement someone has made and then find evidence from a given source to show that the statement is not true.

Give evidence to support …
You will be asked to identify a given statement again, but this time find evidence from a given source to support the person's view.

Compare the views of …
You will be asked to compare the views of two people on a particular topic – make sure you give their views on that topic only.

Selective in the use of facts …
Someone will make a statement or two different statements and you will need to find evidence to support one part of the statement and also evidence to show the other part is not supported. You must find all of this answer to get full marks here.

To what extent …
This is very similar to selective in the use of facts and is likely to ask you to find evidence to support part of a statement and other evidence to oppose part of a statement.

The DME Report

The SQA lays out a number of conditions they expect you to follow if you are going to pass this part of the exam. If you fail to follow these rules, you will not pass the Report. The main rules to follow are:

Report style

The DME must be written in the style of a report. It can have headings and sub-headings, it can have lists, or you can use bullet points. It must not be simply a long essay.

Task box

As part of your report, you must do all of the tasks outlined in the Task Box. This is the box you see after the evaluating questions in the exam paper. The main tasks will have an asterisk (small star) beside them. The Task Box usually asks you to:

◆ Make a decision about the option or choice you have.

◆ Provide arguments to support your choice.

◆ Provide arguments against any opponent's reasons.

Sources

By the time you have finished writing your report you should have used evidence from all of the sources given in the paper. Some of this evidence will be used to back up your case and other evidence might be part of the opposing case that you should try to counter.

Background knowledge

As you go through your report, you should try to include some relevant background knowledge. Background knowledge is any information you know about the topic area that is not in the sources. Bring in background knowledge to support or counter any of the arguments or issues that have been raised by the sources.

Structure

There is no one correct way to write the report but you should have a logical structure. You may want to start with an introduction stating what your report is about, what you have been asked to do in the Task Box and you should make your recommendation clear at the start. Your report may then have two main chapters – your own arguments to support your decision and the opposing arguments and how you would counter them. You may want to sum up at the end, giving the main reasons for choosing your decision.

Practice

The best way to improve your performance in the DME is to practise as many examples as you can. Although the new exam will give you a Report to do on Wealth and Health Inequalities, it might still be useful to tackle some of the DMEs from previous exams, even though they are on the two old topic areas of Income and Wealth and Health Care in the UK. The basic principles of the DME have not really changed and the old ones will still be useful.